Multilane Free-Flow Tolling Systems

Or

Don't panic! It will all flow freely (eventually)

by Rupert W Brown

Second Print Edition

All opinions expressed in this book are the author's own. He does not represent any other agencies, companies or organisations. Rupert W Brown is a Transurban shareholder.

Every reasonable effort has been made to contact copyright holders of material reproduced in this book. If any have inadvertently been overlooked, please contact Rupert W Brown who will be glad to make good in future editions any errors or omissions brought to his attention.

First published by Rupert W Brown in 2018 as an ebook through Amazon Kindle.

This edition released by Rupert W Brown in 2022 as a paperback through Amazon print on demand services.

ISBN: 978-0-9872812-2-7

www.tollingbook.com

Acknowledgements

It would be fair to say that the tolling industry is probably not one of the best loved of human endeavours. But increasingly it provides a vital transport service to millions of people around the world and for that reason alone it is an industry in which we can take some pride. Tolling systems, by doing what they do, enable these great road, tunnel and bridge engineering projects. This book is dedicated to the men and women who get up every day to build and keep operational the world's tolling and road user charging systems and in doing so bring in the cash which is so vital for the ongoing upkeep, maintenance and development of our civil infrastructure.

Table of Contents

Introduction

Multilane Free-Flow (MLFF) tolling systems can now be found all over the planet, from Melbourne to Stockholm, Taiwan to Canada. Their importance is growing as Governments around the world look for ways to fund new road infrastructure and control traffic congestion.

MLFF tolling systems are intended to provide one important service – they allow road operators to charge customers for road use in the most convenient and seamless way possible. This book describes MLFF tolling systems from an Australian perspective. It contains two main parts.

The first discusses some of the most important concepts that drive tolling system design. This includes:

- The Concession Deed, the document that describes the legal framework allowing for the collection of tolls from customers using a road,
- A high level tolling system architecture to provide a framework for the subsequent discussion around system components and functions,
- Road topology and how open and closed toll road configurations have a significant impact on trip reconstruction,
- The issue of correctly determining vehicle class when calculating tolls,
- The functions the tolling system needs to provide to support interoperability,
- Toll products, which includes a detailed look at tags, image processing and other fee and charge structures,
- Considerations for customer self-service through on-line web portals,
- Enforcement arrangements when customers don't have valid arrangements to pay their tolls, and
- Structures to support the tolling system's interactions with a corporate financial system.

The second part takes a more detailed look at the technical architecture of modern tolling systems. This includes:

- A short section on specifying and building a tolling system,
- Tolling system data requirements and some operational considerations,
- Data items. There is no standard tolling system in the world. I'll use data items, which should be generally recognisable, to explain functions in more detail.
- How roadside detection systems operate,
- Structures for Vehicles, Tags and Interoperability Partners,
- Technical detail about image processing,
- Structures for Trips, applying those Trips to Accounts both local and those belonging to Interoperability Partners, producing Statements and Invoices, and,
- A set of metrics I'm proposing for the tolling industry to help us benchmark our tolling system performance.

Let's get to it.

Part 1

Important concepts that drive tolling system design.

Tolling Considerations

Your own personal experience of tolling systems will vary depending on where you live. If you regularly commute by car into Sydney, Australia, paying tolls is probably part of everyday life. It is very hard to move around Sydney and not pay a toll[1]. Conversely, if you live in rural England, you would spend most of your life blissfully toll free.

Cars are a very important part of modern life. They provide people with independence of movement, a sense of freedom and a powerful form of personal expression. We spend a lot of money buying cars, and then more filling them with fuel, and getting them serviced, insured and cleaned. The assumption that every car driver makes is that there will always be roads for them to drive on. For a long time, most roads have been provided by Governments "for free" although there is a significant history of turnpikes and toll gates around the world.

One point of view argues that good road infrastructure drives economic growth. Building roads creates jobs during construction and subsequently in maintenance and repair activities. Roads enable industry and the movement of goods. They facilitate trade. The opposing view is that new roads, rather than alleviate traffic congestion, actually make things worse by generating more traffic and thus more pollution. They take up real estate. They are dangerous. People die on roads all the time, everywhere in the world[2] – more than 1.2 million *every year* - and roads cost a lot of tax money.

What is to be done? Our societies couldn't do without them. At the same time there is a powerful argument that says "Why should my tax money go towards a road I'm never going to use?" Why should somebody living in Horsham (Victoria, Australia) contribute tax money to a motorway in Melbourne, or somebody living in Norwich (England) pay to keep the traffic moving in London?

Governments are increasingly accepting the need to build toll roads on the basis that tolls are the only way to fund and thus get a road built, with the bonus that only those people actually using the road have to pay for it. The "user pays" principle - it can be a workable compromise. Then there is another school of thought that says "tolls are taxes" and do not take into account a person's ability to pay. A Billionaire in a Bentley pays the same as a Pauper in a clapped-out Corolla. But isn't that the same as the public transport system? Ahh yes, but there is such a thing as a concession card! Toll roads are politically sensitive, and as such they have to be ready to face the full gamut of cross-bench scrutiny.

Because of this Governments have to approach the building of new toll roads with a degree of caution. Many voters do perceive tolls as just another tax, and politicians that raise taxes don't always do well at elections. In planning a new toll road, a Government will think about "safeguards" and "considerations" such as:

"Whatever we do, tolls have to be 100% accurate. People don't like paying, but when they do we can't have them being charged incorrect amounts" – this thinking leads to the development of a whole range of financial Key Performance Indicators (KPI) for the toll road operator.

"We've got to make it easy for people to pay their tolls" – which drives the need for a whole range of payment options including retail outlets, a website, with cash through a service centre and over the phone.

"We want to change traffic patterns. We want more people travelling at off-peak times to ease congestion" – which leads to the need for toll rates that vary depending on the time of day and the day of the week.

"Some people drive little cars. They take up less space and do less damage to the road when compared to a huge truck" – this thinking leads to the need for toll rates that vary depending on the class of vehicle a person is driving.

"We can't toll ambulances. We can't charge the ambulance service for trying to save somebody's life" – this results in the creation of a special class of exempt vehicles, for which tolls will not apply. This usually includes public transport.

"It's going to be hard for Taxi drivers to work out how much they should add to their fare to cover the tolls they incur" – this thinking leads to the creation of special rates for some classes of vehicle e.g. charging taxis a flat fee regardless of distance travelled.

"In time we will end up with more than one toll road, but we don't want users having to deal with multiple operators and multiple accounts" – and so the whole concept of interoperable tolling systems is created, where a customer with one account can travel on any toll road.

"Some people will only use the road once or twice a year. We have to make it easy for them" – this thinking leads to the development of casual user toll products like a single trip pass, or a book of trip vouchers.

"You have to be firm. If people use the road and don't pay we see it in the same light as shoplifting or public transport fare evasion. You have to go after them for money" – this leads to the need for some kind of enforcement system, some kind of legal process that allows the road operator to recover money.

"The whole thing has got to be easy to understand" – OK – "*and*",

"You have to keep the cost of collecting toll revenue as low as possible" – Right, I think we get the message. It's going to be a little more complicated than simply charging people and collecting the money.

All of these considerations, and the form and configuration of the road itself, create requirements that drive the detail of the tolling system design.

Concession Deeds

But before we start the discussion on the tolling system itself, it is worth spending a little while looking at the mechanisms that allow toll road operators to do their tolling.

An obvious and simple question is "who actually owns the road?" and the answer of course is not simple at all. In Australia a toll road is defined by its Concession Deed. Two good examples of Concession Deeds are:

- Melbourne City Link, and
- Mitcham-Frankston Freeway – now referred to as EastLink.

Both of these concession deed documents are freely available on the web if you search for them – and you do have to search. Most of the content doesn't relate to the tolling system at all, but rather to the multi-layered and byzantine arrangements concerning the road building project itself, land leases, changes to the road network and where all the money goes. Each concession deed also comes complete with a myriad of schedules, exhibits, appendices and revisions. Table 1 below gives the main headings of the Melbourne City Link deed mentioned above.

1. DEFINITIONS, INTERPRETATION AND GENERAL PRINCIPLES
2. THE PROJECT
3. CONCESSION TERMS
4. PROJECT LAND AND LEASES
5. PLANNING SCHEME REQUIREMENTS AND REMEDIATION
6. INDEPENDENT REVIEWER
7. DESIGN AND CONSTRUCTION
8. TIMING OF THE WORKS
9. OPERATION
10. MAINTENANCE AND REPAIR
11. FINANCE
12. LIABILITY AND RISKS
13. LOSS OR DAMAGE AND INSURANCE
14. REPRESENTATIONS, WARRANTIES AND UNDERTAKINGS
15. TERMINATION
16. DISPUTE RESOLUTION
17. ACCOUNTING AND REPORTING OBLIGATIONS
18. ASSIGNMENT AND MORTGAGE
19. GENERAL

Table 1 – Main headings in the Melbourne City Link Concession Deed

Buried in this document at clause 2.8 is the following text:

> 2.8 Grant of Concession
>
> (a) Subject to clause 12.3, the State grants to the Company the right to:
>
> (i) design;
>
> (ii) construct;
>
> (iii) Commission;
>
> (iv) operate;
>
> (v) impose and collect a toll for the use of Vehicles (within the meaning of the Toll Calculation Schedule) on;
>
> (vi) maintain and repair; and
>
> (vii) raise revenues from other lawful uses of the Link approved by the State under clause 9.4(c) and (d) in respect of,
>
> the Link until the end of the Concession Period, subject to and upon the terms of this Deed.

So there you have it – the deed allows the operator to "impose and collect a toll for the use of Vehicles …". The Mitcham-Frankston Freeway deed has a very similar clause:

> 2.2 Grant of concession
>
> The State grants:
>
> (a) to the Trustee, the right to design, construct and commission its Works and its Temporary Works and to ConnectEast the right to design, construct and commission its Works and its Temporary Works;
>
> (b) to ConnectEast, the right to operate, maintain and repair the Freeway;
>
> (c) to ConnectEast, the right to maintain and repair the Maintained Off-Freeway Facilities; and
>
> (d) to ConnectEast, the right to impose and collect tolls and User Charges for use of, and raise revenues from other lawful uses approved by the State, of the Freeway,
>
> until the end of the Concession Period subject to, and in accordance with, the terms of, and the risk allocation provided for in, this Deed.

The "State" in both these clauses refers to the State of Victoria in Australia. They are the Government in these matters.

Note in both these clauses mention is made of the "Concession Period". The end of the Concession Period brings to an end the right of the operator to charge a toll for using the road. Usually control of the road returns to the Government and it is up to them to decide what to do next. This has actually happened in Australia. The Concession Period on the M4 road in New South Wales (NSW) did come to an end and tolls were removed. Tolling revenue is attractive however and it wasn't too long before the NSW Government announced that tolls would be introduced again to support the development of the WestConnex project[3].

Working out how long a Concession Period should be comes down to a complex financial calculation driven by multiple and sometimes competing sensibilities. The principal driver is the actual cost of the road building project which in turn is driven by:

- Land costs – things like the need to compulsorily acquire land and land leases,
- The design of the road – including the need for bridges and tunnels which can add significant costs, but at the same time may alleviate other problems such as acquiring land in the midst of strong environmental protests,
- The prevailing labour market and competitive forces in the construction industry.

Usually the cost estimate of the project is based on a reference design and then adjusted as bidders work out innovative and hopefully cheaper ways of achieving the desired outcome.

Once the project cost is established, the next input becomes how to finance that cost. It does make sense for Governments to tip money into toll road projects because at the end of the Concession Period they will own the road. The rest has to come from the private sector either as loans or as equity if the toll road operator is listing for this purpose. Both loans and equity (and Governments) require a return from the investment and that return has to come from the tolls.

Enter the Traffic Model, which in recent years has become one of the most controversial elements of toll road building projects in Australia. The traffic model predicts the number of vehicles that will use the road once it has been opened. If there is lots of predicted traffic, the operator can set a reasonable toll, customers will find the road an attractive travel option, and the investors should make money. But then if the actual patronage is very low, that becomes a real problem. Simply charging a higher toll to make up a revenue shortfall is a real disincentive for people to use the road, and you end up with an expensive piece of infrastructure nobody wants to use and a huge debt. Have a look at the story of Sydney's Lane Cove Tunnel and the article in Tolltrans 2016 by Tom Stone[4]. To be fair, traffic modelling for new road infrastructure is very difficult, but the road's financial model needs one to answer the question:

"If we have this many vehicles using the road, and we can charge this toll rate, how long do we need to keep charging the toll to ensure that we make a decent return from the money we invested?"

That drives the length of the Concession Period. At around 35 years or more, these Concession Periods and the relative certainty and pattern of toll revenue has supported long term debt deals and attracted pension funds as investors and lenders to road projects.

Figure 1 – Marsha and Brad

Marsha – look at these figures!
What do they say Brad?
I think they mean our traffic model may have overstated the opportunity by 3000%!
My God! What are we going to do?
Well, I've got two tickets for Mexico – you coming?
Oh Brad! I thought you'd never ask.

The concession deed – and for us this is the important bit – may also contain quite detailed requirements about how the tolling system should work. The following is from the Mitcham-Frankston Freeway deed:

> 33.1 Tolling System requirements
>
> ConnectEast must ensure that the Tolling System:
>
> (a) does not impede the flow of traffic on the Freeway or any Freeway Section or Bypass;

(b) operates so that vehicles can travel at speeds and in the manner as set out in the Project Scope and Project Requirements, when entering, travelling along and leaving the Freeway or any Freeway Section or Bypass without being required to slow down or stop;

(c) is electronic;

(d) operates in a manner which conforms with whichever in each case is the more onerous of all standards and requirements:

(i) as outlined in the Project Scope and Project Requirements; or

(ii) applied by Law from time to time; and

(e) is readily capable of being Interoperable with all other Toll Roads the operation of which is subject to the Tolling Agreement.

This clause specifies two very important design considerations:

- That the road has to be truly free-flow i.e. no entry and exit barriers, and
- That it must be fully interoperable with other toll roads i.e. one customer, one account, travel on any toll road within Australia.

The interesting thing about this concession deed is that it was written several years after the one for Melbourne CityLink. CityLink was a pioneer in true multilane free-flow tolling and at the time nobody was quite sure how it was all going to pan out. That project did carry a lot of risk. By the time the Mitcham-Frankston Freeway concession came round, there was a lot more real experience in industry and Government and the concession deed reflects that. The requirements and conditions for Mitcham-Frankston are a lot more onerous and exacting than they are for CityLink. One area where this becomes very obvious is the Toll Calculation Schedule – the bit of the concession deed that controls the amount by which you can increase toll prices every year. For CityLink this is contained within Schedule 3, is quite complex, but at the heart of it sits these clauses:

2.2 Subject to clause 2.4, the Theoretical Toll for Cars for a Tollable Section for a quarter subsequent to the quarter ending 31 March, 1995 is calculated in accordance with the following formula:

$$\text{Theoretical Toll}_{t+1} = \text{Theoretical Toll}_t \times \text{Index}_t$$

where:

Theoretical Toll_{t+1} is the Theoretical Toll for the Tollable Section to apply to Cars in the relevant quarter

Theoretical Toll_t is the Theoretical Toll for the Tollable Section which applies to Cars in the quarter preceding the relevant quarter

Index_t is:

(a) for a quarter ending before the 15th anniversary of Completion of the last Section to be Completed, the greater of:

(i) the most recently available CPI during the quarter preceding commencement of the relevant quart er (CPI_{t-1}) divided by CPI for the quarter preceding the quarter for which the most recently available CPI applies (CPI_{t-2}); or

(ii) 1.0110650 (that is, 4· 5% per annum converted to a quarterly compound rate plus one); and

(b) for a quarter to which paragraph (a) does not apply, the greater of one and the amount derived under sub-paragraph (a)(i).

For EastLink, the equivalent clauses are in Schedule 4 "Toll Calculation Schedule" of their concession deed and look like this:

3. Theoretical Toll Rate

3.1 Theoretical Toll Rate for Cars

The Theoretical Toll Rate for Cars for a Toll Zone for a Financial Year is calculated in accordance with the following formula:

$$\text{Theoretical Toll Rate for Cars} = \left(\frac{CPI_{FY-1}}{CPI_{Base}} \right) \text{ x Base Toll Rate for Cars}$$

where:

CPI_{FY-1} = at any date in that Financial Year, the CPI for the Quarter expiring on 31 December of the immediately preceding Financial Year.

CPI_{Base} = the CPI for the Quarter expiring on 31 December 2003, being 1.428.

The Base Toll Rate for Cars is as defined in Part 2.1 (Base Toll Rate for Cars) of this Schedule 4 (Toll Calculation Schedule).

Now the keen-eyed amongst you will have noticed a fundamental difference between those two sets of clauses. EastLink have to make do with a once a year CPI increase if they're lucky. CityLink can increase their prices four times a year and over that year it's CPI or 4.5% whichever is greater. Given the low inflation and CPI rates Australia has been enjoying for some time, that clause lets CityLink toll prices gallop ahead. This hasn't gone unnoticed by the media either. A good example of the "unease" some people feel about this arrangement is Stephen Mayne's article of 2014 on Crikey.com[5]. But a deal is a deal.

If prices are laid down in concession deeds, is the idea of "competition" in the road tolling industry ever relevant? In Melbourne, Australia there are the two toll roads EastLink and CityLink. You could get up one morning and say to yourself "I'm sick of the toll prices they charge on CityLink. I'm going to use EastLink instead!" So off you go and of course end up in completely the wrong place because the roads connect different geographical locations - not a very cost-effective consumer decision. In that sense it's rare to find two toll roads that do directly compete with each other. But every toll road argues that it does have competition:

- From the existing non-tolled road network, so the toll road has to provide faster, more predictable journey times,
- From the public transport network, trains and buses – and the tolling industry would argue that they improve the public transport network because buses can benefit from those faster, more predictable journey times,
- From new technology – if you have a super-fast internet connection at home, do you even need to go into the office?

All of which is true to an extent, but is that level of competition enough to keep a toll road company really focussed on things like customer service? Once the road is established and the money is flowing why not outsource the call centre to Buwapbackistax and just be done with it? We'll save a fortune! To help moderate that kind of thinking, Governments can use the concession deed to lay down key performance indicators (KPI), with financial penalties if those KPIs are not met.

A good example of a KPI regime is contained within the Mitcham-Frankston Freeway concession deed. The EastLink KPIs cover the following five service areas:

- Customer service and customer satisfaction,
- Road condition,
- Landscape and architectural features maintenance,
- Tolling accuracy, and
- Environment.

Some of these KPIs have a direct bearing on the tolling system. From the Tolling accuracy section examples of KPIs are given in table 2 below.

The KPIs in themselves are reasonably onerous and have to be considered as *requirements* when the tolling system is being specified and designed. To make the KPI regime work requires a mechanism to be set up and maintained to accurately gather data and report on actual performance. Every breach of a KPI means the operator accrues points. If, at the end of the year, that points total exceeds certain thresholds then the operator has to start giving money back to customers, and another part of the Mitcham-Frankston Freeway concession deed states that that can be up to $15,000,000. Consequently this KPI regime is to be taken seriously. In contrast, CityLink's deed is remarkably KPI free. This is one example of the "more exacting" deed conditions created for EastLink.

13.	Timeframes for charging transactions to Customers' Accounts.	99% within 2 days	1 point for every occurrence outside KPI Benchmark	Assessed monthly
14.	Timeframe for producing statements and invoices.	99% within 3 days of the end of the relevant statement period	1 point for every occurrence outside KPI Benchmark	Assessed monthly
15.	Customer accounts with financial institutions are credited or debited with the correct amounts (excluding Customer errors and omissions).	99.999%	1 point for every occurrence outside KPI Benchmark	Assessed monthly

Table 2 – Example KPIs from the Mitcham-Frankston Freeway concession deed.

The subject of toll road competition is something we will touch on again later. Suffice to say that if your toll road operates within the context of an interoperability group then yes, there can be an element of competition.

The critical message here is **know your concession deed**. Understand what the requirements are and ensure that whatever you build is compliant otherwise almost certainly there will be problems down the track.

It would be a fair question to ask how is the Government going to find out whether the tolling system meets the requirements of the concession deed? Can't we just fudge the KPI reporting? This is where the Independent Verifier (IV) plays a role. On a large toll road project the IV is not normally one person but a team of people, each of whom specialises in a particular area relevant to the project. The IV team will have Civil Engineers, Environmental Scientists, Surveyors and a number of Information Technology (IT) experts who will be taking a keen interest in how the tolling system is being built, including its reporting systems. They are appointed for their skills and experience and are there to take the emotion out of the whole project progress reporting activity. They are expected to take an independent and objective view of what is going on, and then report it to the Government and the toll road operator. It is then up to the management and legal teams on both sides to decide if there is a real problem. Usually a concession deed will require the appointment of an IV and that everybody cooperates fully with the IV when required. Like everything in life, there are good IVs and those that are a pain in the neck. The good ones will always raise issues and problems as they see them, but then will spend time talking to you about why it really is a problem and how to go about fixing things. The bad ones will just stand there and throw rocks for no other reason than they can. If you have any say in the matter, make sure you get a good one, write the need for that good behaviour into their contract, and then cooperate with them. Ironically Governments often make the toll road operator pay for the services of the IV as part of the contract under the concession deed, so you should have a big say in who gets appointed to the role.

Concession deeds are not fixed in stone. They can be and are amended to suit changing circumstances. It is not practical to expect a city's configuration to remain static for the 35 year period of a concession deed. Transurban, who own the CityLink concession, are very good at making the concession work for them and the greater Melbourne road network. They have been willing to put money into developing the road network in return for advantageous changes to their concession deed. In December 2017 the ABC website[6] reported that Transurban had signed an AU$ 6.7 billion deal with the Victorian Government for the development of the West Gate Tunnel in Melbourne. In return for Transurban managing the project and tipping in AU$4 billion, they get to keep charging tolls on CityLink for another decade until 2045, with tolls to rise 4.25% annually from 2019 to 2029. At a time when Governments struggle to find money for infrastructure, this kind of public-private partnership is probably the way of the future.

Cities don't stand still and neither does technology. What would have been a neat way to toll five years ago might not make any sense now. The iPhone appeared in 2007 and changed the way we interact with businesses and each other forever. Customers now expect to be able to deal with a toll road operator using their mobile device, but a concession deed written back in 2005 would have been hard pressed to predict that change. Back then an SMS was a pretty neat trick. The deeds do allow for change but the important consideration is that significant changes have to be approved by Governments and that the approval process is not necessarily quick. It is another significant consideration for a tolling system project and its subsequent operation.

Tolling System Overview

It is important that we orientate ourselves with the components and functions of a tolling system. In this chapter we will take a quick tour of an MLFF tolling system architecture before circling back to look at things in more detail. I'm presenting a model here which I think represents the "state of the art" as we know it today (2018). The experts will probably argue about whether this is correct till the cows come home, but we have to start somewhere. Figure 2 shows the main system components in this MLFF tolling system.

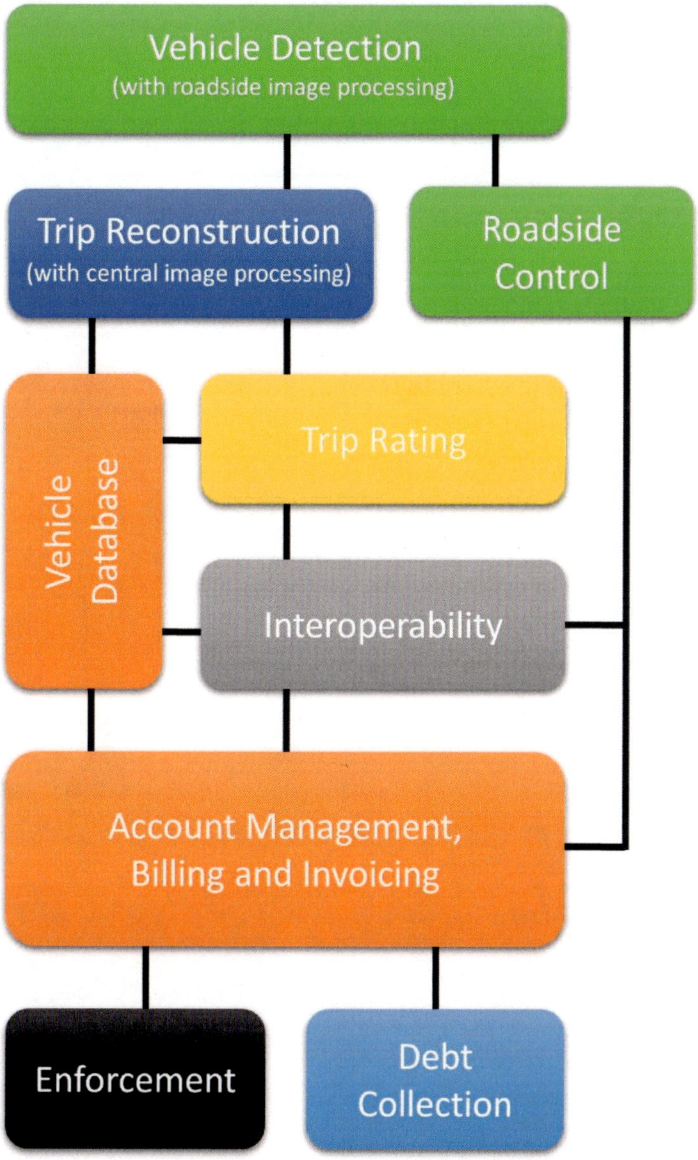

Figure 2 – Main system components in an MLFF tolling system.

Figure 3 then takes these components and puts them in the context of their physical locations.

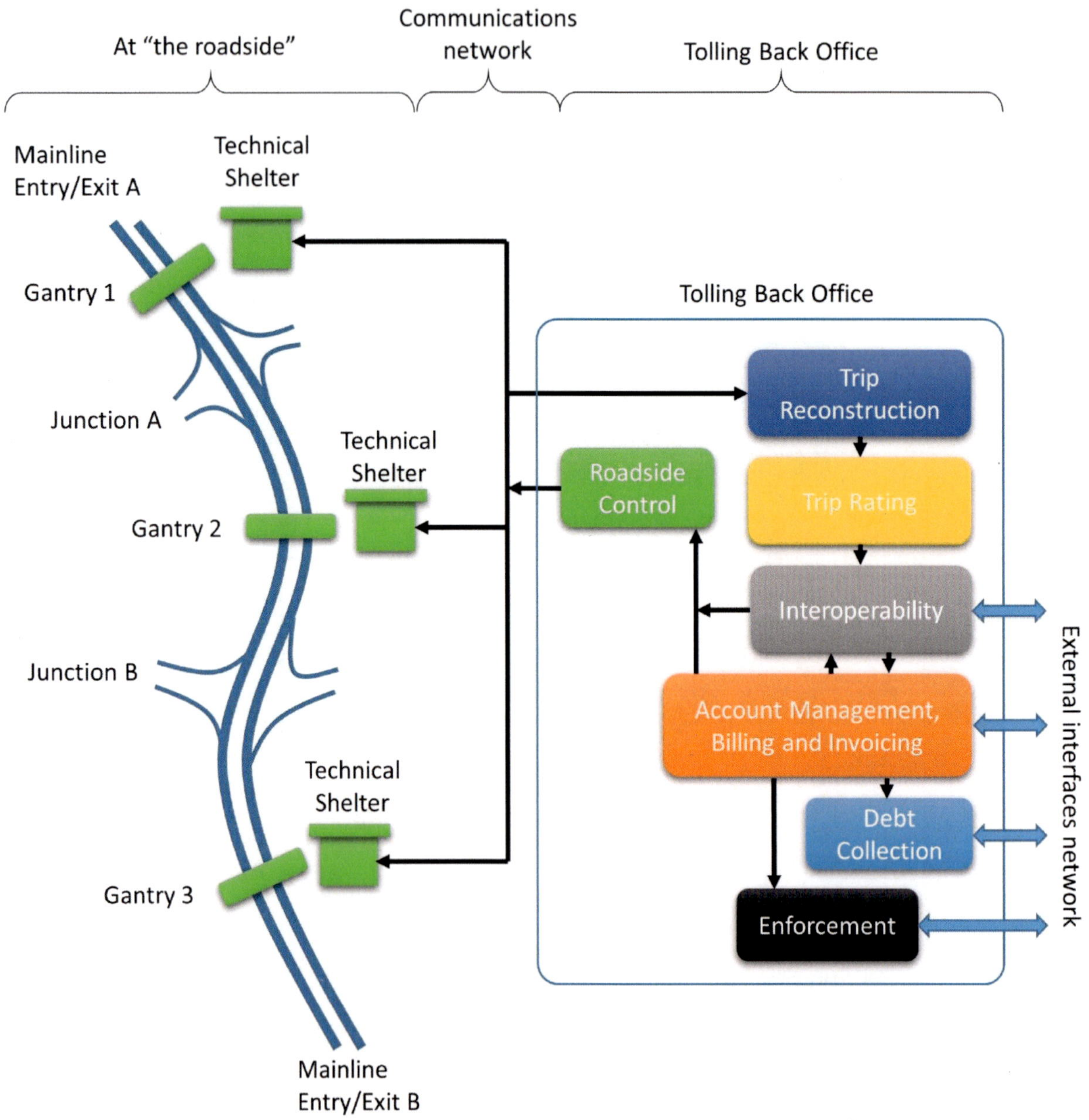

Figure 3 – System components of an MLFF tolling system in the context of their physical locations.

Vehicle Detection

The Vehicle Detection component – often referred to as "the roadside" - covers all the equipment and software necessary to detect vehicles using the road. Vehicle detection includes, but is not limited to items such as:

- On-board Units (OBU), usually referred to as tags. Tags are carried by the vehicles using the road. These tags can use a variety of technologies including Radio Frequency Identification (RFID), Dedicated Short Range Communication (DSRC) and infra-red.
- A gantry or similar structure next to or spanning the road upon which are mounted the vehicle detection sensors. The structure is intended to position the sensors in the best place for vehicle detection, while keeping them out of the way of vehicles and pedestrians.
- The sensors themselves which include tag readers, cameras, vehicle detection systems, vehicle classification systems and illuminators (lights).
- Computer equipment and software which processes and sends on the data from the sensors. This equipment resides in some form of technical shelter – building or cabinet – located close to or inside the gantry structure. Often these technical shelters have air conditioning and some form of back-up power, be that an uninterruptable power supply (UPS) or a standby generator.
- A communications network that allows processed sensor data to be passed back to the tolling back office.
- A power supply to power all the equipment in the technical shelter and on the gantry.

Figure 4 below shows a typical two gantry configuration – looking at it from the side, with vehicles travelling from the left of the page to the right. The structure to the left is the rear gantry which is configured to take images of the vehicle's rear licence plate. The structure to the right is the front gantry which is configured to scan vehicles for classification purposes, take images of the front licence plate and perform tag communications.

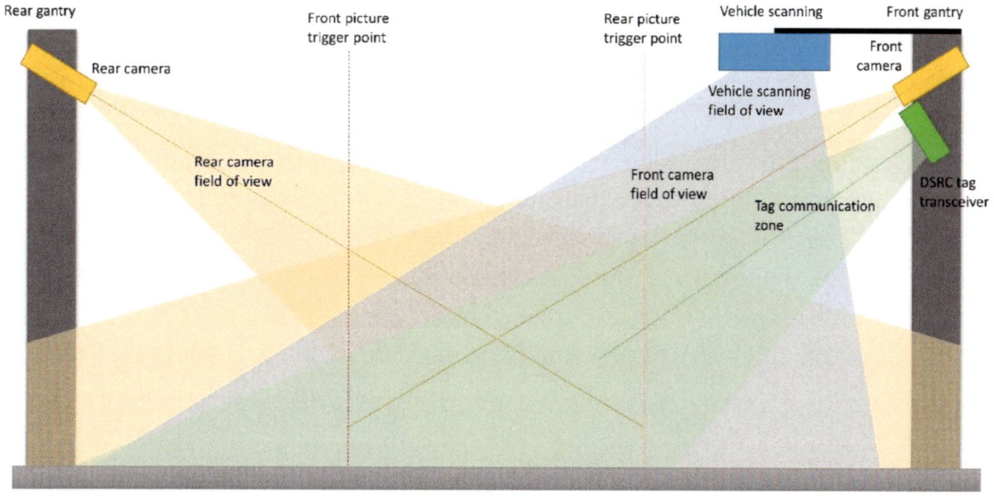

Figure 4 – Typical two gantry configuration of roadside vehicle detection equipment.

As vehicles pass within range of the detection equipment, its role is to send Tag and Vehicle Passages (detection events), and images, back to the Trip Reconstruction component. A Tag Passage captures the unique identification number of the tag in the vehicle. A Vehicle Passage captures the size and position of the vehicle on the road and also the licence plate characters and numbers as a string (computer data type). It is able to do this because the cameras contain optical character recognition (OCR) engines which, in most cases, can read the licence plate string from the images.

These acronyms DSRC and RFID - from Wikipedia:

DSRC - Dedicated short-range communications - one-way or two-way short-range to medium-range wireless communication channels specifically designed for automotive use and a corresponding set of protocols and standards.

RFID - Radio-frequency identification - the wireless use of electromagnetic fields to transfer data, for the purposes of automatically identifying and tracking tags attached to objects. The tags contain electronically stored information. Some tags are powered by energy from the interrogating radio waves and act as a passive transponder. Other types have a local power source such as a battery and may operate at tens of meters from the reader.

For the system to work, tags and tag readers both have to be compliant to the same standards.

Roadside Control

Roadside Control is the control of the behaviour of the roadside equipment. Roadside Control includes the ability to:

- Turn all the equipment on a gantry on or off. Roads do need to be closed for maintenance and if that maintenance happens to be under or near a gantry, the last thing you want is to pick up all the maintenance vehicle traffic. You turn the gantry off.
- Change parameter values. The roadside equipment is usually quite parameter driven, and from time to time the value of parameters need to be changed. One example of this is the set of parameters that define the three dimensional spaces used to classify vehicles into certain classes.
- Synchronise time. As will be seen below, making sure all the gantries are synchronised in time is very important for accurate trip reconstruction.
- Control lists. These lists instruct the roadside equipment to take actions when certain conditions prevail. For example, the roadside equipment is able to communicate with tags and make them "beep". One list is made up of all the tag identifiers which belong to tolling accounts that are in a "low balance" state. The roadside knows that it has to make any tag on that list beep "one plus two" times, when it passes through the gantry, as opposed to the usual one beep.

Trip Reconstruction

I use the words "Trip Reconstruction" simply because our toll road customer has used our road and we're trying to reconstruct their trip based on the Tag and Vehicle Passages we received from the roadside. The Trip Reconstruction component has two principal tasks:

1. Identify *exactly* what was detected and when, to create a transaction with a *unique identifier*,
2. To group transactions with the same *unique identifier* and that conform to a set of reconstruction business rules, so that they can be formed into a *trip*.

In the two statements above there are some important words:

Exactly – the Trip Reconstruction process has to be quite precise in determining what was detected and the time it was detected. It is very important that the system is able to correctly determine *unique identifiers*. Errors at this stage can lead to incorrect charges being applied to customers, which can reduce our tolling revenue through re-work and tolls having to be written off.

Unique identifier – in the context of toll roads, a unique identifier is:

- a licence plate string, the state or country of registration and sometimes the vehicle class, or
- the identification number of the tag carried in the vehicle, or
- both.

Hopefully by the time we get to Trip Reconstruction we have some licence plate string and registration data provided by the roadside. In my architecture, image processing within Trip Reconstruction is the application of business rules to determine if the data we have from the roadside is accurate enough to use without additional image processing and/or manual intervention i.e. getting a human involved to look at images. Trip Reconstruction can use the data as is, pass the images through a second OCR engine to get additional data, or hand it over to a person. In the vast majority of cases, the combined image processing capability (IPC) of the tolling system should be able to automatically confirm the licence plate string and registration details.

Over the years, Tag Passages at the roadside have proven themselves to be consistently reliable. It used to be the case that if a good tag read was picked up by the roadside, then that tag identification number would become the principal unique identifier for the purposes of trip reconstruction. As will be seen later, issues with vehicle class mean that we do need to identify the actual vehicle travelling on the road, which means getting that licence plate string. The tag identification number is by no means redundant. It remains a very useful piece of data for trip reconstruction purposes.

Trip – It may sound odd, but determining what constitutes a trip can be quite complex. Figure 5 below is a representation of a simple toll road. It has two mainline entry and exit points, two junctions and three tolling gantries.

Imagine a vehicle enters the road at Mainline B and passes under Gantry 3. Gantry 3 creates detection events. The vehicle then exits the road at Junction B, and the driver spends five minutes getting a coffee, before re-joining the road at Junction B and driving through Gantries 2 and 1. Does that constitute one trip? The vehicle did actually leave the road, but as far as the tolling system is concerned, there are three sets of detection events, one for each gantry. The system has no way of knowing the vehicle left the road unless it understands the concept that a trip should take a certain amount of *time*. It follows that the definition of a trip obviously involves road topology, but also a sense of time as well, and thus the need to be precise about detection time. These considerations lead to the creation of trip reconstruction business rules.

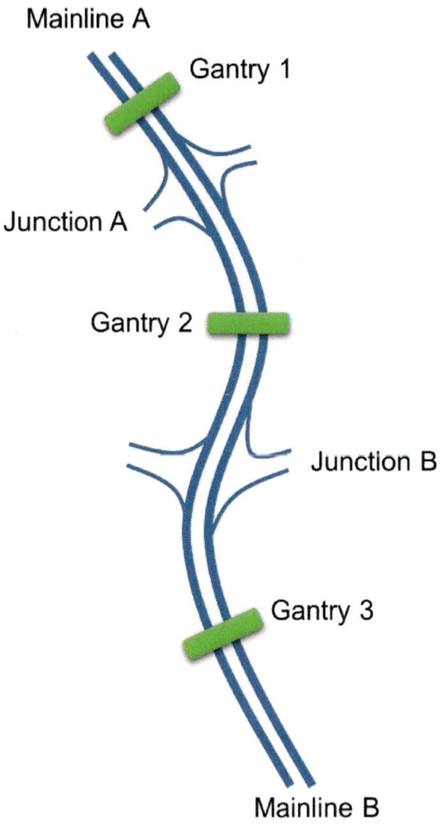

Figure 5 – A simple toll road topology

Trip Rating

Trip rating takes each trip and calculates the appropriate toll. Tolls can be calculated in a variety of ways, but the factors involved in calculating a toll usually include:

- The distance, or the number of toll zones (passages under gantries) travelled by the vehicle,
- The class of the vehicle, be that a motorcycle, car, light commercial vehicle or heavy commercial vehicle – or some other classification scheme,
- A variable toll value, determined by an algorithm, intended to maintain a minimum speed or volume of traffic along the road.

Adjustments may also be applied, such as:

- Discounts for off-peak travel, or premiums for peak time travel,
- A trip cap, which is a maximum amount for any given trip,
- Discounts for short trips, or trips along certain sections of the road.

Interoperability

Interoperability between toll road operators allows a customer to have one tolling account and travel, without the need for other arrangements, on all the toll roads whose operators have signed up to an interoperability agreement. For this to work, interoperability requires the exchange of information between all the toll road operators covered by the agreement.

Firstly, interoperability relies upon the existence and the sharing of details around *arrangements to pay*. An arrangement to pay is said to exist when a toll road customer has opened a valid tolling account with a toll road operator, or bought some kind of casual tolling product such as a trip pass.

This arrangement to pay data can be manifest in the form of *blacklists* and *whitelists*. The easiest way to explain this is to go straight to an example.

- In Australia, all tags are considered valid **unless** they appear on the tag blacklist. They are put on the tag blacklist when there **is no** valid arrangement to pay for that tag.
- Licence plate strings are only considered valid if they are **on** a licence plate whitelist. They are put on the whitelist when there **is** a valid arrangement to pay for that licence plate.

This works because the tag identification number contains details of the toll road operator who issued the tag. If the toll road operator is a member of the interoperability agreement, all their tags are assumed valid by default, unless they're not i.e. on the blacklist. A licence plate has to be on a whitelist so that a toll road operator knows who has the arrangement to pay with that licence plate. The plate on its own can't carry that information.

Every day in Australia, all the toll road operators prepare their own tag blacklists, licence plate whitelists and another list that shows the association between tags and licence plates on their customer accounts. All these lists are shared between all the toll road operators, who then in turn compile master lists. These master lists sit at the heart of the interoperability process.

As trips are created on a toll road, the unique identifier associated with the trip is compared to the master lists and is sorted along the following lines:

- This is my customer travelling on my road – assign that trip to the customer's account.
- This is somebody else's customer (another toll road operator) travelling on my road – assign that trip to the other toll road operator's interoperability account. These other operators are called Interoperable Partners.
- This is recognised as a vehicle that is not required to pay tolls, an exempt vehicle – assign the trip to the exempt vehicle account.

- We see that this vehicle has a licence plate which is not on a whitelist, and/or has a tag which is on a blacklist – assign this trip as a *No Arrangement to Pay* (NATP) trip.

In addition some trips may become disputed. This usually occurs when one operator believes a customer has a valid arrangement to pay and the operator that owns the customer account disagrees.

At the end of the day, all the trips on your road made by customers belonging to other toll road operators are sent off to those toll roads. Similarly, all the trips made by your customers travelling on other toll roads are sent to you. Your tolling system then has to apply those trips to your customers' accounts.

The Australian system works well every day, even though there is a significant amount of duplicated effort between toll road operators. The key point is that it makes it very easy for customers – one tolling account gives them access to all the toll roads in Australia. Figure 6 below summarises this process.

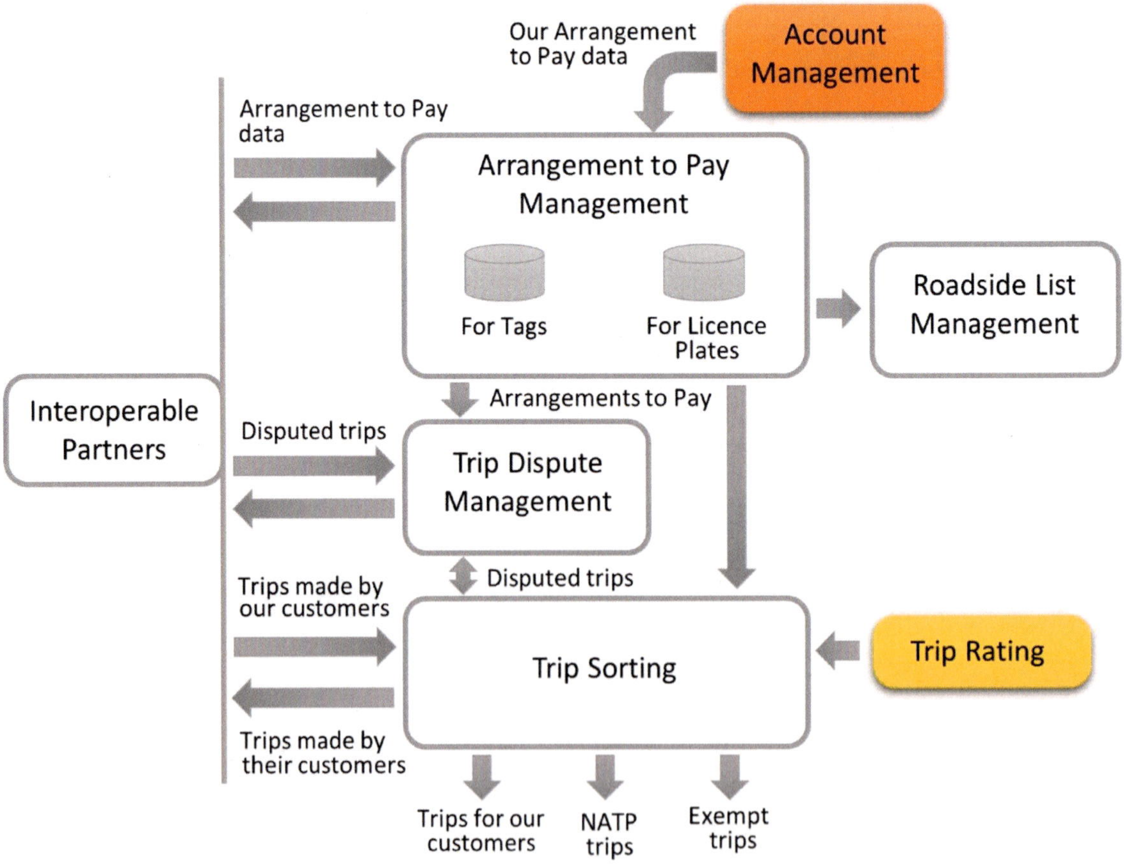

Figure 6 – The basic (Australian) interoperability process

In figure 6 there is a box marked "Roadside List Management". This covers the production of lists that are sent back to the roadside equipment via the Roadside Control component. Lists contain details of tags whose associated account is either in a low balance state or suspended and thus blacklisted. In

Victoria, Australia, the roadside instructs the tag to beep once for a valid arrangement to pay, one plus two beeps for an associated account in low balance, and four beeps for a blacklisted tag which means the associated account has been suspended, or the tag is marked as lost, stolen or destroyed. This beep mechanism provides direct and immediate feedback to customers on the state of their account.

Account Management, Billing and Invoicing

The account management, billing and invoicing component is at the heart of the tolling system back office. Its two critical functions are to manage the accounts of the toll road's customers, along with their personal and contact details, and to manage those NATP trips made by people who have used the road but have no valid arrangement to pay. Principal functions include:

- Maintenance of "toll products". A toll product defines the type of account that a customer uses to create their arrangement to pay with a toll operator. Toll products are typically:
    - Pre-paid – where a customer deposits an amount of money in their account, and the balance reduces over time as they use the road and incur tolls. Once an account low balance threshold is reached, the customer is prompted to manually top-up the account with more money, or an automatic top-up occurs through a direct debit arrangement.
    - Post-paid – where all the tolls incurred by a customer are itemised on an invoice and sent to the customer once a month. The customer pays the invoice.
    - Tag based – where the customer is issued with a tag to place in their vehicle.
    - Video based – where the customer relies on the toll operator reading their licence plate string to correctly apportion the toll. In practice there is little difference between a video and a tag based account save for the fact that video trips incur an additional image processing fee, and there is usually some kind of financial deposit required before a tag is issued.
    - Trip pass – a trip pass represents an arrangement to pay, albeit for a single trip on the road. It is usually a video based, fixed price product that can be purchased up to three days after the date of travel. It is aimed at the very infrequent road user.
- Customer Management. The management of customers' details including their account balance, trip and payment records, contact details and links to vehicle and tag details.
- Channels Management. Inbound and outbound customer contacts, management of enquiries and complaints, and the generation of notifications to customers such as low balance alerts.
- Billing and Invoicing. All the processes involved in creating statements and invoices and mailing them to customers be that via e-mail or regular post.
- The creation of NATP trips. An NATP trip usually results in the creation of an NATP account which treats the value of the NATP trip as a debt. The debt then has to be managed through the enforcement and debt collection processes.
- Tag logistics. The management of tags including their acceptance from the supplier, the allocation to and returns from customers, and their repair or destruction.
- Interfaces. The tolling system requires many external interfaces in order to function. These include:

- A bank interface to handle the vital financial transactions. Increasingly tolling systems are making use of bank tokenisation services to reduce their exposure to the security requirements imposed by the Payment Cards Industry (PCI).
- An interface to the local vehicle registration authority. This interface allows the toll operator to use a licence plate string to look up the name and address of a vehicle owner in order to recover the cost of NATP trips.
- Alternative payment channels such as post offices or payment services in convenience stores.
- Customer self-service channels such as web sites, mobile apps and telephone based interactive voice systems.
- An interface to the toll road operator's corporate financial system to keep track of the money.

Enforcement

Enforcement systems vary greatly around the world. Following is the process toll road operators are allowed to use in Victoria, Australia. Customers are given three days to pay for a NATP trip. The idea is you can travel, and then settle up by buying a trip pass or opening an account. If after those three days no attempt has been made to pay for an NATP trip, then the enforcement process begins. Using the interface to the local vehicle registration authority, the toll operator will attempt to find the registered owner of the vehicle that made the trip based on the recorded licence plate string. The owner will then be sent an NATP Invoice. The NAPT Invoice will be for an amount equal to the tolls plus an administration fee. If the owner does not pay within a certain timeframe, a second NATP Invoice will be issued. This second NATP Invoice includes the original toll amount, but with an increased administration fee. If the owner does not pay this NATP Invoice, the matter becomes a civil offence and passes out of the hands of the toll operator and into the realm of the local enforcement authority. The owner becomes subject to a fine, and if the fine is not paid, the whole matter may end up in court.

The enforcement route is a necessary but painful and time consuming process for everybody concerned. Experience shows that the sooner you are able to communicate with your customers and tell them the situation they are in, the better the outcome.

Some jurisdictions place restrictions on what can be enforced. In some cases, even though a vehicle has been spotted on a road four times in one day, the authority will only accept that one offence has been committed and will therefore only enforce one trip.

Debt Collection

The enforcement process cannot be relied upon to recover all the money owed due to NATP trips. Those trips that cannot be enforced still represent money owed to the toll road operator. Operators will use a variety of techniques to try and recover this debt, including the outsourcing of collection services to professional debt recovery organisations.

Vehicle Database

Lastly we come to the Vehicle Database. This is probably not a feature you will see explicitly addressed in most current tolling systems, but I'm using it as a place holder to remind us that we must be constantly thinking about future-proofing these systems where possible. Every tolling system has some capability for storing vehicle details, and the relationship between Vehicles and Tags which is fine, but it hardly represents the future we are confronted with. Within a couple of decades the majority of our cars will be wirelessly connected, discrete DSRC or RFID tags will probably be redundant and we may not even need to attach licence plates.

The Vehicle Database is there is make us think about what we really need to know in order to be able to accurately and efficiently charge our customers for the use of the infrastructure. Right now it is a licence plate, a state of registration, a tag ID number, a vehicle class, maybe even a photo or two of the vehicle and the signature of the licence plate. In the future will it be a Vehicle Identification Number (VIN), an IP or MAC address and a LIDAR-derived 3D model from which we determine vehicle class?

The Vehicle Database is there to help us keep track of our customers' vehicles, whatever form they take moving into the future. Its purpose is to make robust the link between what we actually observe on the road to the people that pay the money for using the road.

Road Topology

In the context of this book I can't explain why toll roads end up where they do and the reasons behind their final configuration. That is a matter for Governments, Financiers, Architects and Civil Engineers. But I can explain some of the implications of toll road design. The industry describes a toll road as being "open" or "closed" or some combination of the two. The easiest way of understanding this is to consider figure 7 below:

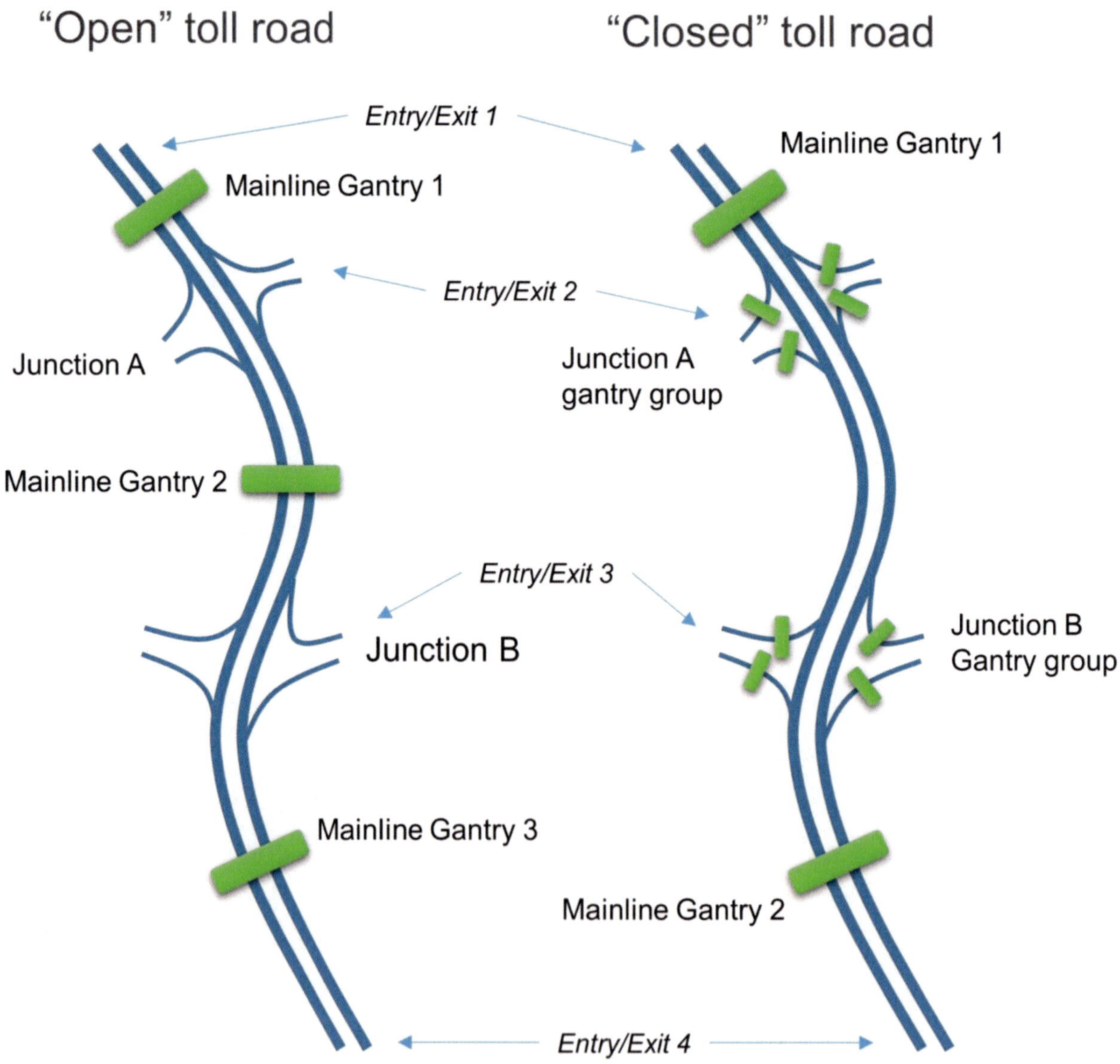

Figure 7 – Differences between open and closed toll roads

In figure 7 the road configuration is the same in both cases, but the gantry locations are quite different. The road has four entry and exit points which are identified in the diagram. These entry and exit points create three "zones" where a zone is defined as the stretch of road between an entry point and the nearest exit point. It is usually the case that a toll road operator would want to charge for every zone travelled by a vehicle, and so would position a tolling gantry (the green rectangle) in each of the zones – thus making them "toll zones". This is the basic principle behind the "open" toll road – a road divided into zones based on entry and exit points, each zone having a tolling gantry that is able to detect the vehicles using that zone. It is important to note that for this to work the road has to be designed to make it physically difficult to avoid driving under a gantry – it's no good if a vehicle can simply drive around a gantry.

Figure 8 below shows a mainline gantry on the Tullamarine Freeway section of Melbourne's CityLink. Note that the concrete barriers make it impossible to avoid travelling under the gantry.

Figure 8 - Toll gantries on the Tullamarine Freeway section of Melbourne's CityLink – by Marcus Wong

The "closed" toll road takes a different approach and focusses on the entry and exit points rather than the zones. The tolling gantries are positioned to detect exactly where a vehicle entered the road and where it left. Figure 9 shows one of the junctions of the 407 ETR toll road in Canada. If you follow the on and off ramps you will notice that each one has a two gantry set, allowing the tolling system to detect vehicles entering and exiting the road.

Both open and closed systems are valid and in use today in Australia and around the world. Both have their advantages and disadvantages.

Figure 9 - Highway 407 and Derry Road, facing southwest - By SimonP

Closed toll road

Reconstructing a trip for a closed toll road should be a simple affair – the system has to find the vehicle's entry point and then look for that vehicle again when it leaves. It's never more than two roadside detection events that have to be married up to create the trip and thus the toll charge. But what happens if the system gets the entry transaction, but then never sees the exit transaction? Or the other way round? Perhaps a tag is working intermittently, or equipment on a gantry has failed. Usually the road's concession deed would only allow the operator to charge the toll relevant for the entry or exit toll zone – the tolls associated with travel in any other zones are effectively lost. So closed toll road trip reconstruction is potentially simpler than that for open, but carries that extra risk that a lost detection event can be a significant loss of revenue for that trip.

Then there is the scenario where the exit detection event turns up 36 hours after the entry detection event, which leads to the interesting question of "how much time do you allow a vehicle to complete a trip?" If you know speed limits and distances between entry and exit points it's fairly straightforward to estimate reasonable amounts of time required to complete trips. The tolling system does need some "allowable time" parameter just so that it can close off uncompleted trips and pass them on to customers.

Open toll road

With the open toll road, it is necessary to define what you actually mean by a trip. As discussed previously, with reference to figure 7, a vehicle could enter the road at Mainline Gantry 1, nick off at Junction A, get back on the road at Junction B and exit again at Mainline Gantry 3. This is easy for the closed toll road – that is two distinct trips – two sets of entry and exit detection events. For the open toll road the system may be left wondering "what happened to the detection event at Mainline Gantry 2?" and "should I treat that as one trip or two?" EastLink answers these questions by defining what a trip means to them. This is taken from EastLink.com.au:

> An EastLink 'trip' is defined as a single trip on EastLink in one direction only.
>
> You can exit and re-enter EastLink in the same trip, provided you keep going in the same direction, don't repeat any section, and complete your trip within 60 minutes. A return trip equals two EastLink trips.

So our example counts as a single trip if the two trips are completed within an hour. This flexibility makes trip reconstruction more complex because the system is looking for an unknown number of detection events to match up and those events aren't necessarily sequential – there may be gaps. On the other hand the nature of the data makes the trip reconstruction process more robust in terms of protecting revenue i.e. one lost detection event doesn't automatically mean a significant loss of revenue for that trip.

Other considerations

Another consideration when thinking about the differences between open and closed tolling configurations is the amount of hardware you need out on the road. The open road in figure 7 would result in six significant gantry structures – three mainline gantries for each direction of travel. The closed road in figure 7 would result in 12 gantry structures, four mainline and then eight on the entry and exit points, the road on/off ramps. The ramp gantries will be smaller structures because a ramp is normally one or two lanes wide at most but still, the closed configuration does result in significantly more structures. These structures need power and communication connections, and ongoing maintenance. The gantry structures themselves however only represent part of the cost of the roadside equipment. The cameras, sensor equipment and associated wiring often drive the cost. Depending on the number of lanes on the road, and assuming that a camera-sensor unit is required for each lane, the difference in the amount of equipment needed for open and closed roads is usually not that great.

Aside from the gantry based equipment, some real estate is needed for technical shelters to house the remaining equipment, and then all of this has to be safely accessible by the people who maintain it. These considerations go into the mix when designing the configuration of a road.

Trip and toll tables

One of the things every toll road has to do is work out, based on the configuration of their road, the set of possible or valid trips that vehicles can make. To make this exercise a bit more interesting, I have created the mythical but magnificent "Peninsula Freeway" as shown in figure 10.

The Peninsula Freeway connects Frankston in the north to Flinders in the south and winds its way through the beautiful east coast of the Mornington Peninsula in Victoria, Australia. The road connects Frankston and Flinders to seven other towns along its route. The towns are listed in the middle of the diagram. The first thing to note though is that not all those towns are equally served by the freeway. At Tyabb it is only possible to join the road and head north, while the opposite is true for Point Leo.

The schematic to the left in figure 10 is the open tolling configuration. The schematic to the right is the closed tolling configuration. The topology of the road results in eight tolling zones.

Using figure 10 it is possible to draw up a number of tables indicating the valid trips vehicles can complete. Tables 3 and 4 are for the open configuration, northbound and southbound. Tables 5 and 6 are for the closed configuration, northbound and southbound (driving Australian style on the left hand side of the road). By looking at these tables you should get a sense of the trip patterns that the different configurations create:

- In both cases, the limited access at Point Leo and Tyabb create "gaps" in the trip combinations,
- The closed configuration trips are quite consistent with two gantry detection events per trip,
- The open configuration trips have a variable number of gantry detection events depending on the length of the trip.

Having established the set of valid trips, the next thing to do is work out the toll charges associated with each. These would be determined long before the road was even built as they are driven by the traffic model and business case, and ultimately set out in the concession deed.

Before we go there though, take a moment to study figure 10 and the trip tables derived from it.

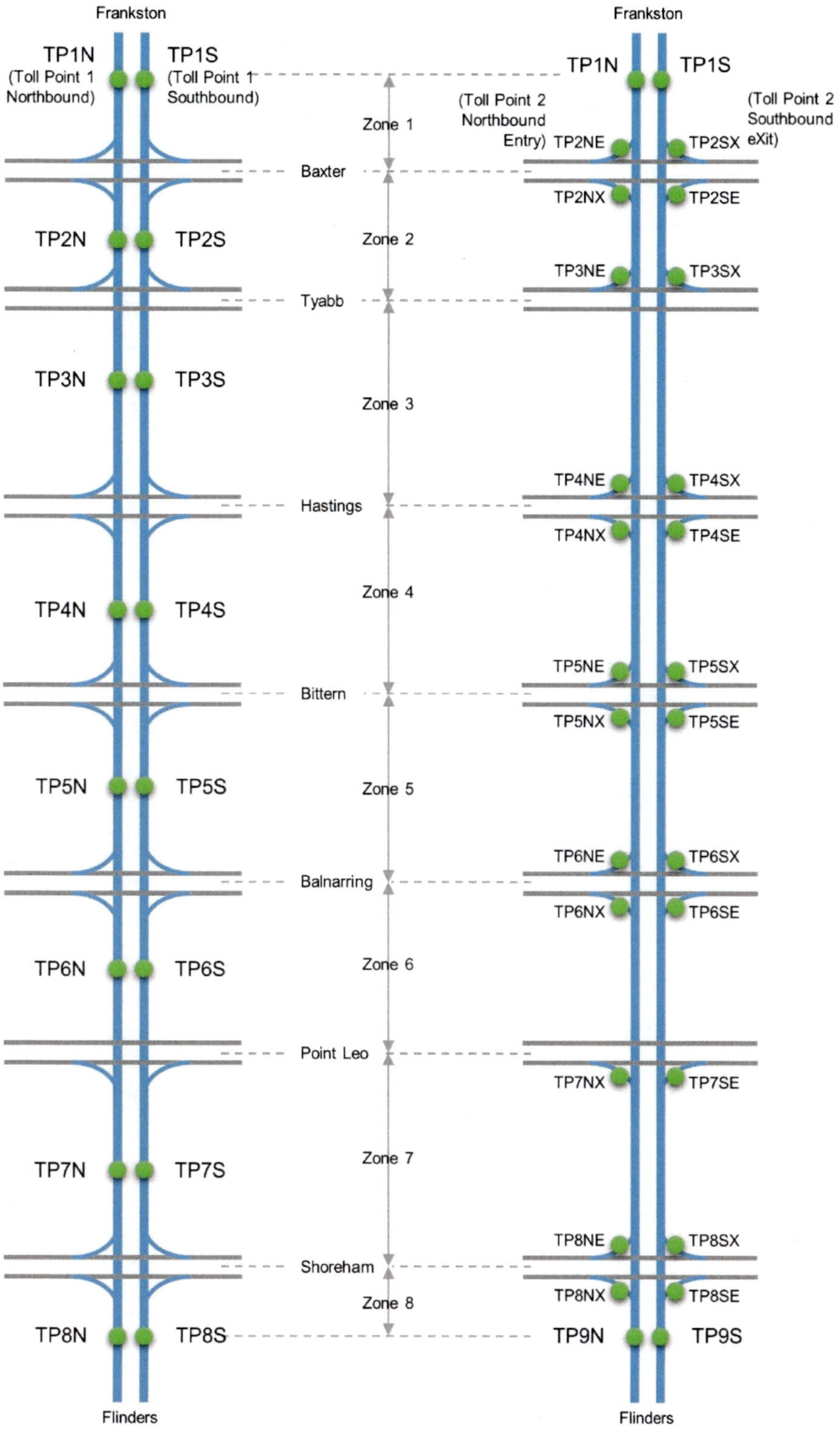

Figure 10 – The Peninsula Freeway

From → / To ↓	Frankston	Baxter	Tyabb	Hastings	Bittern	Balnarring	Point Leo	Shoreham	Flinders
Frankston									
Baxter	TP1S								
Tyabb	TP1S TP2S	TP2S							
Hastings	TP1S TP2S TP3S	TP2S TP3S							
Bittern	TP1S TP2S TP3S TP4S	TP2S TP3S TP4S		TP4S					
Balnarring	TP1S TP2S TP3S TP4S TP5S	TP2S TP3S TP4S TP5S		TP4S TP5S	TP5S				
Point Leo									
Shoreham	TP1S TP2S TP3S TP4S TP5S TP6S TP7S	TP2S TP3S TP4S TP5S TP6S TP7S		TP4S TP5S TP6S TP7S	TP5S TP6S TP7S	TP6S TP7S	TP7S		
Flinders	TP1S TP2S TP3S TP4S TP5S TP6S TP7S TP8S	TP2S TP3S TP4S TP5S TP6S TP7S TP8S		TP4S TP5S TP6S TP7S TP8S	TP5S TP6S TP7S TP8S	TP6S TP7S TP8S	TP7S TP8S	TP8S	

Table 3 – "Peninsula Freeway" as an open toll road, possible southbound trip (gantry passage) combinations

From → To ↓	Flinders	Shoreham	Point Leo	Balnarring	Bittern	Hastings	Tyabb	Baxter	Frankston
Flinders									
Shoreham	TP8N								
Point Leo	TP8N TP7N	TP7N							
Balnarring	TP8N TP7N TP6N	TP7N TP6N							
Bittern	TP8N TP7N TP6N TP5N	TP7N TP6N TP5N		TP5N					
Hastings	TP8N TP7N TP6N TP5N TP4N	TP7N TP6N TP5N TP4N		TP5N TP4N	TP4N				
Tyabb									
Baxter	TP8N TP7N TP6N TP5N TP4N TP3N TP2N	TP7N TP6N TP5N TP4N TP3N TP2N		TP5N TP4N TP3N TP2N	TP4N TP3N TP2N	TP3N TP2N	TP2N		
Frankston	TP8N TP7N TP6N TP5N TP4N TP3N TP2N TP1N	TP7N TP6N TP5N TP4N TP3N TP2N TP1N		TP5N TP4N TP3N TP2N TP1N	TP4N TP3N TP2N TP1N	TP3N TP2N TP1N	TP2N TP1N	TP1N	

Table 4 – "Peninsula Freeway" as an open toll road, possible northbound trip (gantry passage) combinations

From → / To ↓	Frankston	Baxter	Tyabb	Hastings	Bittern	Balnarring	Point Leo	Shoreham	Flinders
Frankston									
Baxter	TP1S TP2SX								
Tyabb	TP1S TP3SX	TP2SE TP3SX							
Hastings	TP1S TP4SX	TP2SE TP4SX							
Bittern	TP1S TP5SX	TP2SE TP5SX		TP4SE TP5SX					
Balnarring	TP1S TP6SX	TP2SE TP6SX		TP4SE TP6SX	TP5SE TP6SX				
Point Leo									
Shoreham	TP1S TP8SX	TP2SE TP8SX		TP4SE TP8SX	TP5SE TP8SX	TP6SE TP8SX	TP7SE TP8SX		
Flinders	TP1S TP9S	TP2SE TP9S		TP4SE TP9S	TP5SE TP9S	TP6SE TP9S	TP7SE TP9S	TP8SE TP9S	

Table 5 – "Peninsula Freeway" as a closed toll road, possible southbound trip (gantry passage) combinations

From → To ↓	Flinders	Shoreham	Point Leo	Balnarring	Bittern	Hastings	Tyabb	Baxter	Frankston
Flinders									
Shoreham	TP9N TP8NX								
Point Leo	TP9N TP7NX	TP8NE TP7NX							
Balnarring	TP9N TP6NX	TP8NE TP6NX							
Bittern	TP9N TP5NX	TP8NE TP5NX		TP6NE TP5NX					
Hastings	TP9N TP4NX	TP8NE TP4NX		TP6NE TP4NX	TP5NE TP4NX				
Tyabb									
Baxter	TP9N TP2NX	TP8NE TP2NX		TP6NE TP2NX	TP5NE TP2NX	TP4NE TP2NX	TP3NE TP2NX		
Frankston	TP9N TP1N	TP8NE TP1N		TP6NE TP1N	TP5NE TP1N	TP4NE TP1N	TP3NE TP1N	TP2NE TP1N	

Table 6 – "Peninsula Freeway" as a closed toll road, possible northbound trip (gantry passage) combinations

Table 7 below identifies the Peninsula Freeway toll zones, their distances in kilometres and a basic toll value. For the purposes of this example I've assigned basic toll values on a "price per kilometre" basis – essentially 10 cents for every (rounded up) kilometre of the zone. The WestLink M7 road in Sydney is a "per kilometre" based toll. Other roads will price their zones in accordance with traffic models and the business case, and will sometimes reflect the cost of building the zone in the zone toll price. For example, at the time of writing, for a car to use the EastLink tunnel costs $2.77, whereas the next section only costs 41 cents. Similarly the CityLink tunnel costs $5.34, while most other sections on CityLink are in the $2 to $3 range. Tunnels cost a lot more to build than regular roads.

Start and end locations	Frankston	Baxter	Tyabb	Hastings	Bittern	Balnarring	Point Leo	Shoreham	Flinders
Frankston		Zone 1 5.1 km BT 50c							
Baxter	Zone 1 5.1 km BT 50c		Zone 2 8.4 km BT 80c						
Tyabb		Zone 2 8.4 km BT 80c		Zone 3 5.7 km BT 60c					
Hastings			Zone 3 5.7 km BT 60c		Zone 4 4.5 km BT 50c				
Bittern				Zone 4 4.5 km BT 50c		Zone 5 7.1 km BT 70c			
Balnarring					Zone 5 7.1 km BT 70c		Zone 6 8.6 km BT 90c		
Point Leo						Zone 6 8.6 km BT 90c		Zone 7 5.6 km BT 60c	
Shoreham							Zone 7 5.6 km BT 60c		Zone 8 7.2 km BT 70c
Flinders								Zone 8 7.2 km BT 70c	

Table 7 – "Peninsula Freeway" toll zone identifications with distances and basic toll prices

I've made reference here to a "basic toll" because as we know, the actual toll price charged can vary depending on:

- The class of the vehicle travelling,
- Time of day,
- Day of week,
- The existence of a "toll cap", and
- Schemes designed to maintain certain levels of traffic flow.

To get a feel for the difference that vehicle class can make to toll prices, Table 8 shows the cost of trip and day passes on EastLink and CityLink for the four available vehicle classes, and then determines the "class multiplier" based on those prices.

	Motorcycle	Car	Light commercial	Heavy Commercial
CityLink 24 Hour Pass	$8.75	$17.51	$37.97	$70.74
EastLink Trip Pass	$3.07	$6.13	$9.80	$16.24
CityLink "multiplier"	0.5	1	2.2	4
EastLink "multiplier"	0.5	1	1.6	2.65

Table 8 – CityLink and EastLink vehicle class "multipliers" based on the cost of their pass products (as of Feb 2018).

In table 8 you can see for example that on CityLink a heavy commercial vehicle attracts a toll that is four times that charged for a car. A good example of variable distance based tolling is Taiwan's toll road network. The price varies depending on the distance you travel as shown in figure 11.

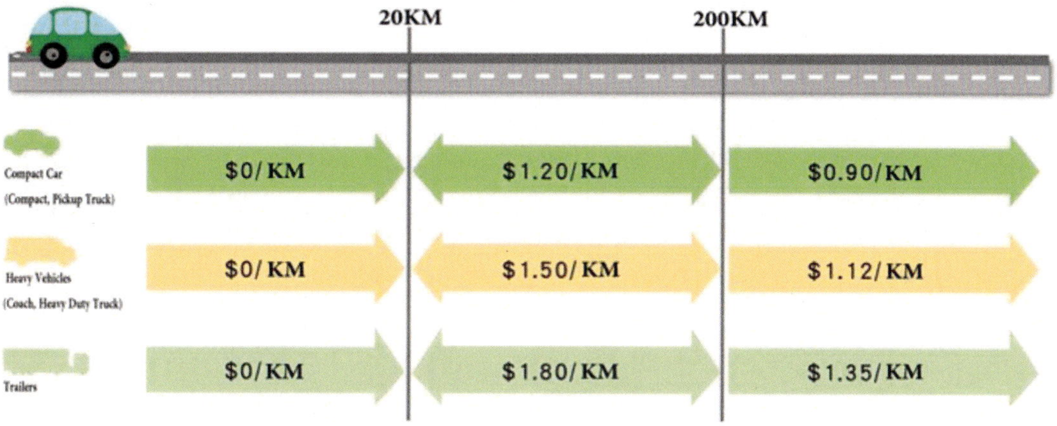

Figure 11 – Taiwan toll road network pricing scheme

The Sydney Harbour Bridge and Tunnel operated by RMS have time of day and day of week toll price variations. Motorists pay the highest toll during the peak morning and afternoon traffic periods during the week, and the lowest toll through the evening and night at the weekend.

The Canadian 407 ETR goes further and combines three vehicle classes with per kilometre pricing that changes depending on which of seven time of day and day of week periods you happen to travel in.

For the sake of the Peninsula Freeway example I won't complicate things with time of day discounts and will use a simple multiplier set of 0.5, 1, 1.6 and 2. This results in a toll table as shown in Table 9.

From → To ↓	Frankston	Baxter	Tyabb	Hastings	Bittern	Balnarring	Point Leo	Shoreham	Flinders
Frankston		MC: $0.25 Car: $0.50 LCV: $0.8 HCV: $1.00	MC: $0.65 Car: $1.30 LCV: $2.08 HCV:$2.60	MC: 0.95 Car: $1.90 LCV: $3.04 HCV:$3.80	MC: $1.20 Car: $2.40 LCV: $3.84 HCV:$4.80	MC: $1.55 Car: $3.10 LCV: $4.96 HCV:$6.20		MC: $2.30 Car: $4.60 LCV: $7.36 HCV:$9.20	MC: $2.65 Car: $5.30 LCV: $8.48 HCV:$10.60
Baxter	MC: $0.25 Car: $0.50 LCV: $0.8 HCV: $1.00		MC: $0.40 Car: $0.80 LCV: $1.28 HCV:$1.60	MC: $0.70 Car: $1.40 LCV: $2.24 HCV:$2.80	MC: $0.95 Car: $1.90 LCV: $3.04 HCV:$3.80	MC: $1.30 Car: $2.60 LCV: $4.16 HCV:$5.20		MC: $2.05 Car: $4.10 LCV: $6.56 HCV:$8.20	MC: $2.40 Car: $4.80 LCV: $7.68 HCV:$9.60
Tyabb	MC: $0.65 Car: $1.30 LCV: $2.08 HCV:$2.60	MC: $0.40 Car: $0.80 LCV: $1.28 HCV:$1.60							
Hastings	MC: 0.95 Car: $1.90 LCV: $3.04 HCV:$3.80	MC: $0.70 Car: $1.40 LCV: $2.24 HCV:$2.80			MC: $0.25 Car: $0.50 LCV: $0.80 HCV:$1.00	MC: $0.60 Car: $1.20 LCV: $1.92 HCV:$2.40		MC: $1.35 Car: $2.70 LCV: $4.32 HCV:$5.40	MC: $1.70 Car: $3.40 LCV: $5.44 HCV:$6.80
Bittern	MC: $1.20 Car: $2.40 LCV: $3.84 HCV:$4.80	MC: $0.95 Car: $1.90 LCV: $3.04 HCV:$3.80		MC: $0.25 Car: $0.50 LCV: $0.80 HCV:$1.00		MC: $0.35 Car: $0.70 LCV: $1.12 HCV:$1.40		MC: $1.10 Car: $2.20 LCV: $3.52 HCV:$4.40	MC: $1.45 Car: $2.90 LCV: $4.64 HCV:$5.80
Balnarring	MC: $1.55 Car: $3.10 LCV: $4.96 HCV:$6.20	MC: $1.30 Car: $2.60 LCV: $4.16 HCV:$5.20		MC: $0.60 Car: $1.20 LCV: $1.92 HCV:$2.40	MC: $0.35 Car: $0.70 LCV: $1.12 HCV:$1.40			MC: $0.75 Car: $1.50 LCV: $2.40 HCV:$3.00	MC: $1.10 Car: $2.20 LCV: $3.52 HCV:$4.40
Point Leo								MC: $0.30 Car: $0.60 LCV: $0.96 HCV:$1.20	MC: $0.65 Car: $1.30 LCV: $2.08 HCV:$2.60
Shoreham	MC: $2.30 Car: $4.60 LCV: $7.36 HCV:$9.20	MC: $2.05 Car: $4.10 LCV: $6.56 HCV:$8.20		MC: $1.35 Car: $2.70 LCV: $4.32 HCV:$5.40	MC: $1.10 Car: $2.20 LCV: $3.52 HCV:$4.40	MC: $0.75 Car: $1.50 LCV: $2.40 HCV:$3.00	MC: $0.30 Car: $0.60 LCV: $0.96 HCV:$1.20		MC: 0.35 Car: $0.70 LCV: $1.12 HCV:$1.40
Flinders	MC: $2.65 Car: $5.30 LCV: $8.48 HCV:$10.60	MC: $2.40 Car: $4.80 LCV: $7.68 HCV:$9.60		MC: $1.70 Car: $3.40 LCV: $5.44 HCV:$6.80	MC: $1.45 Car: $2.90 LCV: $4.64 HCV:$5.80	MC: $1.10 Car: $2.20 LCV: $3.52 HCV:$4.40	MC: $0.65 Car: $1.30 LCV: $2.08 HCV:$2.60	MC: 0.35 Car: $0.70 LCV: $1.12 HCV:$1.40	

Table 9 – "Peninsula Freeway" toll table.

The toll table is created by:

- Taking the basic toll values for each of the toll zones (Table 7), then
- Summing them to determine the basic trip toll based on the toll zones covered by the trip (Tables 3 to 6), then
- Using the multiplier set (0.5, 1, 1.6 and 2) to determine final trip tolls for each of the vehicle classes.

Simple really. If a road does have time of day or day of week variable pricing, then it's a good idea to have a separate table for each time zone. If you are a Microsoft Excel Wizard, developing toll tables will provide you with hours of entertainment. You can lose yourself in pivot tables, and VLOOKUPs and write macros to do "what if" calculations. The possibilities are endless.

It's time to apply a toll cap. The toll cap effectively represents a discount to customers who make long trips along the road. In practise what it says to customers is "Once your toll for a trip reaches the toll cap value, you won't be charged anymore". It sets an upper limit on the toll for any given trip. The actual value of a toll cap will be determined by the business case and the traffic model. The value of a toll cap often drives the cost of a casual user toll product such as a trip pass and vice versa. If a road is offering a trip pass:

- It's not fair that a regular account customer ends up paying more for a trip than a casual user, so the toll cap and the trip pass price are often set at the same value,
- A casual user may buy a trip pass for a trip that, with a regular account, would cost less than the trip pass cost. Fair enough you say, get a proper account, but giving that casual user a discount on the price of a full trip shows some goodwill.

For my toll table I've set the toll cap price for a car at $4.00, and then used the multiplier set to work out the toll cap for the other vehicle classes. Applying the toll cap to the trip tolls results in Table 10.

From → To ↓	Frankston	Baxter	Tyabb	Hastings	Bittern	Balnarring	Point Leo	Shoreham	Flinders
Frankston		MC: $0.25 Car: $0.50 LCV: $0.8 HCV: $1.00	MC: $0.65 Car: $1.30 LCV: $2.08 HCV:$2.60	MC: 0.95 Car: $1.90 LCV: $3.04 HCV:$3.80	MC: $1.20 Car: $2.40 LCV: $3.84 HCV:$4.80	MC: $1.55 Car: $3.10 LCV: $4.96 HCV:$6.20		MC: $2.00 Car: $4.00 LCV: $6.40 HCV:$8.00	MC: $2.00 Car: $4.00 LCV: $6.40 HCV:$8.00
Baxter	MC: $0.25 Car: $0.50 LCV: $0.8 HCV: $1.00		MC: $0.40 Car: $0.80 LCV: $1.28 HCV:$1.60	MC: $0.70 Car: $1.40 LCV: $2.24 HCV:$2.80	MC: $0.95 Car: $1.90 LCV: $3.04 HCV:$3.80	MC: $1.30 Car: $2.60 LCV: $4.16 HCV:$5.20		MC: $2.00 Car: $4.00 LCV: $6.40 HCV:$8.00	MC: $2.00 Car: $4.00 LCV: $6.40 HCV:$8.00
Tyabb	MC: $0.65 Car: $1.30 LCV: $2.08 HCV:$2.60	MC: $0.40 Car: $0.80 LCV: $1.28 HCV:$1.60							
Hastings	MC: 0.95 Car: $1.90 LCV: $3.04 HCV:$3.80	MC: $0.70 Car: $1.40 LCV: $2.24 HCV:$2.80			MC: $0.25 Car: $0.50 LCV: $0.80 HCV:$1.00	MC: $0.60 Car: $1.20 LCV: $1.92 HCV:$2.40		MC: $1.35 Car: $2.70 LCV: $4.32 HCV:$5.40	MC: $1.70 Car: $3.40 LCV: $5.44 HCV:$6.80
Bittern	MC: $1.20 Car: $2.40 LCV: $3.84 HCV:$4.80	MC: $0.95 Car: $1.90 LCV: $3.04 HCV:$3.80		MC: $0.25 Car: $0.50 LCV: $0.80 HCV:$1.00		MC: $0.35 Car: $0.70 LCV: $1.12 HCV:$1.40		MC: $1.10 Car: $2.20 LCV: $3.52 HCV:$4.40	MC: $1.45 Car: $2.90 LCV: $4.64 HCV:$5.80
Balnarring	MC: $1.55 Car: $3.10 LCV: $4.96 HCV:$6.20	MC: $1.30 Car: $2.60 LCV: $4.16 HCV:$5.20		MC: $0.60 Car: $1.20 LCV: $1.92 HCV:$2.40	MC: $0.35 Car: $0.70 LCV: $1.12 HCV:$1.40			MC: $0.75 Car: $1.50 LCV: $2.40 HCV:$3.00	MC: $1.10 Car: $2.20 LCV: $3.52 HCV:$4.40
Point Leo								MC: $0.30 Car: $0.60 LCV: $0.96 HCV:$1.20	MC: $0.65 Car: $1.30 LCV: $2.08 HCV:$2.60
Shoreham	MC: $2.00 Car: $4.00 LCV: $6.40 HCV:$8.00	MC: $2.00 Car: $4.00 LCV: $6.40 HCV:$8.00		MC: $1.35 Car: $2.70 LCV: $4.32 HCV:$5.40	MC: $1.10 Car: $2.20 LCV: $3.52 HCV:$4.40	MC: $0.75 Car: $1.50 LCV: $2.40 HCV:$3.00	MC: $0.30 Car: $0.60 LCV: $0.96 HCV:$1.20		MC: 0.35 Car: $0.70 LCV: $1.12 HCV:$1.40
Flinders	MC: $2.00 Car: $4.00 LCV: $6.40 HCV:$8.00	MC: $2.00 Car: $4.00 LCV: $6.40 HCV:$8.00		MC: $1.70 Car: $3.40 LCV: $5.44 HCV:$6.80	MC: $1.45 Car: $2.90 LCV: $4.64 HCV:$5.80	MC: $1.10 Car: $2.20 LCV: $3.52 HCV:$4.40	MC: $0.65 Car: $1.30 LCV: $2.08 HCV:$2.60	MC: 0.35 Car: $0.70 LCV: $1.12 HCV:$1.40	

Table 10 – "Peninsula Freeway" toll table, with the toll caps applied

As we'll see later, this toll calculation function is the role of your tolling system's Trip Reconstruction and Trip Rating components – taking roadside transactions, reconstructing trips and then coming up with toll charges that match your toll tables. Further, given that most toll road operators do not have a lot of exciting material to play with on their customer facing websites, having a super swish toll calculator – with cute user interaction features – has to be a must. It sounds obvious but just make sure what it tells your customers matches the output from your tolling system and your own toll tables taking taxes (like GST in Australia) into account. Figure 12 below is a screen grab from the magnificent multi-toll road toll calculator by RMS featuring the toll roads around Sydney, Australia.

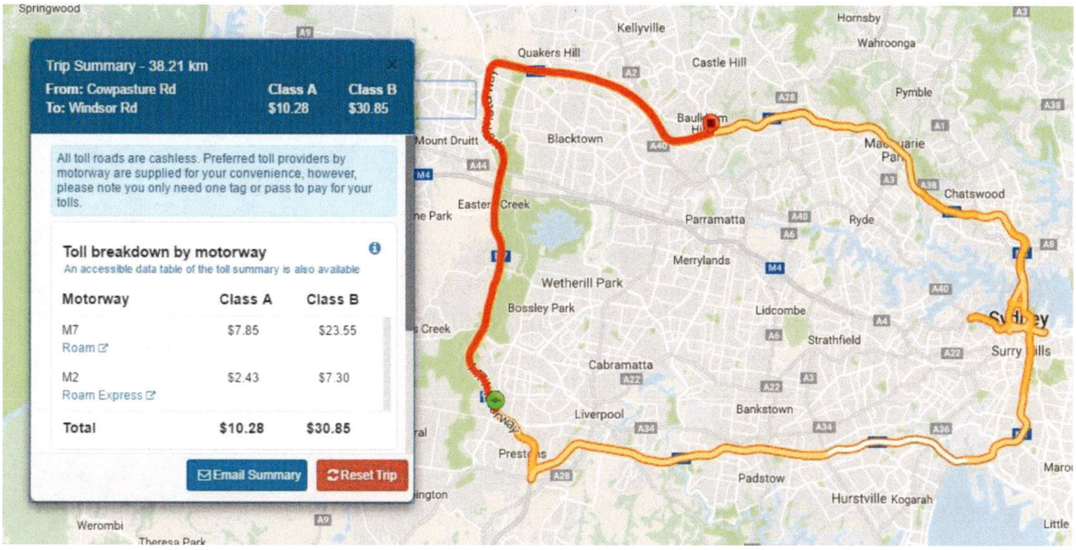

Figure 12 – A web based toll calculator from RMS.

If you want to take defining your road topology to the next level you can consider using directed graphs. See Appendix A for some ideas in this area.

Vehicle Classifications

Vehicle classification is very important because, as we've just seen, it drives the rate at which you can toll vehicles using your toll road – but at the same time the rules which you have to apply can drive you quite mad. By way of introduction, let's have a look at the vehicle classification rules that apply in the State of Victoria, Australia.

One place where vehicle classes are defined is within Schedule 4 – the Toll Calculation Schedule – of the Mitcham-Frankston Freeway concession deed. With some editing (for simplicity's sake) the classes are defined as:

- LCV - Light Commercial Vehicles have two axles, cab-chassis construction, and a gross vehicle mass greater than 1.5 tonnes but not exceeding 4.5 tonnes.
- HCV - Heavy Commercial Vehicles include all of the following vehicles:
  - Vehicles with three or more axles, cab-chassis construction, and a gross vehicle mass greater than 1.5 tonnes;
  - Articulated Vehicles with cab-chassis construction, and a gross vehicle mass greater than 1.5 tonnes;
  - Buses with more than 12 seating positions (including the driver);
  - Vehicles with two axles, cab-chassis construction, and a gross vehicle mass greater than 4.5 tonnes; and
  - All other vehicles with a gross vehicle mass greater than 30 tonnes.
- Motorcycles (no tag required) are two wheeled motor vehicles (including those with side cars).
- Taxis are motor vehicles licensed for operation as a taxi-cab under the Transport Act 1983 (Vic).
- CAR - Cars are motor vehicles other than those that comply with the motorcycle, light commercial vehicle, heavy commercial vehicle or taxi classifications. Cars include those Cars towing trailers and caravans.

  A Bus with less than 12 seating positions is classed as a Car.

Exempt vehicles can be any of the above and are another matter entirely.

Well, that is all very clear. But it actually throws up some interesting outcomes, as shown by figure 13 below.

The fact that the Mercedes Sprinter Extralong with Super high roof is a monocoque and not a cab chassis construction means that, despite being a true behemoth of the road, it is still technically a car for tolling purposes. Similarly the Holden Ute is a car, but the Ford Falcon Ute, which is a cab chassis construction, falls into the Light Commercial Vehicle class and thus attracts a more expensive tolling class.

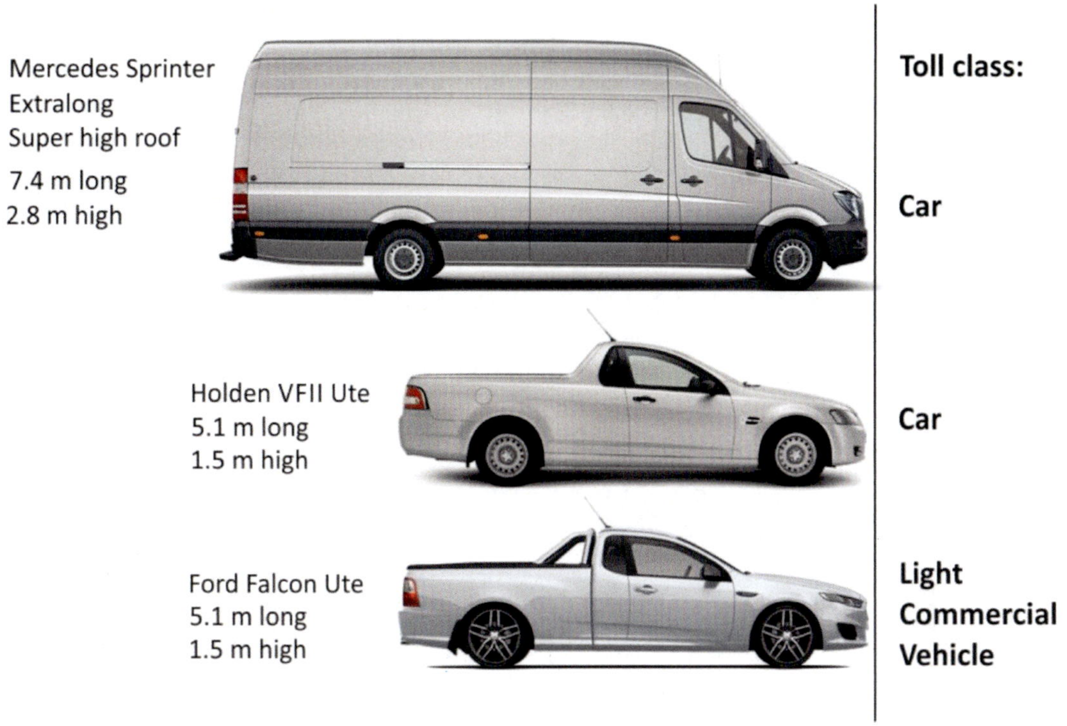

Figure 13 – Tolling class rule outcomes

This results in two things:

- A lot of very annoyed Ford Falcon Ute drivers – especially if their best drinking buddies all have Holdens. Be prepared to field a few spirited phone calls about that one.
- Havoc when it comes to deciding the true tolling class of a vehicle based on physical vehicle dimensions alone. Basically you can't do it, which has serious implications for your roadside detection equipment.

A note about Utes and Australia: Ute is an Australian abbreviation for utility vehicle. Way back in the day, Australian farmers wanted a vehicle that could move sheep around during the week, and was still decent enough to use to drive the wife to church on Sunday. Utes are a much loved part of Australian life. You can even go to "Ute musters". Holden is the Australian brand of General Motors and, like Ford, for many years manufactured some quite unique vehicles for the Australian market. Recently all that came to end as all the big car manufacturers ceased production in Australia. That doesn't stop an ongoing rivalry that culminates in the V8 Supercar racing series – you're either a Holden or Ford fanatic. There is very little room in the middle.

To make it simple, surely all our Australian interoperable toll road partners follow the same vehicle classification rules don't they? Nothing could be further from the truth.

In New South Wales (NSW), every toll road has a classification system[7] that is kind of the same but different and nothing like the Victorian scheme. Table 11 elaborates.

Toll road	Class A	Class B
M5 South-West Motorway	A three axle vehicle under 2.0 metres in height or a two axle vehicle under 2.8 metres in height	Any vehicle that exceeds the dimensions for a Class A vehicle
Eastern Distributor	A three axle vehicle under 2.0 metres in height or a two axle vehicle under 2.8 metres in height	Any vehicle that exceeds the dimensions for a Class A vehicle
Hills M2 Motorway	A vehicle that is: 12.5 metres or less in length; and 2.8 metres or less in height	Any vehicle that exceeds the dimensions for a Class A vehicle
Cross City Tunnel	A vehicle that is: 12.5 metres or less in length; and 2.8 metres or less in height	Any vehicle that exceeds the dimensions for a Class A vehicle
Lane Cove Tunnel	A vehicle that is: 12.5 metres or less in length; and 2.8 metres or less in height	Any vehicle that exceeds the dimensions for a Class A vehicle
Westlink M7 Motorway	A vehicle that is: 12.5 metres or less in length; and 2.8 metres or less in height	Any vehicle that exceeds the dimensions for a Class A vehicle

Table 11 – Vehicle tolling classification on NSW toll roads

Queensland[8] has a scheme which is like Victoria but slightly different again and shown in table 12 below. To add to the fun, Queensland introduces the concept of a vehicle "registered for commercial use". This implies that you can have Utes that are private cars and the same type of Utes that are LCVs. Just by looking at them you would never know, so you have to pay a look-up fee to the Queensland Government to find out. What might be described as a "nice little earner".

Class 1	Class 2	Class 3	Class 4

Motorcycles Two wheeled motor vehicles (including vehicles with a trailer, fore car or side car attached).	Cars Four-wheeled motor vehicles, including taxis which are not commercial vehicles (including vehicles towing a trailer or caravan).	Light commercial vehicles Motor vehicles that are registered for commercial use and: (a) are two-axle rigid trucks or load carrying vans or utilities, having a gross vehicle mass greater than 1.5 tonnes but not exceeding 4.5 tonnes or (b) have spatial dimensions which are substantially consistent with the criteria in paragraph (a) above	Heavy commercial vehicles Motor vehicles that: (a) are rigid trucks with 3 or more axles (b) are articulated trucks (c) are buses (d) are two axle rigid trucks having a gross vehicle mass greater than 4.5 tonnes (e) are motor vehicles having a gross vehicle mass greater than 30 tonnes, or (f) have spatial dimensions which are substantially consistent with the criteria in any of paragraphs (a) to (e) above.

Table 12 – Queensland's govia toll vehicle classifications

But we shouldn't panic. At some point in time, somewhere in a public service office far, far away this all made sense. All that matters is that when a vehicle travels on *your* toll road, the tolling system works out the correct class for that vehicle according to *your* rules and charges the appropriate amount. Simple. Except it's not.

> A Sydney toll road may issue the equivalent of a car tag to a class A vehicle that then travels on a Victorian toll road. Under the Victorian scheme the vehicle is actually an LCV but we charge car prices because of the class of the tag. Strictly speaking the Victorian road loses money on the deal.
>
> A Ford Ute driver realises that if he gets a car tag, the roadside equipment on his Victorian toll road isn't sensitive enough to tell the difference between his Ute and every other Holden Ute on

the road. He gets car prices which, by the way, he feels is natural justice, and again the Victorian road loses money.

The driver of a Mercedes Sprinter Extralong Super high roof just accepts now that every time she uses the toll road she is going to get charged at HCV rates. After all it is a big van, and the roadside detection equipment also thinks it's a big thing and registers it that way. But the truth is she is being over charged every time and deserves some money refunded.

The reason why we are interested in vehicle class is to ensure that we charge the right toll amount and maximise our toll revenue, while not incorrectly charging our customers. Remember those KPIs about tolling accuracy? So what sources of class information do we have available? There are several.

Customer supplied information

When a customer wants to open a tolling account, a toll road operator will ask them for the licence plate strings and other details of the vehicles to be included on the account. There are commercial organisations that for a fee, will provide vehicle make, model and class information, and keep this data up to date as new vehicles are released into the market. This can be a useful service for a toll road operator as it provides a consistent reference source of data to check a make and model and derive the appropriate class. A Customer Service Operator (CSO), when opening an account for a customer over the phone, can check the make and model against the reference data and determine the right class of vehicle to apply to the account.

This concept can also be applied when a customer is using a website or App to open their account. The website won't expect the customer to work out the vehicle class, but just supply the make and model information. The system will do the rest.

There are some scenarios however that do require a customer to directly select a class. The most common is when they are buying a trip pass at a retail outlet that is effectively off-line from the tolling system.

Class measured by the roadside

As we've seen the roadside equipment includes a vehicle scanning system. This uses technology to both detect vehicles and measure their physical dimensions.

Based on the measured physical dimensions, the roadside equipment will derive a vehicle class. This class is determined by comparing the measured vehicle dimensions against the dimensions for each vehicle class stored at the roadside.

In the Victorian context, the roadside can determine between Motorcycles, Cars/LCVs and HCVs with a good degree of confidence. However it struggles to accurately determine the difference between Cars and LCVs because, as has been outlined above, the difference between these two classes is not a simple matter of a difference in size. And that Sprinter Extralong is just out there.

Consequently information from the roadside can only be used as a guide to vehicle class.

Class measured by image processing

The data provided by the roadside OCR engines, when combined with the business rules in Trip Reconstruction and the second central OCR engines mean that the tolling system should be able to automatically read over 90% of the licence plates presented in roadside images. When a licence plate and registration details are determined automatically, the class assigned to the vehicle is usually based on the class detected by the roadside or the customer supplied class for that licence plate, because that is the information available in the tolling system.

When a licence plate string cannot be automatically determined, the image is forwarded to a Human Image Processor for review. The role of that person is to record through a special image processing interface the licence plate string, state of registration and class of the vehicle in the image. The issue here is that Image Processors have to assess their images quickly and accurately in terms of licence plate and registration details. Often vehicle class becomes a secondary consideration that takes additional handling time and also relies on the Image Processor knowing the vehicle class rules, the accurate application of which can be problematic given the time pressure they are under.

Information from other toll roads

Information on vehicle class also comes in to the tolling system from other toll road operators via the interoperability interface. If they have comparable systems, then all the problems relating to vehicle class being experienced by your road will be the same for them. Let's examine some of these problems.

Vehicle class problems

To be fair to the travelling public, most people, most of the time are honest about what they're doing and pay their bills on time. A tolling system, on the one hand, is a serious business system responsible for the accurate collection of millions of dollars of revenue every day. On the other hand it's like a giant technology driven social experiment with hundreds of moving parts, thousands of inputs that change constantly – new vehicles appearing as old ones disappear - and is subject to some weird behaviours exhibited by its customer base. Its users learn its behaviour from each other. For example, it doesn't take long for people to realise:

- They can register their Toyota Hilux cab chassis (LCV) as a Toyota Corolla (Car) on the website simply by playing with the make and model options. That's great because Car tolls are a lot less that LCVs – and nothing seems to happen to them because the roadside equipment can't really detect the difference.
- They can move tags between vehicles. I can put my Car tag in the Isuzu truck and it still seems to work, and I pay less. This is brilliant!
- And then there is the "Hey Barnie! What happens if I hold the tag out of the window when we go under the gantry?" – but let's not go there.

So regardless of who tells us anything including the tag read, we need a way of accurately determining the class of the vehicle at the time of travel.

Enter the Vehicle Identification Number (VIN). Every car since the late 1980s has been given a 17 digit alphanumeric VIN which follows an international standard. It is possible to decode a VIN and find out where and when the vehicle was made, but more crucially in this case the very specific details about the vehicle's model and body type. In short, being able to decode a VIN lets a tolling company work out the true class for tolling purposes.

The next step then is to find an organisation that keeps track of the licence plates issued to specific vehicles and thus the licence plate issued for a specific VIN. In Victoria it turns out this is exactly what the Government agency VicRoads does when vehicles are registered, and they have become willing to share this information for a fee with the toll road companies.

So in this tolling system architecture, I am recommending that we make full use of that VIN data and take a brute force approach to determining vehicle class. In essence that we:

- Take pictures of every vehicle using the road,
- Use our image processing technology to derive a licence plate string and registration details,
- Match our licence plate data to a VIN,
- Decode the VIN to get the true vehicle class and then toll appropriately.

Later I'll refer to this as my "Class Model". As we'll see it isn't quite that simple, but the basic premise is sound. One of the first problems is decoding the VIN. Although it is a standard, within that standard the manufacturers have some licence to use character combinations of their own design to represent data. Thus to decode a VIN you have to be aware of all those designs. If you are willing to put in the research it is possible to build your own application to do this. Alternatively you can buy a service from a company that has already done it such as IHS Automotive. Buying a service is going to get expensive if you decide to decode every VIN and you don't really have to. The data from the vehicle registration authority should come with some basic make and model information, and you can use this to get selective about the VINs you send for decoding.

In the State of Victoria, Australia, the problematic vehicles are those that are caught up in the Car – LCV conundrum. But not all car manufacturers are problematic. If a customer registers a Jaguar, there is a very slim chance that it is anything but a car. Jaguar have been known to make the occasional Shooting Brake, but they still don't fit the criteria for LCV. Similarly for Aston Martin, Porsche, Ferrari, Lexus, Tesla, Citroen and Volvo. Toyota, Ford, Nissan and Volkswagen, to name a few, are a lot more interesting because they produce models of very similar sizes but different configurations which fall into the Car – LCV conundrum. So you limit your need for VIN decoding to certain vehicle makes.

The other thing to be aware of with VINs is that the first 12 digits are all you need to identify the make, model, body type and thus the class. The remaining digits are there to identify a unique vehicle. Paying close attention to those first 12 digits, and putting them in a suitable place for future reference can be a very valuable thing to do.

This all sounds very bothersome and difficult. Do I really need to do it? Well, for your own benefit do a data analysis exercise to see if you are losing revenue through the incorrect application of vehicle class – or regularly over charging certain customers. The truth will lie in the business case.

Tolling Interoperability

The great thing about misguided self-interest combined with a lack of foresight is that it leads people, who in every other way may appear intelligent, to do really silly things. But we mustn't be too harsh a judge of history with the glorious benefit of hindsight. The following is taken from the Australian Government infrastructure history website[9].

> By Federation in 1901, all States except Western Australia were 'linked' by rail and more than 20,000 km of track had been laid. Sadly, those who envisaged a nation had not contemplated a national rail network. Three different gauges had been used.
>
> New South Wales adopted the European standard gauge of 1435 mm, Victoria and South Australia built with the broad Irish gauge of 1600 mm, and Tasmania, Queensland, Western Australia and parts of South Australia used the narrow 1067 mm gauge. For many years, the different gauges handicapped the effective operation of interstate rail services.
>
> In 1917, a person wanting to travel from Perth to Brisbane on an east-west crossing of the continent had to change trains six times.

I think it is very impressive that by 1917 you could cross the continent at all. It's huge! The process of standardising Australia's interstate track to a standard 1435 mm gauge commenced in the 1930s, and was only completed in 1995! This throws into sharp relief just what a massive achievement it was for Sir Tim Berners-Lee to get up one standard for the World Wide Web. Just imagine if we had to switch web browser applications to access different websites. In Australia we can claim a similar, if not quite as significant an achievement when it comes to toll road interoperability.

Toll roads in Australia go back many years with a history that spans the available technology of the time, including coins "into the bucket", payment cards and then the "eTag". The story of toll road interoperability starts in 2001 with the Sydney toll roads coming together to develop an interoperable eTag standard for New South Wales. The original parties included the NSW Government Department (now Roads and Maritime Services) which owns the Sydney Harbour Bridge and Tunnel, and the Macquarie owned roads – M2, M4, M5 and the Eastern Distributor. Together they created the interoperability Memorandum of Understanding (MoU) which laid the foundations for true toll road interoperability – and I for one are very glad they did.

By 2003 the MoU was a fully-fledged committee with monthly meetings. It was initially NSW centric in its discussions but in 2003 Transurban with CityLink weighed into the deal and it has grown ever since to cover every toll road in Australia.

Why is this important? If we didn't have the MoU and interoperability the average motorist in Sydney would probably be driving around with three tags stuck to their windscreen, have to manage three separate toll road accounts and the whole thing would be a nightmare for everybody. At every level, interoperability is a really good thing. It is interesting to note however that from being something toll road operators wanted to do, it is now something new operators have to do by way of their concession deed obligations.

That's not to say there aren't problems. The principles laid down in 2001 are still very sound but the technological ideas driving their implementation are way overdue for reform. In this section we'll look at the way Australian interoperability works now, and then examine how it could be made better – and some of the problems associated with those "better" ideas.

For interoperability to work, all the toll road operators have to agree on two basic things:

- That they are all going to use the same tag technology, and
- They are all going to agree on the way to share arrangement to pay and trip data.

The tag technology is very important. If operators use different standards then you end up with the rail gauge problem. Australia produced AS 4962(INT)-2001 "Electronic toll collection - Transaction specification for Australian interoperability on the DSRC link" amongst others. These were based on the similar European standards of the time. In practice what AS 4962 does is to specify:

- The frequencies that tags and tag readers should use,
- The communication and security protocols, and
- The message structures.

Tag equipment manufacturers wishing to sell into Australia have to be able to show compliance with this standard.

Under the MoU, every toll road operator is also given a "concession identification number" which uniquely identifies them, is embedded as part of the data within the tags they issue and is used to identify where trips made using those tags should be charged back to. An example of these concession or issuer IDs is given in table 13 below. These are allocated by and agreed upon by the MoU committee.

Issuer ID	Allocation to Tollways
060	Melbourne Citylink
076	EastLink
100	SHB & SHT
101	M1 Eastern Distributor
102	M2 Hills Motorway
104	M4 Western Motorway
105	M5 South West Motorway
107	Westlink M7 Motorway
108	Cross City Tunnel
109	Lane Cove Tunnel / Falcon Street Gateway

Table 13 – Toll road concession or issuer IDs

Now that we've got the roadside bit sorted out, the next challenge is the data exchange. The MoU has an Appendix C. This document – "TOLLROAD OWNERS MEMORANDUM OF UNDERSTANDING FOR ELECTRONIC TOLL COLLECTION - APPENDIX C: DATA TRANSFER AGREEMENT" defines itself as:

> The format to be used for the transfer of data between Operators will be in accordance with the following file formats. These formats make reference to, but are not in conformance with Australian Standard AS 4588 – 1999 "Automatic fee collection – Interface specification for clearing between operators."

There is another one of those standards – AS4588, and the MoU Committee have decided not to conform to it. That is fair enough, just so long as everybody is conforming to Appendix C. Appendix C goes on to describe some twenty different file formats covering arrangement to pay, trip and trip dispute data. We won't cover all of those formats here because some relate to the specific enforcement process that operates in NSW. Figure 14 below shows the main file formats of interest.

Within the Australian industry people refer to these files using their "F" file numbers. If you are going to be working in the interoperability space it really helps to learn the "F numbers".

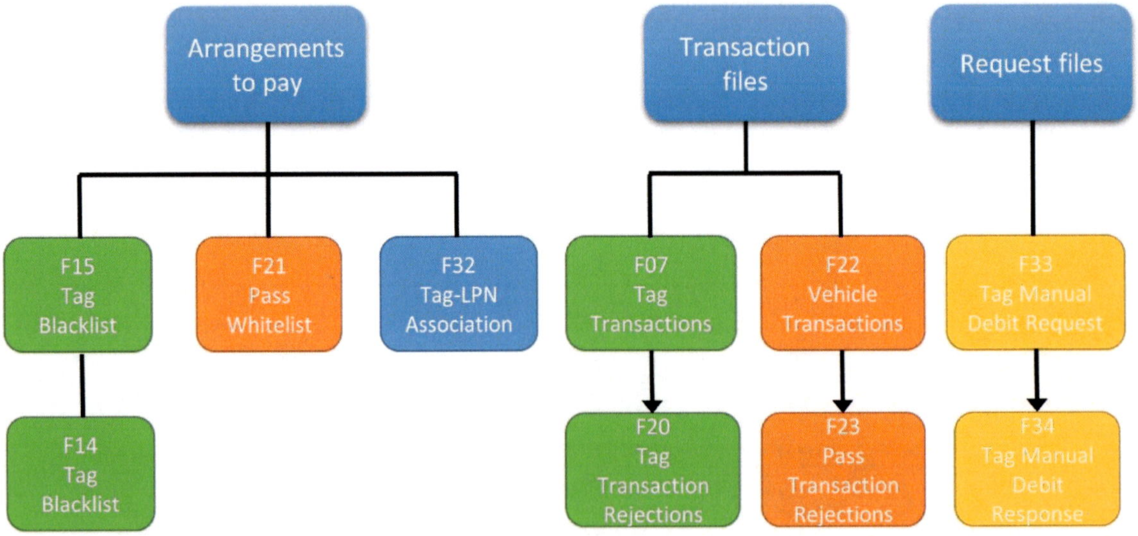

Figure 14 – Main interoperability file formats

File distribution

Files have to be created, shared between operators, and processed in accordance with a schedule. This part of the process is dictated by the MoU.

As a consequence of history – the NSW origins – the NSW Government Roads and Maritime Services (RMS) operates "The RMS Hub". This is an sftp server which all of the MoU parties can access. Every day they upload files to and download files from the Hub

Every MoU member uploads the F07, F20, F22, F23, F33 and F34 to the Hub starting from 10 am each day. At 11 am they start downloading those same files from the other operators, and start processing the files in their tolling systems.

A similar process starts at 4 pm for the F14, F15, F21 and F32 – an upload to the Hub, and then the downloading starts at 5 pm.

Note however that not every operator uploads and downloads all the files for every other operator. What actually gets produced and used depends on the specific roaming agreements the operators have with each other. This is discussed later.

The Interoperability process works every day for millions of toll road customers across Australia. But as we will see later, when we get in to the contents of each of these files, not everything goes right 100% of the time. That is because it is a batch process that takes a tolling system time to work through. The operators' tolling systems may start generating these files several hours before they have to be uploaded. Processing the files that are subsequently downloaded again can take several hours.

Time again becomes an important factor because of the grace period, that three days allowed for people to make an arrangement to pay. This implies that the arrangement to pay data for interoperability purposes also has to be back dated for three days. The F15, F14, F21 and F32 are not that crash hot at the whole "back dating" concept, so tolling systems use other business rules to try and iron out the wrinkles. It's this timeliness, time shifting and the batch processing nature of the operation that can result in a few problems.

Arrangement to pay files

There are four main files in this group:

F15 (and F14) – the principal purpose of this file is to be that tag blacklist mentioned earlier. The message to other tollways is – "yes this is our tag and our customer, but we no longer have a valid arrangement to pay with them, we won't be paying for their travel on your road, so do what you must."

A tag usually ends up in the F15 file when the customer has an account that has been suspended for some reason, although there are other reasons listed below. An operator seeing a blacklisted tag in the F15 file would set their roadside equipment to take a picture of the vehicle carrying the tag, get the licence plate string and then go down their own enforcement processes.

To give you a sense of MoU Appendix C, the following text is how it describes the format of the F15 and F14 file:

6.1 Header Record

The first record in the Data Transfer File shall be a Header Record with the following format.

Starting Position	Field Length	Field Type	Description
1	1	a	Record Type = “H” for Header
2	3	n	Sender ID
5	3	n	Receiver ID (eg: 000 for Broadcast Blacklist)
8	2	n	Message Type = “14/15” for Blacklist Data
10	4	n	Message ID
14	8	n	Reference Date
22	8	n	Reference Time

6.2 Tag Blacklist Record

The blacklist records, which constitute all the records in the file except for the Header and Trailer Records, shall have the following Format:

Starting Position	Field Length	Field Type	Description
1	1	a	Record type = “D” for Detail
2	10	n	Contract Serial No.
12	3	n	Home Operator ID
15	1	a	Blacklist Reason Code (refer to Section 25.9)

6.3 Trailer Record

The last record in the Data Transfer File shall be a Trailer Record with the following Format:

Starting Position	Field Length	Field Type	Description
1	1	a	Record Type = “T” for Trailer
2	3	n	Sender ID
5	3	n	Receiver ID (eg: 000 for Broadcast Blacklist)
8	2	n	Message Type = “14/15” for Blacklist Data
10	4	n	Message ID
14	8	n	Reference Date
22	8	n	Reference Time
30	6	n	No. of Detail Records in File

6.4 File Naming Convention

The file naming convention for the Data File shall be as follows:

AAABBBCCDDDD.TXT

AAA	Sender ID	Issuer sending the file
BBB	Receiver ID	Motorway Operator to receive the file
CC	Message Type	"14/15" for Tag Blacklist Data File
DDDD	Message ID	Message ID (refer to Section 25.7)

You may have spotted that there is a reference to Section 25.9. The "Blacklist Reason" codes given in this section are as follows:

L	=	Lost
S	=	Stolen
D	=	Delinquent
A	=	Address Required
C	=	Closed
T	=	Terminated
W	=	Warning of low account balance

Note that in the header section of the file there is a field for "Receiver ID". This is analogous with the concession ID, so if I was producing a file for CityLink, I would identify that file by inserting 060 in that field. Similarly I would put my own ID in the previous field. I won't share with you all the file formats in Appendix C. I'll let you discover the joys of that document for yourself.

The F15 and F14 files are identical save for the fact that the F14 doesn't carry the "W" code, which lets toll operators know if a tag belongs to an account which is in a low balance state. Whether an operator uses the F14 or F15 file is a choice and really comes down to how often they see each other's customers. In Melbourne it makes sense for CityLink and EastLink to share the F15 file (with account low balance information) because a lot of their customers regularly use both roads. It becomes less useful for CityLink to share the F15 with a Queensland motorway. On a daily basis both roads would only see a handful of each other's account holders and they can avoid the processing overhead of all those low balance account tags.

F21 – the principal purpose of this file is to be that licence plate whitelist mentioned earlier. The message to other tollways is – "yes, this licence plate string belongs to one of our customers, and they do have a valid arrangement to pay with us, so we will be paying for their travel on your road."

The F21 file comes into own for people with tolling accounts that are video based i.e. no tags, all tolling is done by recognising their licence plate string. This includes the idea of "pass accounts" where a customer has set up a temporary arrangement to pay for tolls.

Whereas at the time of writing all toll roads in Australia are genuinely tag interoperable, not all are licence plate interoperable. Different arrangements exist between different operators in different states.

F32 – it can be argued that the F32 file is not strictly an arrangements to pay file because all of that information is covered by the F15 and F21 files, but it is still very useful nonetheless. It contains all the relationships between tags, licence plates and accounts for tag based accounts. So if a tag fails to work for whatever reason, and you do get a licence plate string which isn't in the F21 file, you can check the F32 file using the logic in table 14 below.

> Find the account number associated with that licence plate string,
>
> Find the tags associated with that account number,
>
> Check whether those tags are in the F15 file,
>
> If they are *not* in the F15 file then,
>
> > The licence plate is associated with an account that does have an arrangement to pay, (but the tag didn't work or wasn't in the vehicle) so charge the trip to the operator who owns the account. Curiously the trip ends up in the F33 file – see below.
>
> Else if they are in the F15 file then,
>
> > The licence plate is most probably associated with a no arrangement to pay situation, and you can take the appropriate enforcement action. Note, strictly speaking we shouldn't be here. Tags should not be in the F15 and F32 files at the same time.

Table 14 – Basic logic for using the F32 interoperability file

There are two points to note about the F32 file:

- If an account doesn't have an arrangement to pay, do you take it out of the F32 file altogether? The answer is yes. If there is no arrangement to pay then the tags should end up in the F14/F15 file, and the licence plates won't appear in the F21 file, so any trips should go down the enforcement process. In that scenario you shouldn't find the licence plate in the F32. You should be using the latest information from the F32 file, but there is no harm in keeping history data of interoperable account movements from previous files so you get a sense of what those customers are doing.
- By sharing an F32 file, an operator is sharing a view into their entire account customer database. In practice this isn't really a problem. An operator's primary concern is collecting toll revenue from users. Anything that assists in that process is usually good for business.

Transaction files

There are four main files in this group:

F07 – when an operator generates this file and sends it to you, it contains all the tag based trips made by your account holders on their road. When you generate this file it contains all the trips made on your road by the account holders of another operator. The trips are identified by the concession ID that is part of the Tag Passage. Before putting a trip into an F07 file you have to check that the tag ID is **not** in the F14 or F15 file i.e. blacklisted from relevant operator. If it is then you have to assume that the tag has no valid arrangement to pay and has to be treated as a NATP trip.

F22 – the F22 file is very similar to the F07 but contains trips made by customers with video accounts. The trips are based on the observed licence plate string and registration details, and crucially that licence plate-registration combination **must be present** in a valid F21 file for the trip to make it into an F22 file. If the licence plate-registration combination cannot be located in any operator's F21 file then the assumption is that vehicle has no valid arrangement to pay and has to be treated as a NATP trip – given that you've done the F32 check described in table 14 above.

F20 and F23 – these files are used to indicate that a trip will not be accepted by an operator. Your tolling system may have created a tag or video trip and with the information available at the time through the F15 and F21 files, decided that the associated arrangement to pay was valid and so added the trip to the relevant F07 or F22 file. The other operator has received and analysed the file, and for whatever reason decided that the arrangement to pay was not valid and so sent you the trip back in an F20 or F23 file. Two questions follow:

- What do we do with the trip now?
- Why did the trip come back to us?

In reality the number of trips that get rejected in this way is very small. Each trip might have a value that ranges between 50 cents to a few dollars. How much time and therefore money do you want to spend analysing a trip like that to find out who is in the right? As an operator you can:

- Get into an argument with the other operator about their decision,
- Just the write the trip off and forego the revenue,
- Send the trip down the enforcement path and see what happens.

What you actually do at that point is really a business decision. You always have to balance maximising toll revenue coming in against the cost of collecting that toll revenue.

Thinking about "Why did the trip come back to us?" – different circumstances produce different outcomes, but in most cases these situations arise because of the timelines issues mentioned previously. In the time it takes to create (and stuff around back-dating things), send and then process F15 and F21 files it is conceivable that the "arrangement to pay" status of some accounts has changed, and thus some valid or chargeable trips are eventually deemed not to be. Similarly during that same period, vehicles and tags can be linked to and un-linked from accounts and the tolling systems themselves are not infallible when it comes to reading tags and licence plates.

There are two things to note here:

- There is no "Tolling for Windows". Every tolling system is different and works in a slightly different manner. There are rules within the MoU about most aspects of the process, but those rules can be implemented in ways which lead to interesting outcomes.
- Tolling systems, in terms of their accuracy, are as good as banking systems (or certainly should be), but even banking systems are not infallible. The crucial thing is to ensure that your tolling system's audit capabilities are such that an error can be found and corrected in good time.

Request files

There are two main files in this group:

F33 – the Tag Manual Debit Request file. This file is useful in several situations. It allows operators to resolve situations that fall outside the normal arrangement to pay and trip reporting functions. The principal benefit of this file is that it lets operators associate a fee along with the trip. This is why trips made by customers with tag accounts held by other operators, where the tag was not detected, end up in this file – because an image processing (or video matching) fee can be associated with the trip. Similarly, if you were to a receive a toll invoice from an operator, but have an account with another operator, the value of that toll invoice – trips plus fees – can be transferred to your account via the F33. The F33 allows an operator to specify both why the trip and fee are included in the file, and what the fees represent.

F34 – the F34 file serves much the same purpose as the F20 and F23 in that it informs those manual debit requests that have been accepted and those that have been rejected. And much like the F20 and F23, what an operator does with the rejections becomes a business decision.

In addition, Appendix C still makes reference to an F35 and F36 file:

- **F35 –** Pass Manual debit request, and
- **F36 –** Pass Manual Debit Response.

These are not used any more. Everything that needs to be done can be achieved using the F33 and F34.

Interoperability invoice and roaming fee

The interoperability files deal with arrangements to pay and trips, but it is the Interoperability Invoice, known locally as the *daily notice*, which sorts out all the money. An Interoperability Invoice is an invoice that one operator sends to another to request payment for those trips made on their road by the operator's customers. It is based on the contents of the F07 and F22 files, and has to take in to account all the rejections within the F20, F23 and F34 files. Every day across Australia all the MoU operators exchange their Interoperability Invoices to make real in money terms all the transactions on the road.

The other thing that the Interoperability Invoice contains are details of the roaming fees. The best way to think about a roaming fee is to imagine that it is an "account keeping fee". It goes something like this – "Yes, my customer did travel on your road, so we need to pay you the toll, BUT we should get some financial recognition for maintaining their account – so we're going to hang on to a bit of that toll". Roaming fees are negotiated individually between operators and are typically either a flat fee of around 20 cents, or a combination of a flat fee and a small percentage of the trip value. The roaming fees are written down in a roaming agreement between two operators. It is also in this roaming agreement that the operators decide whether they want to be licence plate interoperable in addition to tags.

Roaming fees and competition

As I mentioned before, toll roads rarely compete directly with each other because more often than not they are geographically separated and serve different travel routes. But if two toll roads are in an interoperability group, there is the notion of competition. Imagine this scenario: There are two toll roads in your city – DriveHard and TransportFuture. You have an account with DriveHard, use their road on a regular basis but they have outsourced their customer service centre to Buwapbackistax. Now every time you phone up you have no idea what anybody is saying to you, and can never get anything done. Plus DriveHard seem to charge "a little bit extra" for everything, including paper statements and additional tag holders. But the DriveHard road and TransportFuture's road are interoperable. Although you never use TransportFuture, you can have a working account with them, and their fees and charges seem to be a bit more reasonable. So you close your DriveHard account and open a new one with TransportFuture. The tolls you pay won't change, but you feel better with the customer service. At that level there is a sense of competition between toll road operators.

The brutal question is "does TransportFuture want you as a customer"? Do they want any customers at all? What value do customers have in the context of an interoperability group?

What I mean by this is:

- Is it better for TransportFuture to pay the roaming fee to somebody else and get rid of all those costs associated with servicing customers?
- Does TransportFuture earn any extra revenue by having the relationship with customers? Does its concession deed allow it to make money from its customers from fees, charges and other services?

In truth, if you're the first toll road in your city or county you have to have a customer service function. It's unlikely anybody will do it for you, unless you have a Department of Transport (DOT) with big plans. You have to get those accounts opened, register vehicles and issue tags. But if you're the third toll road coming in to an established market with an interoperability agreement, then maybe you don't. But you do the sums and think on this – how would you stop your interoperability partners arbitrarily doubling their roaming fee?

Roaming fees make interoperability work

In practical terms the roaming fee represents a financial incentive to make the whole interoperability system work. It is problems in this area of cost and incentive that, in part, appear to be holding back other interoperability schemes around the world. Certainly in Europe the EU mandated that toll roads should be interoperable in 2009 with the system up and running by 2014. That just hasn't happened in the way they wanted it to[10] partly I understand because their financial model isn't working well for them. Making interoperability work means either charging customers more or foregoing toll revenue to pay for the interoperability service. In established toll markets without interoperability that transition can be difficult. You would need to be convinced that interoperability would bring significant benefits in other areas, most noticeably an uplift in toll revenue.

But if not the EU, then over in France they do seem to have got their act together. France has over nine thousand kilometres of tolled autoroute which is run by twenty two companies[11]. For all the time I can remember to use the Péage you had to stop at a toll booth. This was always a great experience. Being in a right hand drive car (over from the UK) meant there was no way you could reach the toll booth – designed for their left hand drive cars. You would have to stop, get out of the car, go round to the other side and pay at the window. An old woman, a direct descendant of the crones who delighted in the work of Madame Guillotine during the French Revolution would take your money, but only after she had sucked once again on her Gaulois Blonde. Then as you turned to leave you would hear her mutter "stupide" under her nicotine stained breath as she raised the barrier while you were still fighting with your seat belt. Ahh, happy days. But you can't stop progress, and now France has the Liber-t tag system spruiked by Sanef[12] as:

> Liber-t is the French national télépéage scheme for light vehicles operated by the members of ASFA, the association of French motorway operators on behalf of the French government. The scheme operates across the entire autoroute network and a Liber-t tag can even be used to pay for parking at some car parks.

So a good example of a national interoperability scheme, albeit one that is financed by extra service charges. Strictly speaking though I shouldn't be talking about France at all because even with Liber-t their roads are not true multilane free-flow. Liber-t is a restricted entry scheme represented in figure 15.

Figure 15 – Liber-t tag lanes on French Autoroutes

But what can you do? *J'adore la belle France.*

Interoperability implications

Interoperability (the Australian process) is a big deal because it touches just about every part of your tolling system:

- The back office has to keep a detailed audit trail of every account and every trip pass. This means keeping a history of:
    - when tags and vehicles were added to and removed from accounts.
    - when things were reported lost or stolen,
    - all the account status transitions from active to suspended and vice versa.

  A good tolling system should do this anyway, but with interoperability it is especially important to help sort out arrangement to pay issues.

- Trips made by your customers will enter the tolling system as the interoperability files are processed. An operator has very little control over the number of trips coming in for a customer on any given day – it may be none, but for large commercial accounts it may be hundreds. The tolling system has to be able to cope with that processing load and react sensibly to changes in account status – such as low balance – and fire off downstream processes in a controlled way. A good example of a downstream process is an automatic account top-up payment request. Firing off fifteen automatic payment requests in quick succession is not a good look from a customer's point of view.

- The system has to produce and process interoperable files in a timely manner. Everything has to be completed in a twenty four hour cycle. Taking forty eight hours to process a six million line F32 file just doesn't cut it. The download from and upload to the Hub has to occur every day – if there is a problem then you need another process to inform the other operators as to what to expect.
- As well as customer accounts, the tolling system has to manage accounts for the other interoperable operators so that the various trip files can be accurately produced.
- The company's corporate financial system has to be able to take data from and reconcile with interoperable data so that Interoperability Invoices can be produced correctly and the real money reconciled in company bank accounts.
- The company has to have processes and procedures for dealing with rejected trips and manual debit requests.
- The company has to have processes and procedures for installing new operator tag keys in the roadside equipment.
- As an operator you have to be able to explain to your customers what interoperability actually means for them.

There is a lot to think about and a lot to get right. To make for an even richer tapestry, some of your interoperable partners may use the system in unexpected ways. Consider a NATP trip. We could go down the enforcement path or we could just hang on to it for a bit and wait to see if that account comes good again. Surely there is no harm in resubmitting the trip if the account is back in an active status? Would anybody notice? Now of course I couldn't condone any actions that run contrary to the spirit of the MoU agreement; that just wouldn't be right.

In conclusion, figure 16 shows "Big Jag" – a happy toll road customer who is roaming freely across a couple of toll roads. Big Jag gets one statement from the operator who has his account. The diagram gives an indication of all the other transactions that go on to support that process. I've restricted the processes to an ideal case where Big Jag is a good customer who regularly puts money into his tag based account – the diagram does not show all the other things that happen if Big Jag were to end up on a blacklist for example.

Alternative models

Surely in this age of the Internet of Things we can do better than moving around and processing huge flat files that, in terms of arrangements to pay, contain a lot of data we'll never actually use. The answer is almost certainly yes. The technology needed to get computers to talk to each on-line and in real-time is well known and proven, so why don't we get rid of these files and use simple web services instead? With any complex system involving multiple independent parties, standards need to be developed, reviewed, agreed upon and then finally implemented within a timescale everybody can cope with and at a cost everybody is willing to bear. So it will happen, it will just take time to organise and needs a "champion" to emerge to drive it through.

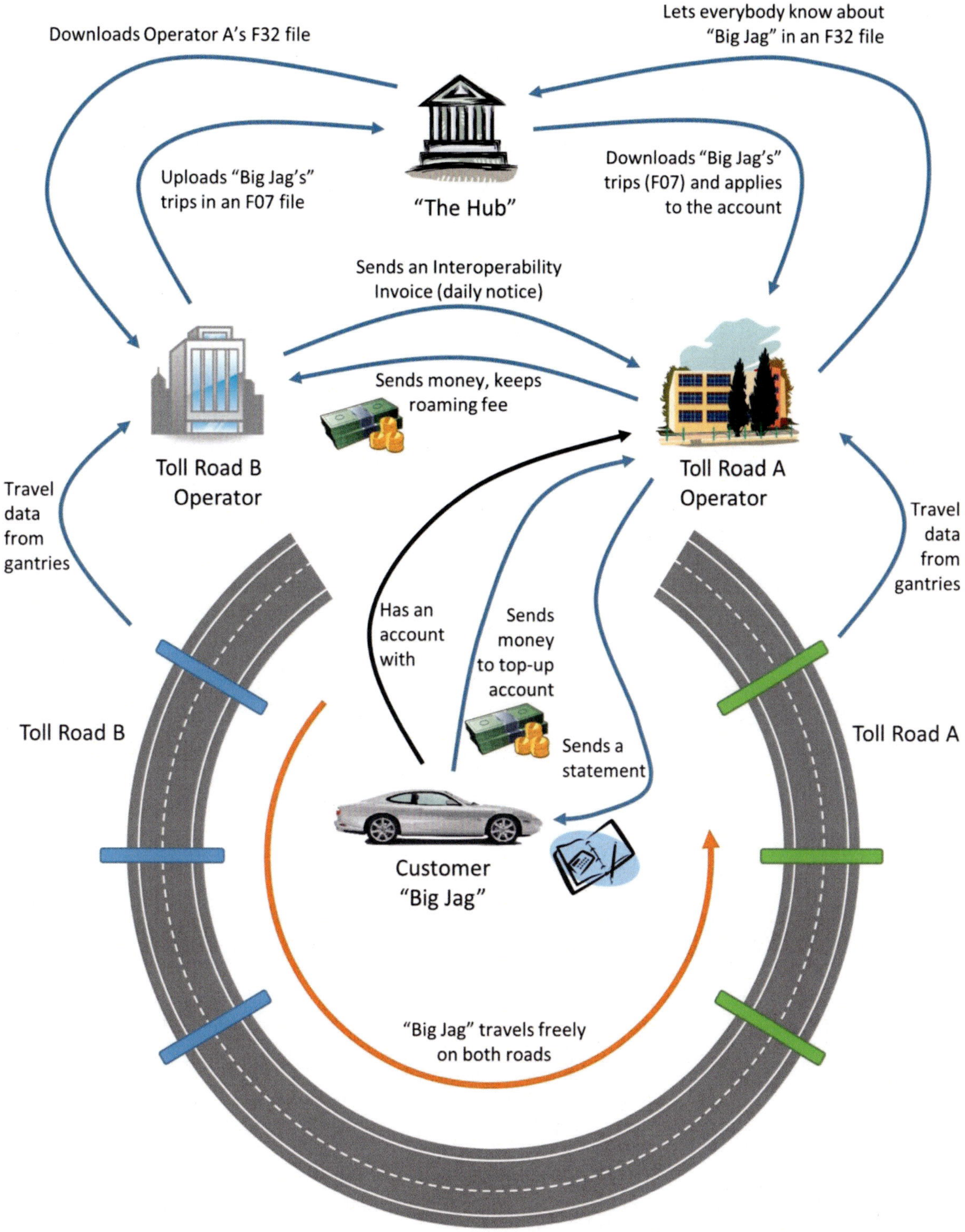

Figure 16 – Big Jag and his interoperability experience

Potential benefits of a more real-time on-line system include:

- Real-time arrangement to pay data – with the aim of minimising those rejections in the F20, F23 and F34 files, and reducing the number of incorrect toll invoices that get issued – removing all the subsequent remedial work they cause.
- Near real-time allocation of trips to accounts owned by other operators to give customers a better indication of their account status on-demand.
- The removal of the need to process data that hasn't changed or relates to customers that are never seen on your road.

If we think about a technology like web services, what we're trying to achieve is the creation of a few simple on-line interfaces that can push out and be interrogated for information. Within this context, there are two possible models:

- Peer to peer, where every toll road operator talks to every other toll road operator, and
- Central clearing house, where all the toll road operators talk to one central place.

In both cases, our requirements for data sharing remain consistent with the requirements that are currently satisfied with the flat files; the need to share arrangement to pay data, to pass over trip details, and some mechanism to handle data inconsistencies.

Peer to peer

For the peer to peer model the basic protocols could look something like this:

Arrangements to pay interactions

For arrangement to pay details, the account owner would assume responsibility for pushing out changes to those details to all the members of the interoperability group:

Toll Operator 1: Initiate: *Yo, fellow tolling system.*

Toll Operator 2: Response1: *What up!*

Toll Operator 1: Response1: *Yo, this tag/[licence plate string and state] is good to travel. I'll honour its trips.*

Alternatively:

Toll Operator 1: Response2: Yo, *this tag/[licence plate string and state] is one bad mother. Bring righteousness down upon it because* [include a reason code].

Toll Operator 2: Response2: *Got it.*

Given that these complex systems have to deal with the random acts of the general population, there will be times when we have to check specific details. This would require a similar interaction but initiated the other way round:

Toll Operator 2: Initiate: *Yo, fellow tolling system.*

Toll Operator 1: Response1: *What up!*

Toll Operator 2: Response1: *What is the current arrangement to pay status for this tag/[licence plate string and state]?*

Toll Operator 1: Response2: *Yo, that tag/[licence plate string and state] is good to travel. I'll honour its trips.*

Alternatively:

Toll Operator 1: Response3: *Yo, that tag/[licence plate string and state] is one bad mother. Bring righteousness down upon it because* [include a reason code].

Alternatively:

Toll Operator 1: Response4: *Yo, you shouldn't be seeing that tag/[licence plate string and state] – its marked as lost/stolen/destroyed. Do what you will.*

Alternatively:

Toll Operator 1: Response5: *Yo, I have no knowledge of that tag/[licence plate string and state] – try somebody else.*

If the first interaction type was working well – the simple push of data out, the second interaction type should be needed only rarely in situations where there is some conflict or confusion in the data. Even then, hopefully the response just confirms a position.

Initiate and then **Response5** for a tag would be unusual if you're sure that you got the concession ID correct. It implies that there is a data error in somebody's system or might indicate fraudulent activity in that tags are out in the open that haven't been registered by an operator i.e. pinched from the warehouse.

Initiate and then **Response5** for a licence plate string and state leads to the NATP Invoice and enforcement process – unless that is, you do want to check with everybody just in case.

Trip interactions

For trip details, the toll road operator (where the trip was made) would assume responsibility for pushing out trip details to the operator that owns the account:

Toll Operator 1: Initiate: *Yo, fellow tolling system.*

Toll Operator 2: Response1: *What up!*

Toll Operator 1: Response1: *Yo, fellow tolling system, here is a trip for this tag/[licence plate string and state].*

Toll Operator 2: Response2: *Yo, thanks, for that tag/[licence plate string and state] all is good. I'll honour that trip and take my roaming fee.*

Things could get a little tricky though:

Toll Operator 1: Initiate: *Yo, fellow tolling system.*

Toll Operator 2: Response1: *What up!*

Toll Operator 1: Response1: *Yo, fellow tolling system, here is a trip for this tag/[licence plate string and state].*

Toll Operator 2: Response 2: *Yo, thanks, for that tag/[licence plate string and state] all is not good. That account is currently suspended.*

Toll Operator 1: Response 2: *Hang on, not two hours ago you said everything was OK with that tag/[licence plate string and State].*

Toll Operator 2: Response 3: *Yes, but two hours ago – that is like so in the past. The situation has changed.*

Toll Operator 1: Response 3: *Now just wait a minute, did you tell me about that change? No! You can't go changing the rules when it suits you ….*

If you're familiar with your Douglas Adams, that exchange could quickly degenerate into the kind of conversation enjoyed by Marvin the Paranoid Android leading to silicon suicide. To spare our systems from that doom, much like we currently have with the flat files today, there would have to be rules, and decent records kept, as to when arrangements to pay were valid and when they weren't.

The transaction interaction would have to be able to deal with timings issues. It may take a tolling system several hours between first seeing the tag or vehicle and then finally sending over the trip. If the trip involves the manual viewing of images the delay in passing over the trip could be a couple of days, and the trip itself may need to be adjusted. None of this is impossible, but just needs careful design.

Then there has to be yet another interaction to replace the F33 and F34 files, although you would hope that if the other interactions were working well and in near real-time, the number of F33-F34 interactions would be minimal. And of course, as soon as we open up on-line interfaces we have to be very mindful of security.

Central clearing house

The Central clearing house model is essentially about replacing the current Hub with a more dynamic and interactive central data repository.

With the Central clearing house model, all the interactions of the peer to peer model would remain, with the big difference being that every toll operator would only need to communicate with the clearing house – rather than with individual operators. The transactions required are those that allow operators to push data to the clearing house which would include:

- Details of new accounts – associated tags, vehicles and account status,
- Details of pass arrangements,
- Account status changes – tags and vehicles associated with accounts that have gone low balance, suspended or closed.
- Lost, stolen and destroyed tags, and stolen vehicles,
- Trips made by tags and vehicles.

The Central clearing house would then assume responsibility for pushing that data out to the relevant operator. This model is attractive because it could be developed to be much more than just a tolling data repository. It could be combined with vehicle classification data and so remove any ambiguities around a vehicle's true class. Further, why not become the national customer centre for tolling across Australia? Do toll road operators actually want to deal with customers anyway? It's not a great leap to go from that to becoming the centre for managing Australian road user charging.

The complication with the Central clearing house model comes down to finance. The existing roaming fee concept isn't really threatened by the peer to peer model, but with the Central clearing house model who pays for what and when? Such a system wouldn't come free, so who owns it and how much does the service cost – and is that in addition to a roaming fee? Does the Central clearing house play a role in the arbitration of arrangement to pay disputes, and is it financially liable for data errors? And we're only going to pay for a service if we have service level agreements, and penalties for non-performance, and ... so it goes on. This is one of those situations where the technology is relatively straightforward, but the corporate and organizational aspects may be quite complex.

Finally many thanks to the Australian Tollroad Owners MOU Group for the use of their standards. Given what we now know about vehicle classifications and interoperability, I'll leave you with a question. Can a customer living in one state of Australia reduce the amount they pay in tolls by opening an account with a toll road operator in another state?

Toll Products and Casual Users

Toll products are about as exciting as a gas bill, or that bill you got from the dentist for the root canal you really didn't want. In the general taxonomy of exciting things, toll products come under the heading of "Others", right at the bottom. But that said, for a toll road operator they are a *very important thing* because they are the vehicle we use to collect the money. So we have to talk about them – at some length.

Some people do get excited about toll products, but usually they are paid to do it, have a scary look in their eyes and stand too close to you at toll road conferences. They enthuse about the toll product innovations that they have just introduced – which usually amounts to an increase in the lease fee based on the colour of the tag you ordered, or they are developing the killer "tolling app". But hey, there is a place in the Universe for everyone and if it gets their kids through school, so be it. I've just given up going to toll road conferences.

Think about this. There are a huge number of free roads in the world. Roads where you don't have to worry about a "toll product". Who cares! I can just drive. Then there is your toll road which has all this weird stuff associated with it. All these rules about tags, and registering licence plates and "what happens if I don't pay"! And then I have to think about your time of day charging, and things are cheaper when there is a full moon and meanwhile your Chairman just rolled over twenty million in his super fund – like seriously, whatever!

There are some toll roads where the advantages of using the road and paying the toll obviously bring benefits to the user in terms of shorter and more consistent travelling times, safer journeys and a less stressful trip. Then there are cases where that just isn't the user experience. There is nothing worse than being stuck in a toll road car park when you are late for a meeting and paying some arse of a company for the privilege. So above all your toll products have to be simple to understand, the fees and charges have to be reasonable and relate to real costs you incur, and you have to give people a mechanism to dispute tolls they think are incorrect. Unless you have a serious monopoly situation and the Government backs you all the way – in which case go for your life.

I define a "toll product" as an aggregation of the following:

- The mechanism(s) used to identify the individual or entity (**Customer**) who engages in a commercial arrangement with a toll road,
- The mechanism(s) used to identify the vehicles (**Vehicles**) for which the **Customer** is responsible and which are to use the toll road,
- The toll rate table and fees and charges that the **Customer** is subject to when the **Vehicles** use the road,
- The payment method the **Customer** agrees to use to pay tolls, fees and charges, and
- All other terms and conditions pursuant to the **Customer** using the road.

These five characteristics represent a good guide to defining any toll product. We are going to start on this journey by considering the "mechanism(s) used to identify the vehicles", and to do that we have to discuss tags. Love them or hate them, tags are amongst us, millions of them. Certainly in the Australian Eastern States most people know what they are and what they do.

Tags

When I refer to a tag in this chapter, what I mean is a 5.8 GHz, DSRC tag that conforms to the CEN (European) and Australian standards. This is the type of tag that Australia picked to use. There are other types of tags that are used very successfully in tolling, but we'll look at those later. A standard tag looks like this one from the Norwegian manufacturer Norbit:

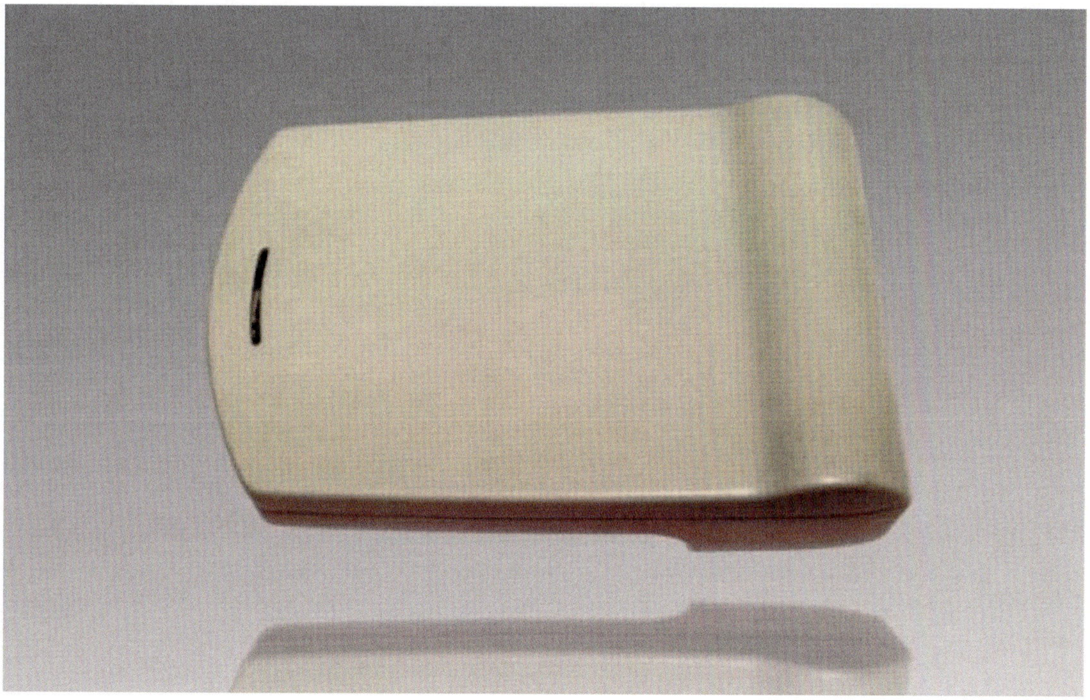

Figure 17 – A Norbit DSRC 5.8 GHz tolling tag

They're in the order of 5 to 6 cm long and 3 to 4 cm wide and always seem to be made in that dull white-fawn colour, as though they come in to this world without the will to live but with a desire to suck the life out of everything around them. However, now you can get them in a range of exciting colours, and have special things printed on them too. That's something to look forward to! The world has become a brighter place.

On the one hand tags are great. As described previously, if they all follow the same technical standards they can enable true interoperability. They are a reasonably secure identification mechanism. They are reliable. Not only do they give very accurate roadside readings, but they also last a long time, and by a long time practical experience is that a tag will normally operate for at least seven years before it starts causing problems.

On the other hand they are a pain. They are relatively inexpensive in their own right, but if you are buying millions of them they cost millions of dollars to purchase. They need a logistics team to move them about from manufacturer to customer and back again. They are usually encoded with a vehicle class and, unless you go out to the car park with your customer and nail the tag to the bonnet of their Bentley (which is not advisable), they will move tags between vehicles – and then we get into the whole vehicle class issue we discussed previously. HCV tags in Holden Barinas and Car tags in Mack trucks because "I didn't realise there was a difference your Honour". Then customers come in to your service centre and say things like:

- "I'm a musician, an artiste! Your tag beeps in b# which is an offence, an aural disgrace! Nothing should make that noise. It's atonal – I thought the ghost of Schoenberg was in the car with me. I want one that beeps in a pure clear C or you be damned!"
- "Eeer, yeah, like I had a tag, but I lent it to my mate who got done for doing doughnuts in front of the cop shop. He's in prison and the car has been trashed but none of these trips are mine yeah."
- "This tag keeps beeping at us as we go under your gantries and Mildred and I don't understand why."
- "This tag doesn't work." "Have you put it in the centre of your windscreen behind the rear view mirror?" "Good Lord no, it's in the glove box." "Why didn't you put it on the windscreen like we told you to?" "Because I own a bloody Porsche! I'm not having that piece of plastic anywhere near my windscreen."
- "Hello, how are you? Yeah, look, the dog ate my tag."
- "Barney, my mate, well he's a bit of a Sheldon. He stuck the tag on the end of a pole and stuck the pole out of the window as we were going under the gantry and like hit a truck. Barney's fine, once we got him to Casualty but as far as we can tell the tag's cactus."
- "Uuum, my tag's been beeping four times for months. Is that OK?"
- "You filled the tag with perfume and now it doesn't beep. Why perfume?" "To make the car smell nice."

No matter what scenarios you can think up for tags, real customers will do something much, much weirder, to the point where you shouldn't be surprised if the opening gambit is "Yes, sorry it's sticky, KY Jelly ......"

But let's not go there. Just to say that you have decided that your toll road will supply customers with tags and you've done a really good deal with a supplier and you've bought half a million ready to distribute to an eager public. In terms of your toll product, what are you going to do? You want your customers to take a tag because they are very good at helping to identify vehicles on the road and your interoperability agreements require them, but how are you going to recover the cost of buying the tags and the organisation and infrastructure in subsequently managing them? There are three basic options, and then any number of variations that you might like to think of:

Lease – just tell your customer that the tag comes with a monthly lease fee, but because a tag transaction is cheaper than anything else (no image processing fee) they will save in the long run. This is great for you – say the tag cost $20 to buy. You lease it out for $2 a month and the tag lasts for seven years. That is $168 in revenue before you have to replace the tag. If you really want to stick the boot in you can insist there is a $40 replacement fee if they lose or destroy their tag. The great part of this scheme is that there is *no refund of any kind* if they close their account and return their tags. You can only get away with this type of scheme if you exist in a monopoly situation – or everybody else in your interoperability group is as evil as you are Darth. Oh, and extra tags cost extra lease fees! But if your tag breaks, and it's not your fault, we will give you a new one. I sense the good in you Darth, the conflict. The Emperor hasn't driven it from you completely.

Deposit – simply that when each tag is issued, the toll road company takes a deposit which is refunded when the tag is returned. Any number of tags can be issued if they are covered by deposits. The deposit is lost if the tag is lost or destroyed. As an operator, you get to use that deposit money how you see fit. This approach is wavering between the light and dark side.

Toll credits – that yes, if you want a tag you have to pay this much up front (say $40), but you can use that money as toll credits i.e. you can make trips with that money. If you lose or destroy your tag you have to pay us the up-front cost to get another one, but then again, you can use that money as toll credits. No refund when you return the tags. Fully Jedi Knight.

You can mix and match these ideas as much as you want – lease fees, deposits, toll credits, refunds for returns. It all depends on how you view the usefulness of tags to your tolling business, what costs you want to recover and what your concession deed lets you do.

Tag costs

Tags cost you money, both in their acquisition and then in their management. They are not a "set and forget" item. With tags you have to:

- Understand the technical specifications you want or have to comply with – which takes a specialist team of engineers.
- You have to find a supplier that is able to deliver those tags to you at the right price, which takes purchasing and negotiation skills.
- You have to work out how you are going to test that the tags work with your roadside equipment. This can be everything from getting Gazza to waive one or two in front of a transceiver, to testing them at high speed under your test gantry using your boss' AMG. Once you've proven the specification, you can't test every tag you purchase, so you have to have SLAs with your supplier.
- You have to build a supply chain model so that when you need tags you have them in the right place.
- Your tolling system has to be integrated so that it knows what tags you have issued to which customers.
- Your roadside has to be able to read tag identifiers, which means somebody has to know how to load "keys", the things that decrypt the tag signals.

- Your customer service staff have to be able to explain to the general public what this tag thing is and how it works – and why the thing beeps when it does – and how to stick it to the windscreen of their car – and field endless stupid and abusive questions as to why it doesn't work, or what to do when it hasn't reacted well to KY Jelly.
- You have to take them back when people close their accounts – or do something about the fact you didn't get them back.
- When you get them back you have to clean them before you can re-issue them, and then you have to convince the tolling system that you have actually re-issued them, and they belong to somebody new.
- Eventually, when they die, you have to find an environmentally friendly way of getting rid of them.

So tags are great, and a source of constant aggravation at the same time.

Beeping

The one thing a tag does that is rather cute is that it beeps. At the toll road conferences that I no longer attend I've heard people disparage "the beep" along the lines of "Guys, why do we need the beep when everybody has a smart phone and they can check the state of their tolling account instantly anyway". Well that argument is flawed on a number of levels. For a start if we are driving we shouldn't be going anywhere near our mobile phones. Secondly you have to accept that you are a road tolling company – people aren't going to be logging into your website for fun – only when they really have to. And is your website mobile friendly anyway? Thirdly most tolling systems are not hard real-time when it comes to updating the status of accounts so the phone is going to be no better than the beep anyway. But the tag beep is a real presence, in their car. I think it's a good compromise between an intrusion and giving customers some valuable information. I described before the beeping convention in Victoria, Australia. Tags can be programmed to respond in any number of ways depending on the signals sent from the roadside equipment, so you are quite at liberty to set your own beeping patterns. But for your customers' sake, consistency is a good thing. Everybody in an interoperability group is best off using the same convention. On the whole I think beeping is a good thing.

Now there is the possibility of making the whole beeping thing a lot more exciting. With modern electronics, why just beep? Why not have different tunes for different scenarios? A few bars of Beethoven's 5th for suspended! Why not let people upload their own beeps to the tag? Well, you probably can do that now and good luck to you. I think you will find that just explaining the "beep" concept to the great unwashed of your city will tax your customer service staff to limit, let alone asking them to explain why a tag won't accept the whole of a Justin Bieber number.

More exciting tags

If being totally thrilled at the prospect of ordering and distributing your first batch of 100,000 tags wasn't enough, there is more. Over in California they have tags that not only can you stick to windscreen, not only beep at you, but have switches and everything!

I am of course referring to FasTrak Flex. Great name; makes me think I'm going fast on a bendy race track somewhere. Ironic given the speed limits in the USA. Anyway, this tag has a switch on it with three settings:

Figure 18 – the FasTrak Flex tag.

The FasTrak is a regular tag that you can use on a number of roads in California. The Flex bit allows you access to the "High Occupancy Vehicle" (HOV) or Express lanes available on some motorways. This from the Santa Clare Transportation Authority website[13]:

> During normal Express Lane operations, solo drivers can use the Express Lanes with a FasTrak® transponder. Solo drivers will be charged the posted toll amount, which varies dynamically based on the level of congestion. The minimum toll amount is $0.30, and the maximum is $7.00.
>
> When traffic is heavy on the 237-880 interchange, the Express Lanes can go into "HOV ONLY mode". This means the lane is no longer open to solo drivers paying the toll with FasTrak®.
>
> During HOV ONLY mode, only vehicles with 2 or more passengers, motorcycles, and clean air vehicles with appropriate decals can use the Express Lanes. When "HOV ONLY" is posted on the toll message sign, a solo driver who enters the Express Lane can be issued an HOV lane violation citation of $491.
>
> Solo drivers who enter the HOV/carpool/diamond lane too early, or fail to exit the Express Lanes promptly, risk being cited for a carpool violation by the California Highway Patrol (CHP).
>
> ……………..
>
> FasTrak Flex® is a new FasTrak® transponder that is convenient for carpoolers on I-580 in Contra Costa County and on SR 237 in Santa Clara County. It allows drivers to move a switch to indicate how many occupants are in their vehicle. FasTrak Flex®, when used properly, will allow drivers to use the Express Lanes and be charged the appropriate toll for solo drivers, or no toll at all for carpoolers and motorcyclists.

Those few paragraphs reveal that there is a huge amount going – it's quite impressive:

- You set the switch to match the number of people in the car, and that controls the toll amount you pay,
- The road has variable toll pricing in an attempt to control congestion on the HOV lanes, and the HOV lanes can be closed for single occupancy vehicles at times of high congestion,
- "Eligible clean air vehicles" can use the HOV lanes which is a nod to environmental concerns, and
- If you don't get on and off when you should the California Highway Patrol is going to *run ya down*!

Plus these guys only want a simple deposit of US$20 for a FasTrak tag. No lease fees in sight. But to be serious for a second, behind those simple statements is a huge amount of sophisticated technology making it all possible.

What makes FasTrak even more impressive is that within California it enables its own asset interoperability scheme covering all of the following:

Toll Bridges

Antioch Bridge
Benicia-Martinez Bridge
Carquinez Bridge
Dumbarton Bridge
Golden Gate Bridge
Richmond-San Rafael Bridge
San Francisco-Oakland Bay Bridge
San Mateo-Hayward Bridge

Express Lanes

I-680 Sunol Express Lanes
SR-237 Express Lanes
I-580 Express Lanes
I-680 Contra Costa Express Lanes (Opening Spring 2017)
Southern California Express Lanes

Parking

San Francisco International Airport (SFO)

Now personally I have no idea where any of these things are, *but they all sound great!* Check out the Caltrans website[14].

Let's finish this with a picture of the California Highway Patrol who will *hunt you down* if you get it wrong:

Figure 19 – California Highway Patrol

Slugging

If you want to use the HOV lanes there is an obvious benefit to having more than one person in the car. If you don't know of anybody who wants to make the same trip as you, what do you do? Well people have resorted to all sorts of schemes to make it at least look like there is more than one person in the car, including sitting shop mannequins and those blow up rubber dolls in the passenger seat – and if you've been married as long as I have you'll know somebody with one of those dolls. I think these schemes have a variable success rate. From a technology point of view though it is difficult to produce a system that works at highway speeds, and can accurately tell how many people are actually in the car i.e. real people, not rubber dolls. There have been attempts made using infra-red cameras (to detect body heat) but I don't know at this time of a system in production that works reliably, although I'm sure somebody claims to be able to do it.

Just to illustrate the point, the picture below is from the New York Daily News site – so this isn't California, rather Suffolk County New York, but you get the idea.

Figure 20 – HOV lane dummy.

There is an alternative – get more real people! In America there is a movement called "Slugging" based on the concept of "Slug-lines". These are people who queue up at various places on the highway to get picked up by drivers who want to use the HOV lanes. A whole culture and etiquette has developed around this concept. The following is from the Slugging Wikipedia page[15].

> Some Washington D.C. rules are:
>
> - Drivers are not to pick up sluggers en route to or standing outside the line, a practice referred to as "body snatching".
> - A woman is not to be left in the line alone, for her safety.
> - No eating, smoking, or putting on makeup.
> - The driver has full control of the radio and climate controls.
> - No open windows unless the driver approves.
> - No money is exchanged or requested, as the driver and slugs all benefit from slugging.
> - Driver and passengers say "Thank you" at the end.

If you want to become part of this movement, check out the website Slug-Lines.com[16]. I wonder how many long term relationships have started with a Slug-line? It's possibly even Hollywood movie material.

Sticker tags

Up in Taiwan they have had great success with a simple RFID sticker tag. In fact the MLFF toll road transformation of Taiwan's road network is at the same time huge, award winning[17] and worth taking a good look at if you are planning something similar. They had operated a free-flow system of sorts for a while based on the "constrained" entry idea and infra-red tags as shown in figure 21.

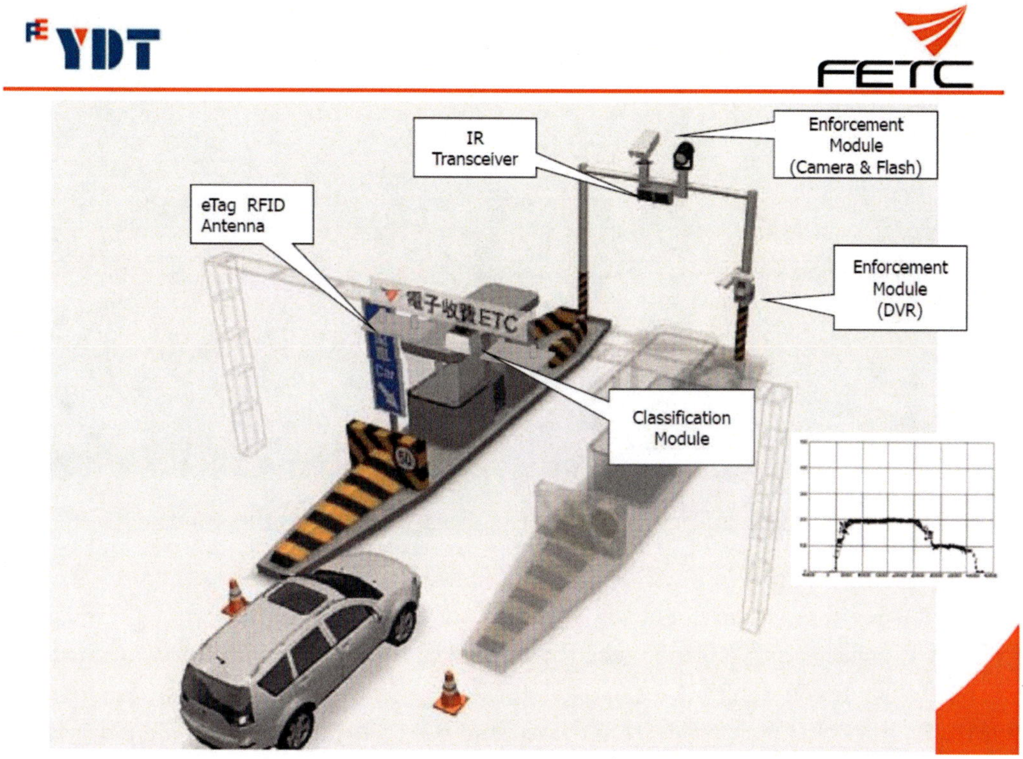

Figure 21 – Taiwan's infra-red tag tolling gantry, with RFID sensor.

They came to the conclusion that the infra-red tag was actually holding them back. It was expensive for the customer and the uptake was poor. To get real progress, they had to change and made the decision to go with an RFID solution. This tag is literally a thin piece of plastic a few centimetres long with an embedded RFID aerial and chip in it – no battery.

But the other thing they worked out was the service element – how could they make it simple and easy for people to get hold of these new sticker tags? They set up a significant network of centres based out of service stations and convenience stores. You rock up, a couple of highly efficient chaps wack a sticker tag on your windscreen or headlight (which is free), register you, relieve you of some money and off you go. The whole process takes a few minutes. See figure 22.

Figure 22 – Applying a sticker tag to a car headlight in Taiwan.

These sticker tags cost a couple of bucks or less to buy and it is tricky moving them between vehicles – why aren't we all using them? I'm not absolutely sure but I think when the various standards were being written in Europe, the DSRC tag was considered a better technical solution for Australia back at the end of the 1990s. If you don't have a battery in the tag you have to up the power of your roadside transmitter to give the RFID tag enough energy to send back a reliable signal. You don't want that transmitter frying your customers every time they use the road. But Taiwan demonstrates that the technology does work.

The uptake of this sticker tag over the infra-red unit is quite impressive. The following graph is from the Taiwan Area National Freeway Bureau[18].

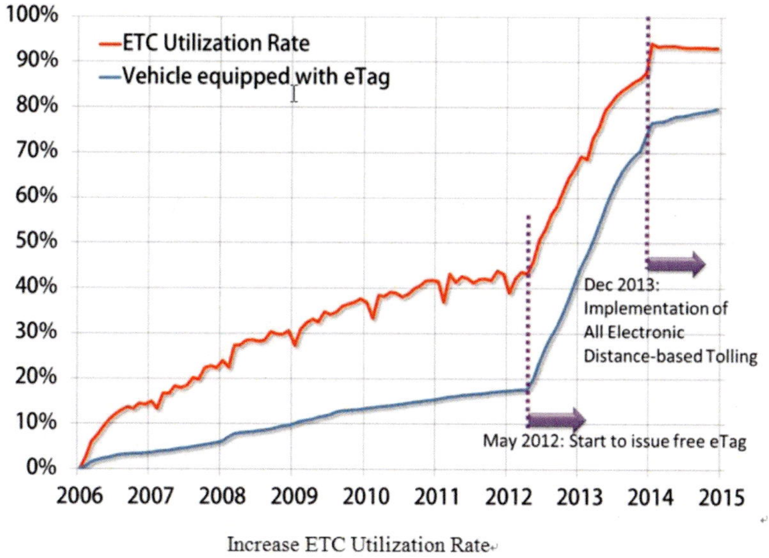

Figure 23 – Taiwan's sticker tag uptake.

My information on the Taiwan system comes from a presentation (NeTC 2013) given by the most excellent Mr Y C Chang and Fah Siang Ho. FETC and YTD are both part of the Far Eastern Group headquartered in Taipei, Taiwan.

The Mother of all tags

If you thought the FasTrak Flex was pretty exciting, have a look at this one:

Figure 24 – The Sitraffic Sensus Unit from Siemens

This is the Sitraffic Sensus Unit from Siemens installed in a German heavy commercial vehicle. Not only is this tag fully DSRC compliant, it also:

- Has a built in GPS unit that determines when the vehicle is on a tolled road,
- Calculates internally the route the vehicle takes and the toll cost, then
- Transmits the toll data in a secure form back across the mobile phone network to the toll operator.

In this case the DSRC bit (and in effect the gantry) is only used to demonstrate that the vehicle is equipped with the tag, for compliance purposes. This heavy vehicle tolling scheme operates right across Germany but no further – till Europe can solve their interoperability problems. This tag, and the operation behind, could be said to be MLFF tolling, but really this a full blown road user charging scheme.

This tag is physically wired into the power within the vehicle, and the unit itself is not cheap. The tag and its fitting cost upwards of $200. That price makes it problematic for adoption across the full fleet of private cars for now.

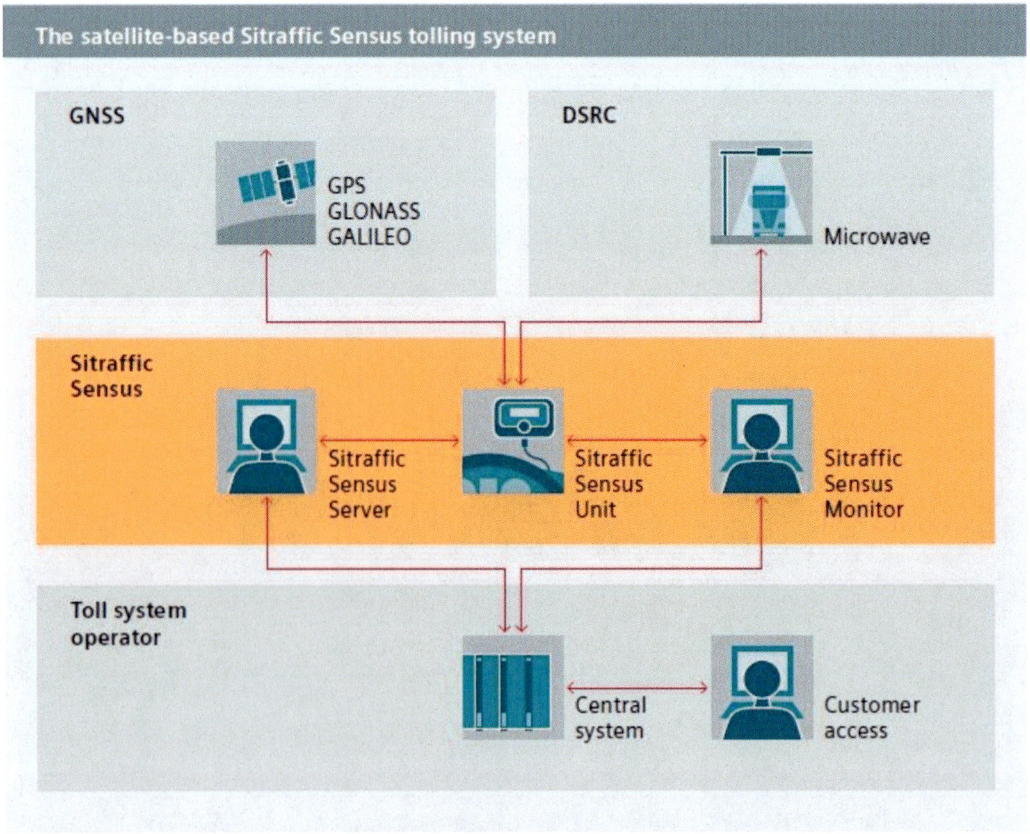

Figure 25 – The Sitraffic Sensus system from Siemens. The Sensus server is the tolling part, the Monitor is the enforcement part.

When we think about road user charging on a massive scale we will probably find technology, like the Siemens unit, sitting at the heart of the solution. Most cars now come with GPS built in to drive the on-board navigation system. Increasingly cars are connected to the mobile phone network and carry enough computing power to run apps. It is not a great leap of technology to add that DSRC tag for compliance purposes and everything we need will be there in the vehicle. I would hazard a guess that the incremental cost will not be that great either.

Tag mass extinction events

If you were a new toll road and a new tag supplier, and you issued most of your active (battery powered) tags in the first year or two of your operations, you can look forward to a "mass extinction event". This is when, after seven or eight years, all of your tags start dying, all at once. It starts with a few people complaining that their tag doesn't beep anymore and ends up with you scrambling to issue thousands of new tags and refunding image processing fees. I exaggerate. If you keep an eye on certain key business metrics you can plan for such events, and the nature of tags and tag usage means that it is rarely a "huge spike" problem, but be mindful of that one.

Oh, and just a little reminder. Don't let the truck that is delivering your next batch of 100,000 tags drive under one of your gantries unless you are sure that:

- None of the tag batteries have been activated, or
- Every tag is in its own Faraday cage, or
- The whole truck is one big Faraday cage (unlikely). This conversation with the driver is likely to go along the following lines "Faraday cage! Yes mate, got one of them in the glove box. 'Ang on a minute and I'll get it for ya."
- You've turned the gantry off.

Physics serves no master other than itself.

Video

The Video Account, or the Tag-less Account, is an account which uses a licence plate string to identify the vehicle and thus the owner of the account, and charges them accordingly. I'm going to have to give you a lot of anecdotal information because toll road companies and equipment manufacturers rarely publish hard data on their image processing systems' performance for valid commercial reasons, and in this game the performance of your Image Processing Capability (IPC) is everything.

In this section I'm going to introduce two image processing models, the Standard Model and the Class model. The Standard Model treats tag passages at face value i.e. if we get a good tag read we use it to reconstruct trips and do nothing to try and determine the licence plate of the vehicle carrying the tag. The Class Model on the other hand is designed to allow us to identify the class of the vehicle regardless of whether we have a tag read or not. The Class Model pulls in that VIN data we discussed earlier and is intended to ensure we are tolling correctly at all times with respect to vehicle class. It has some significant implications for image processing.

Standard Model

In the Standard Model only those passages which:

- Do not have tag data, and
- Those that do have tag data and those tags are on the roadside blacklist or have some other anomaly,

end up in the image processing stream. I am also making the assumption that the Standard Model is serviced by a discrete image processing system within the Trip Reconstruction component of the tolling system. Within the context of this model there are a few parameters that help to define the performance of your IPC:

Tag Penetration Rate: the percentage of your roadside transactions that are tag based [**T%**]. This is not the same as the percentage of your customer accounts that are tag based.

Standard Automation Rate: the percentage of all the images presented to the discrete image processing system from which can be determined the licence plate string and registration details – referred to as "automatically validated" images [**A%**]. Closely linked to this is:

False Confirmed Result Rate: the percentage of those licence plate strings that are automatically validated but where the licence plate string is wrong [**F%**].

Operator Error Rate: similar to the False Confirmed Result Rate, this is the percentage of licence plates that are incorrectly read by your Human Image Processors [**E%**].

Validation Loss Rate: despite all your best efforts, both machine and human, this is the percentage of images viewed by Human Image Processors from which a licence plate string cannot be determined [**L%**].

It's all a bit abstract presented in that form. Hopefully figure 26 makes it clearer.

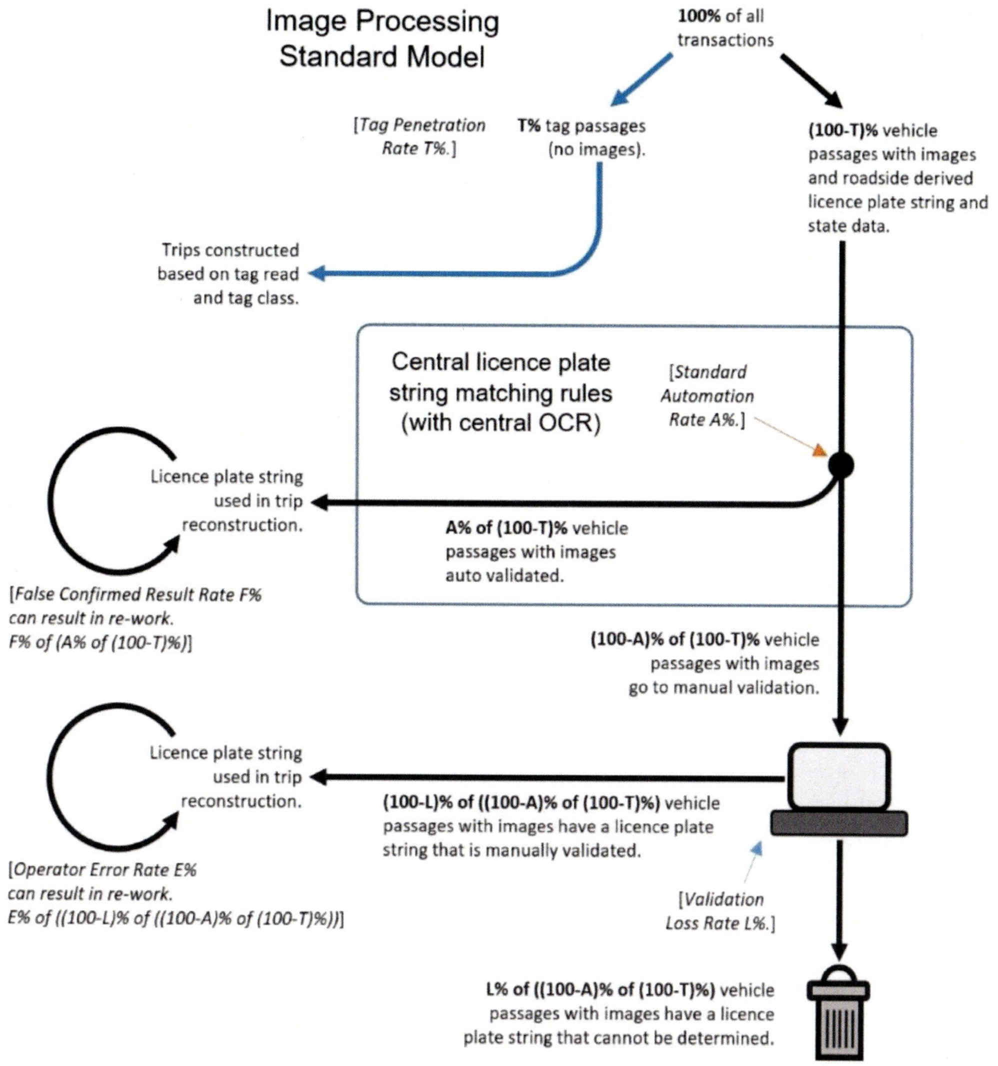

Figure 26 – Image processing Standard Model

Strictly speaking the Tag Penetration Rate isn't really about image processing performance per say. Rather it helps you define performance requirements for your image processing system. For example, say you have a road that generates a million individual detection events under all your gantries each day – but 85% [**T%**] of those events are made with a tag. So that would leave you with a basic processing requirement of: 100% - 85% = 15% * 1,000,000 gives 150,000 image based detection events (Vehicle Passages) a day to process. But hang on – each of those events contains a front and rear vehicle image – two images per event – so that makes 300,000 images. But that is today's traffic. You have a traffic forecast model that grows at a healthy 5% each year for the next three years – that is 347,288 images a day after three years. And there is more. That is a normal day's processing load. What happens if we have a system outage and have to recover a number of days – let's say 48 hours of images in 24 hours. Suddenly your image processing system has to be able to process the best part of 700,000 images a day. That number gives you an image processing system throughput requirement. The cloud, with scalable compute power, starts looking like a good option. Ultimately the Tag Penetration Rate you achieve is up to your business and how hard you push the tag based account over the video account (if you offer one).

Obviously you want a high Standard Automation Rate [A%]. The automation rate your system can achieve is based on a number of factors including, but not limited to:

- The clarity of the licence plates you are having to process,
- How good the OCR engines are,
- The presence or otherwise of a secondary vehicle identification system – sometimes referred to as a signature, and
- The business rules for matching vehicles.

Most these things can be tuned and tweaked to suit the licence plates you encounter on your road, and it's really up to the vendors of these systems to convince you of their various merits. But with a modern image processing system, an automation rate of 90% [**A%**] or better should be achievable.

Closely linked to automation rate is the False Confirmed Result Rate [**F%**]. It is usually the case that the harder you push for a higher Standard Automation Rate the higher will be your False Confirmed Result Rate. This comes about because as you search for that higher automation rate, it tends to mean that you are relaxing the matching business rules, leading to a greater False Confirmed Result Rate. As fixing up the mess caused by false confirmed results costs you money and potentially some public embarrassment, and manually validated images cost you money to process, in time you will find an equilibrium where the two rates are just about right for your business. Ideally your False Confirmed Result Rate should be less than 0.1%. You do the sums – if you are dealing with 150,000 Vehicle Passages a day, even 0.1% is quite a lot of errors.

The Operator Error Rate [**E%**] is similar to the False Confirmed Result Rate, but these are errors made by the real people viewing your images. Well trained Human Image Processors are remarkably accurate given the nature of the job, but occasionally they do make mistakes.

Finally there is the Validation Loss Rate [**L%**]. If a plate is particularly difficult to read, almost certainly the OCR engines will have given up and passed it to a Human Image Processor. With the best will in the world some plates just can't be read. They might be covered in mud, bent, obscured or just not there. There is always a loss rate when reading licence plates. Anecdotally, New Zealand achieves one of the highest licence plate reading automation rates in the world. This is due in part to the fact that they have clear licence plates, but also the agency that does the licence plate reading also controls the registration of those plates. If you have a dodgy set of plates they send you a new set and tell you to get yourself sorted out.

Image processing fee

The trick with the Video Account is a wonderful thing called the "Image Processing Fee" – a fee you can slap on to every customer's toll the minute they travel on your road without a tag account or an arrangement to pay. Around the world the image processing fee ranges from what some might describe as something approaching reasonable to sheer daylight robbery. Just for fun let's set up a very crude financial model and see how it all pans out. I'll assume we're looking at costs over a three year period. Table 15 sets up our basic system costs:

Item	Unit cost	Total
Acquisition of a central image processing system, including your own internal project costs	$3,000,000	$3,000,000
IT infrastructure maintenance	$100,000	$300,000
Internal support personnel	$200,000	$600,000
Vendor support contract	$70,000	$210,000
Image processing desktop equipment	$10,000	$30,000
Others, project lunch, misc.	$20,000	$60,000
	Total	$4,200,00

Table 15 – Basic image processing system costs

So over those three years we could be up for $4,200,000 to have the image processing system up and running. Now to the basic operational cost model:

1. Let's say we get 1,000,000 detection events a day now, and we have a 5% annual traffic growth rate. Over three years that equates to a total of 1,150,662,500 events to be processed.
2. Our tag trip penetration rate T% is 85%. That means that 172,599,375 of those events are without a tag.
3. Assume our Standard Automation Rate A% is 90%. That means that of those tag-less detection events 155,339,438 will be automatically processed with some 155,339 errors assuming a False Confirmed Result Rate F% of 0.1%.
4. This leaves us with 17,259,938 passages to process manually. If we assume that in a five hour shift our Human Image Processors can work through 1,500 Vehicle Passages, over those three years we will need 11,507 image processing shifts. Assuming an hourly rate of $30, each shift costs $150 so that manual processing effort costs $1,725,994. Round that up to a nice $2,000,000 to take into account supervisors, training and recruitment.
5. Let's assume the Operator Error Rate E% is again 0.1%. Of those human processed passages we can expect some 17,260 errors.
6. Between machine and humans we end up with a total of 172,599 errors. But of these only half ever get noticed. You struggle to find them, and half the time the customers don't even notice! When we do find them though we have to take remedial action and that costs on average around

$20 a time. The errors therefore cost us about $1,726,000 over those three years. That is quite a lot thank you.

7. For the sake of trying to keep this simple I won't add validation losses in at this point.

Putting all those figures together, table 16, gives us a total image processing cost over the three of $7,926,000.

Cost component	Value
IPS system	$4,200,000
Human image processing operators	$2,000,000
Errors and re-work	$1,726,000
Total	$7,926,000

Table 16 – "Total" Standard Model image processing costs

So how do we want to scope our image processing fee? To start with let's simply divide the total cost of image processing by the number of transactions processed:

$7,926,000/172,599,375 = **4.6 cents** a transaction to process. That is pretty cheap. Feels too cheap!

But hang on, in a business sense the real effort in terms of management time and effort is getting those Human Image Processors recruited, trained and organised. Let's set the baseline cost as the cost for them to process a transaction:

$2,000,000 / 17,259,938 = **12 cents**. That's more like it. If we actually charge 24 cents a pop we start making money!

To hell with it, let's load all the image processing costs on to those manually viewed images.

$7,926,000 / 17,259,938 = **46 cents**. Triffic, but let's charge them 90 cents! Kerching!!

Now I've made all those numbers up. It would be interesting to see how your real road stacks up against them. To finish this, let's do a quick review as to what some toll roads actually charge – you be the judge:

Road	Fee (2017 prices)	Cost
EastLink (Australia)	Image Processing Fee	AU$0.29
M6 Toll (UK)	Tag accounts get 5% discount over non-tag accounts	AU$0.48 (~£0.28)
CityLink (Australia)	Access Account – Vehicle Matching Fee	AU$0.75
407 ETR (Canada)	Camera Charge per trip	AU$4.10 (C$4.10)

Table 17 – Actual image processing fees

Class Model

In the Class Model the aim is to get a licence plate string and registration details for every detection event on the road. Through the licence plate, via the VIN, we can derive vehicle make and model and thus class for tolling purposes. This means we want images of everything passing under the gantries.

We could just push all the images through the central image processing system and be done with it. But we are effectively increasing the number of images to be processed by an order of magnitude. OCR engines have a finite processing throughput. Increasing the image volume by that amount means building a much bigger central image processing system. OCR engines usually come with a licence fee, so you have to weigh up whether the additional costs in upgrading the central image processing system are justified by the benefits you get through the precise knowledge of vehicle class.

There is a halfway house which is the concept I'm presenting here. That is to make better use of the roadside OCR engine output, by putting in business rules to automatically process images before they get to the central image processing system. Depending on those business rules, that "first pass" should greatly reduce the number of images having to go through the central system, thus keeping down costs.

I've been referring to business rules and automation rates, and you may be wondering what are these things and how are they determined? Well, we'll get in to that discussion in part 2. In the meantime, my Class Model is shown in figure 27.

For completeness, the class model changes a couple of our IPC parameters:

The Standard Automation Rate [A%] and False Confirmed Result Rate [F%] are both replaced by two associated pairs of parameters:

Roadside Automation Rate: the percentage of all the images presented to the roadside matching rules from which can be determined the licence plate string and registration details [**RA%**]. Closely linked to this is:

Roadside False Confirmed Result Rate: the percentage of those licence plate strings that are automatically validated but where the licence plate string is wrong [**RF%**].

And

Central Automation Rate: the percentage of all the images presented to the central matching rules from which can be determined the licence plate string and registration details [**CA%**]. Closely linked to this is:

Central False Confirmed Result Rate: the percentage of those licence plate strings that are automatically validated but where the licence plate string is wrong [**CF%**].

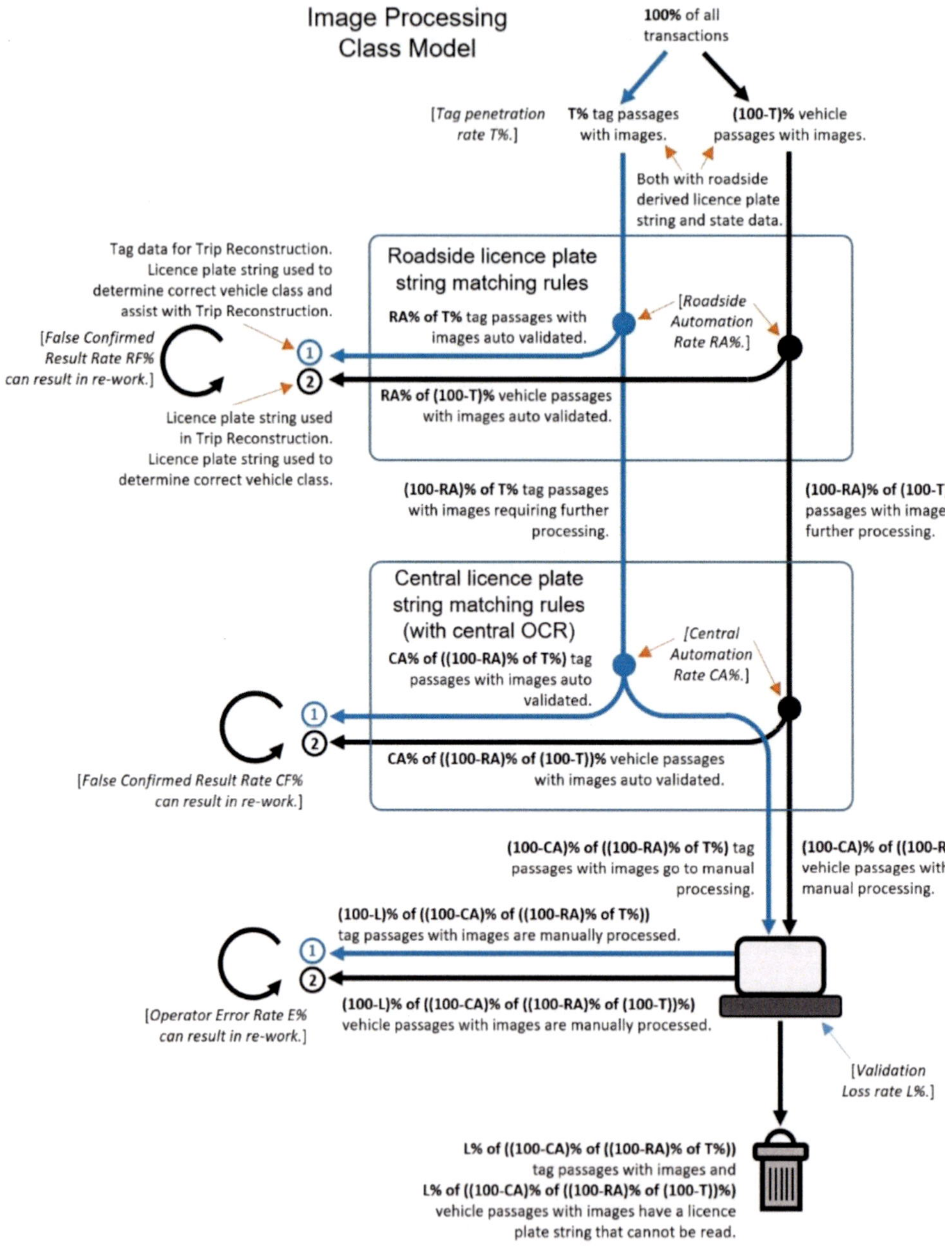

Figure 27 – Image processing Class Model

From an image processing perspective the Class Model is obviously more complex and will attract additional costs to set up and operate. The benefit is that it should deliver the correct vehicle class in the vast majority of cases. An additional benefit is that it delivers a lot more data on our customers (that licence plate string) which can only help to improve our Trip Reconstruction function and give us further insights into how customers use the road.

Human image processors

The fact that there are many websites[19] active today dedicated to the collecting of licence plates should not be taken as evidence that the human race is a failed experiment. The members of these sites are as passionate about their collecting as anybody. If you are running an image processing operation you should find these people, employ them, nurture them and ultimately grow to love them.

In your image processing office, it can be quite disconcerting to hear conversations along these lines:

> *"Did you see Vicious Housewives last night?"*
> *"Oh, my, God!"*
> *"I mean what was she thinking?"*
> *"OMG, OMG!"*
> *"Who would even think to do that with a lobster?"*
> *"OMG, OMG, OMG!!!"*

Far better to hear the conversation of two licence plate recognition professionals:

> *"That my friend is an original Victorian vitreous enamel number plate issued by the Chief Commissioner of Police under the 1932 Motor Car Act between 1932 and 1939."*
> *"Oh yeah."*
> *"Further, it is attached to a Series 1 E-type Jaguar. VIC, Car, sorted!"*
> *"How can you tell?'*
> *"The shape of the headlights. The car that Enzo Ferrari called the most beautiful ever made."*
> *"Who is Enzo Ferrari?"*
> *"The Main Man, the Big Cheese, the Huge Kahoona Burger of the Prancing Horse."*
> *"You're weird."*
> *"You're right, weird but brilliant Baldrick ... "*

You see, that is much better. There is a view that image processing is a commodity activity, that it doesn't really matter who does it so long as it gets done, so farm it out to Buwapbackistax at 3 Zlotys an image. I do have sympathy for that approach if your IPC has a weak and feeble Standard Automation Rate of between 60 to 70%. If you have a lot of traffic on your road, then the image volumes really can be problematic.

Figure 28 – This is an E-Type Jaguar. There is no reason for showing you a picture of this car at this point in time. It is a gratuitous waste of space – except for the fact that it is a stunningly beautiful car.

But I don't think outsourcing is such a good idea if you have 90%+ automation rates, and you are trying to confirm vehicle class. As the automation rates get better, the plates that are presented to people are by definition the problematic ones that the IPC can't read. So I would argue that you need people who do possess some knowledge and skill in deciphering tricky plates with accuracy. That only comes through training, the experience gained actually doing the job and the sharing of information amongst people who consider themselves to be a team. In that case make them a team. Keep them briefed on changes to licence plates. Send them off to car shows. Get dealerships to give them new model track days, and above all listen to their feedback regarding your image processing user interface and act on it. They are a valuable part of your tolling organisation.

Following is an apocryphal tale from when things go wrong. Every toll road has their own version of this story.

> The image processor that we met earlier, the one who had issues with the lobster, is presented with the heritage plate 1O1 (one oh one). Being in a somewhat distracted state of mind, but diligent nonetheless, she enters 101 (one zero one), because the general rule is that heritage plates only contain numbers. However, this becomes problematic because the plate 101 (one zero one) is attached to a 1950s vintage grey Massey-Fergusson currently resting in a paddock in the Victorian High Country. The tractor is owned by a farmer, Charlie Bludger. The last time it moved anywhere was twenty years ago. Charlie and some friends had spent the day drinking beer and shooting wild pigs and decided that they needed more beer. So they climbed aboard and drove the Massey-Fergusson the full round trip of 20km to the Dargo pub. By the time they got back they decided that, no matter how much beer they'd drunk, they were never ever doing that again. The tractor remains in the field to this day.

Figure 29 - Grey Massey-Ferguson

One morning Charlie opens his mail to find NATP Invoice for $15.96 from NextLink alleging that he and his tractor had been spotted on NextLink just the week before without a valid arrangement to pay. Somewhat bemused by this demand, Charlie does what he always does in times of crisis and goes to the Dargo pub. It so happened that in the pub that day was Pamela Scribble, the only journalist currently working for the Dargo Tribune. It was a slow day for news in Dargo, but when Pamela hears about Charlie's NATP Invoice, she knows she has the cover story for next week's edition.

A couple of days later Charlie, armed with his pig rifle and invoice, is standing in the paddock in front of the Massey-Fergusson. Charlie growls at the camera while Pamela snaps away. Charlie's dog, a Kelpie, is also in the picture. He is sitting down looking at Pamela, his head slightly cocked to one side with an expression on his face which says only one thing – "I'm a dog, but even I wouldn't screw up like you guys". Charlie, and the Kelpie, make the front page of the Dargo Tribune.

The plate 1O1 (one oh one) happens to be attached to a Maserati GranTurismo that, at the time the picture was taken, was doing 160 km/hr down the toll road. It belongs to Stephane, a male model, who having just done three lines of coke decided it was a good idea to get across town to see his new squeeze, a Slovenian pole vaulter going by the name of Vlad. Stephane does actually own the plate 1O1, but in the VicRoads custom plate format. Working in an industry where appearance is everything, and having just taken delivery of the GranTurismo, Stephane decides that VicRoads could do a lot better in the styling department. He engages a friend, who crafts decorative pieces in enamel, to make him his own custom "heritage" plates.

Figure 30 - Maserati GranTurismo

Meanwhile ABC Melbourne Radio has got hold of the Charlie tractor story and Mac McTollface (PR for NextLink) is having to front up and explain why anybody should trust NextLink ever again. The situation is resolved by returning to the paddock so that Pamela can take another picture, this time of Mac McTollface handing over a letter of apology and a slab of beer to Charlie. Charlie calls his friends over. They drink the beer and fail miserably to shoot anything, let alone a pig. Mac McTollface drives back to Melbourne from the High Country truly believing that the human race *is* a failed experiment. In those quiet moments of solitude Pamela still dreams of that Pulitzer Prize, if only she could tear herself away from Dargo.

[Public safety announcements:

Do not take drugs and drive. You are a danger to yourself and those around you.

Do not drink alcohol and operate firearms. You are a danger to yourself and every living thing around you.

Observe the signposted speed limits at all times, even if you do have a Maserati GranTurismo.

In fact don't do anything described in that story apart from image processing and possibly journalism – because depending on where you live, even that can be dangerous.]

Would your team be able to correctly interpret a "fake heritage" plate 1O1? And why did the IPC pass on it in the first place? Maybe deep down in its silicony logic cells it had a doubt about that O.

Accounts

Tolling accounts in themselves are just like any other retail utility account. They resemble your telephone bill. Replace calls with trips on roads and your phone number with a tag ID, and you're pretty much there. However, there are two distinct models in tolling when it comes to getting hold of the money – the *pre-paid* and *post-paid* account.

It makes sense that every toll road prefers the pre-paid model. The customer loads up their account with money, and then draws down on that positive balance every time they make a trip. When the account reaches a *low balance threshold*, if the customer has set up a direct debit order, money is automatically taken from their bank account to top up the tolling account. So long as there is enough money in the bank account when the direct debit instruction comes through, a customer can drive on the road to their heart's content and doesn't need to do anything else. It's very simple, very efficient and is working all over the world today.

The only downside to this type of arrangement is that the date when money is taken from a customer's bank account bears no relationship to the date when they put money into their account e.g. when they get paid. When a direct debit gets fired off depends entirely on how much they've been using the road. So some customers appreciate a notification – an SMS or e-mail – just to let them know that money is to be taken and their tolling account topped up. If there is no direct debit instruction set up against the account then it becomes very important to notify the customer that they need to top up their account manually. Figure 31 below demonstrates the basic mechanism of the pre-paid account.

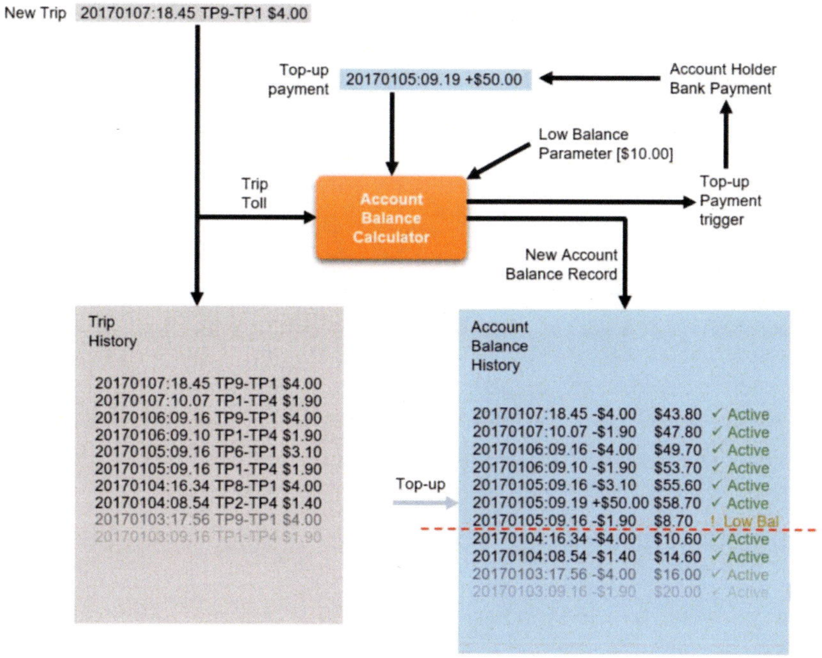

Figure 31 – Pre-paid tolling account

Some people, and most businesses, don't like the idea of this pre-paid model. They want more control over who they're paying, what they are paying for and when they pay it. The post-paid tolling account is a good alternative.

With a post-paid account there is no concept of a low balance threshold because the account balance by definition is always negative. Instead there is an invoicing frequency which is usually monthly. At the end of the invoicing period a line is drawn across the account and the value owing sent to the customer in the form of an invoice. Ideally the customer pays the invoice within the term and all is good. Figure 32 below demonstrates the basic mechanism of the post-paid account. It makes sense in some situations for customers to set up direct debit instructions against post-paid accounts i.e. the invoice is paid automatically by direct debit. This arrangement removes the timeliness problem with the pre-paid account.

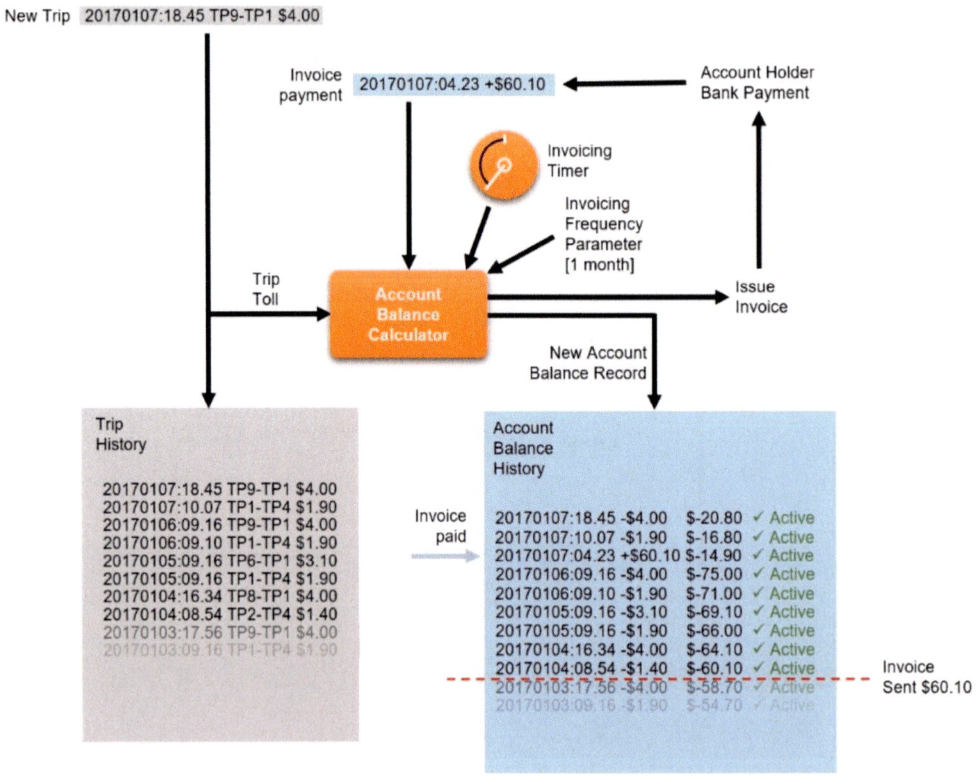

Figure 32 – Post-paid tolling accounts

With the pre-paid account a customer can set up a fixed top-up amount but they're not sure when the top-up is going to occur. With the post-paid account they know when they have to pay but they can't be sure about how much, because that depends on their usage of the road during the invoicing period.

There can be any number of variations on these two account types. For example a very "light weight" tolling account might simply be a licence plate string and a credit card number. At the end of the month all the trips against that licence plate are charged against the credit card.

The account component gives a toll product a further four basic options:

- Pre-paid with an automatic top-up arrangement,
- Pre-paid with a manual top-up arrangement,
- Post-paid with an automatic invoice payment arrangement,
- Post-paid with a manual invoice payment arrangement.

Summary of Toll Product Features and Charges

In addition to our pre-paid/post-paid and auto/manual top-up options, following is a summary list of the other features and charges you can build into your toll products.

Toll modifiers

We've met some of these already on our journey, but just to recap:

Name	Description
Toll free period	A period after the road opens when tolls are not charged. It lets your customers get to know the road and see the benefits before they start having to pay. "Try before you buy".
Flagfall	A fee for just turning up on the road, charged before you have even been anywhere. Seriously? Yes, but not common.
Short trip allowance or discount	The first few kilometres of travel are free or offered at a discount. Your toll road you might have subsumed an existing free road and so you have to keep the locals happy, or you have obligations to take traffic off parallel local roads. Can also be a way of letting people get used to the idea that paying for using a great road isn't that bad after all.
Time of day or day of week discounts	Every road has a finite capacity which when reached leads to traffic congestion and then using the road and paying for it becomes an annoying and frustrating activity. Charging less for road travel outside of peak times and at weekends may help to move traffic out of those peak times and so increase the overall efficiency of the road.
Toll cap	A maximum amount a customer can be charged for a trip on the road. Is often related to the price of a trip pass, a casual user product.
High occupancy	Discounts or free travel for vehicles carrying more than one person. Aimed at encouraging drivers to transport as many people as possible in a vehicle.
Green vehicle discounts	Discounts or free travel for vehicles with very low or zero emissions. Aimed at encouraging customers to buy and use those vehicles.

Table 18 – Toll modifiers

Tag related

Fees and charges associated with tags:

Name	Description
Lease fee	An amount payable every month or year for the use of each tag.
Deposit	An amount held as a deposit for each tag issued. Refundable upon return of the tag.
Deposit as toll credits	An amount required to be deposited in the account for each tag issued. But becomes toll credits.
Tag annual minimum usage fee	The minimum amount of toll fee activity that has to pass through an account each year. For example if you only incurred $20 in tolls, but the Tag annual minimum usage fee was $30, you would pay an additional $10 for that year. It recognises the fact that even if you don't use the road much it still costs money to maintain an account.
Missing tag fee	Payable when a customer closes an account and then doesn't return the tag. If they paid a tag deposit obviously they don't get the deposit back, so an additional fee probably isn't necessary. For some other tag arrangements however this becomes valid.
Missing tag waiver amount	If a missing tag is associated with an account that has pushed through thousands of dollars of toll charges which have been paid, it can appear churlish to charge a tag non-return fee. This sets the value for when the missing fee can be waived.

Table 19 – Tag related fees

Account related

Finally all the things you need to consider with account operations:

Name	Description
Account minimum opening amount	The minimum amount of money you need to deposit in your account at the time of opening. Often linked to the way you want to handle tag charges.
Account low balance threshold	For pre-paid accounts – the account balance level that triggers a top-up request.
Minimum top-up amount	Again for pre-paid accounts you might want to specify that people are only allowed to top-up their account by an amount greater than the minimum amount. Ironically you may also wish to specify that there is a maximum top-up amount. If your tolling system is smart enough, it can suggest to customers a top-up amount that helps to align their payments with monthly cycles based on average usage.

Top-up amount fee	It makes sense that if customers are putting money into their account you shouldn't charge them to do that. But there may be situations where a fee for topping up an account is appropriate – perhaps chargeable on top-up amounts that are below the Minimum top-up amount or related to the channel that people use to make the top-up. Some third party provider fees may have to be passed through to the customer.
Payment methods	Rules around how customers can pay their toll charges. Some accounts may be credit card and direct debit only; some maybe credit card, electronic bank transfer and PayPal. You may or may not want to accept cheques.
Statements and invoices	Rules around how customers will receive statements and invoices. You may decide that the basic account has all statements delivered by e-mail and that paper costs more. A quarterly paper statement may be the baseline. For a business customer an invoice may be a spreadsheet that can be read directly into their accounting system.
Additional statement fee	A fee charged when customers want more statements than their basic account provisions allow for. This often occurs around tax return time, when everybody is scrambling to find records.
Dishonour fee	A fee when the customer's bank rejects a payment request. The bank will usually charge a dishonour fee. This can be passed on to the customer as is or with a loading.
Invoice terms	For post-paid accounts the number of days you are prepared to wait for payment.
Account management fee	Business accounts may attract a management fee, especially if the account is large, involves a constant "churn" of tags and vehicles, and has special reporting and invoicing requirements.
Account re-activation fee	Accounts do get suspended when payment systems fail and toll fees begin to rack up. You may or may not decide to charge a re-activation fee when the customer puts the account back into credit.
Image processing fee	Our friend the image processing or "vehicle matching" fee.

Table 20 – Account related considerations

Your toll products will be a wonderful combination of some or all of those items.

The one thing not covered in this section are the fees and charges associated with when things go wrong – enforcement. We'll look at that in a later section.

Casual Users

As a toll road operator, how do you see yourself? Is your road itself a beacon of efficient, sustainable architecture that is to be enjoyed as much as any of the other city's attractions? Or is it just another transport corridor, but one that needs to be squeezed for every dime it can make? How you answer that question will speak volumes about how you treat visitors to your toll road.

There are many different types of casual user. There are people who live in rural areas who will only make a trip once or twice a year. There are people who live in the city but for most of the time leave the car at home and move around on public transport. There are business people who jet in for meetings and might have to travel around for site visits. There are tourists who just want to fossick about and see what is going on. All of these groups share the following requirements:

- They need to know that there is a tolling scheme in force on some roads,
- They need to know that they have to take some positive action in order to comply with the rules,
- They need access to the retail outlets that will let them purchase something to comply with the rules.

Some obvious things to do are:

- Make the signage on the road very clear i.e. "This is a toll road. You need to do X Y Z".
- Have information on display at ports and airports,
- Be on good terms with the hire car companies so they can spread the message when people are picking up cars. Make it easy for them to make it easy for the customer.
- Have casual user products available on-line but also in post offices and convenience stores.

The principal reason for making an effort in this regard is because going through the enforcement process later is painful and expensive. You can end up issuing NATP Invoices to hire car companies (legal owner of the vehicle) who rented it to a guy who has gone back to Finland after his holiday. Somebody along the way may have a working credit card number you can charge, but it turns into a real administrative problem.

Casual user products fall into four basic types, with all the usual variations along the way:

- **Trip pass** – a "one payment per trip" product based on the vehicle's licence plate string. One trip pass allows the vehicle to make one trip of any length on the road.
- **Time pass** – again a product based on the vehicle's licence plate string. This product allows the vehicle unlimited travel on the road for a set period of time, be it over a weekend or for a number of days.
- **Light post-paid account** – a simple account linked to a vehicle's licence plate string and a credit card. At the end of every month the trips made are simply charged to the credit card.

- **Temporary tag account** – some roads, especially in Europe, do offer temporary tag accounts. You can pick up a tag at a country's border, use it, pay for the travel and then return the tag when you leave.

All of these solutions have fees and charges associated with them based around such things as fees charged by retail outlets and account administration costs.

Taxis

Taxis, private hire cars, Uber and Lyft drivers all share the requirement for passing on their toll charges to their customers. If you have a super tolling system that can create rated trips in real-time and stream that data wirelessly to a taxi on-demand then there is no issue. But given that tolling systems are rarely real-time in that sense, we have to come up with other ways for the drivers to work out the tolls they need to charge their customers.

We have several options here:

- Let them travel for free – but seriously that is so not going to happen,
- Develop a simplified toll structure for taxis, one based on a small number of "zone charges" that is easy for drivers and customers to understand,
- Do nothing and let them work it out for themselves,
- Collaborate on a toll charge calculator app of some kind.

Thanks to companies like Uber and Lyft, this whole area is going to get bigger and more complicated in the future. Looking forward, there are many predictions that within a few years a lot of us will be moving about in shared autonomous vehicles. Now by definition those vehicles will be packing a lot of on-board computing power and they will be connected to central servers, each other and roadside infrastructure. Given that they have a detailed map, a positioning system and the tolling rules for each of the toll roads they use, it should be straight forward for them to work out what to charge and to who.

That raises an interesting point. In making that possible for shared autonomous vehicles we are effectively moving or sharing part of a traditional tolling system with the vehicle itself. We can already see this happening with some of the more sophisticated on-board units deployed in heavy vehicles, such as the Sitraffic Sensus. As we enable vehicles to calculate their own tolls, which in itself is not a bad thing, it begins to open up possibilities for Governments to go that next step – full road user charging. That might be a long bow going from a simple scheme for taxis to road user charging, but the truth is it is no longer a technology issue. It is now a policy issue.

Exempt Vehicles

Every toll road has to deal with some form of exempt vehicle. It makes sense that we don't impose an additional financial burden on the people who come and rescue us in times of crisis. The issue becomes recognising true exempt vehicles and then managing them against an exempt vehicle account.

There are two options:

- Issue tags – as soon as you send out a box of exempt tags you begin to lose control as to where those tags go. Most of them will end up in fire trucks, ambulances and police cars. Some will end up in other places. Getting them back will be next to impossible.
- Maintain a list of exempt vehicle licence plates. This is slightly easier to manage because if you need to check that an exempt vehicle is what it says it is, you can always check what you're seeing through the image processing system. A public transport bus is pretty obvious. But an unmarked police car by definition isn't.

If your concession deed or Government regulations require exemption for certain vehicles, so be it. Just be aware though that these vehicles will need managing.

Customers Doing It For Themselves

Figure 33 – Madi, customer service professional

"Hello. You've called NextLink. You pay to use our tarmac. Your call will be recorded for quality assurance and training purposes. Hi, my name is Madi. I hope you're having a great day. How may I help you?"

"Oh, sorry, I think I've got the wrong number. I was after the taxidermist's in George Street."

"Oh … well … I hope you have a great dead animal stuffing day! Is there anything else I can help you with at this time?"

"Um, not really, unless you know how to embalm a stoat?"

"No, we're a turnpike. Is there anything else I can do for you today?"

"No, thanks.

"No, thank you. Goodbye."

Toll roads must have customers, and like or not we have to interact with those customers to make sure everything is running smoothly and the money keeps coming in. I know very little about running call centres, but I have the greatest admiration for those that run them well. Like a top flight image processing team, a good call centre and customer reception centre can make a huge difference to the way your customers perceive you. But they come at a cost, and the truth is that unless a customer has a difficult or unusual problem, most customer interactions could and should be dealt with on-line. This section is about how we can give our tolling system a friendly face and present that to customers so that they can do things for themselves.

To understand how to do that we have to identify with our customers and they fall into several different types:

New-comers – they may never have used a toll road before. They need information to help them decide what they have to do.

Casuals – they know about the toll road – they've used it before. They don't want an account, just one of those pass things to cover them for a trip they are going to make.

Disgruntled – they've received a NATP Invoice telling them they have to pay. They are on the site to pay. They don't like you.

Regulars – your customers who use the road on a regular basis. They have an account and want to perform some action.

Informers – they just want to tell you that there is an embalmed stoat on the road and they want to take it home, or the lights on your tolling gantries keep them awake at night, or that there has been a terrible accident at Junction 6. They want to pass on information. They may or may not expect a reply.

Then there are two more types of customer. We can define these as:

Angry – they aren't going to use your website because they want to shout at somebody. They don't care – they're angry and they just want to shout, lots.

Lonely – they aren't going to use your website because they just want to talk – about anything – for a long time, with a real person.

I can't really help you with Angry and Lonely, but it is probably a good idea to get policies in place to handle those people.

For our other customers, to help guide them to right places there are two golden rules:

- Don't assume that they know anything about what you do or how you operate. If you work in the tolling industry you will come to this with a whole set of hidden assumptions and a vocabulary that may not mean anything to the lay person. To this end,
- Employ the best user experience designer (UXD) you can find (regardless of how much they cost) that has never worked on a toll road website or app before, and let him or her translate your crazy talk into a meaningful flow of actions.

Without trying to second guess what your UXD will tell, you have to think about three distinct aspects of your on-line experience:

- Areas that inform, educate and advise,
- Areas that let people transact with you i.e. actually do something with the tolling system,
- Areas that let people interact with you, sometimes in real time.

Inform, educate, advise for new-comers

Take a moment to think about it – if you're going on a road trip, somewhere you've never been before, how do you work out the route you're going to take? In the past you would have had to dust off the road atlas (remember those) and spend some time pouring over curious cartographical symbols to work out a journey plan. Then, halfway through the trip you discover that your atlas was so out of date your planning is meaningless and you have to wing it anyway. Now you can jump on a super service like Google Maps. It's up to date and it does all the hard work in devising a route for you. It even lets you print out directions. Then there are some people who don't make a plan at all. They get in the car, turn on the satellite navigation system (sat nav), type in a destination and drive. And then they bump into your toll road.

Most services like Google Maps and good sat navs do alert people to the fact that they will be using a toll road and so hopefully that prompts them to do something about it. But who do they contact? In some cases it is quite straight forward. Google Maps shows EastLink as a toll road, and a quick search for Eastlink gets you to the right website. That is the first thing to get right – that the way your road is referred to by third parties matches up with the way your own website refers to the road. It doesn't matter if somebody is wrong in some way, just so long as everybody is consistent.

There will be people who look at their sat nav, see the toll road alert and just blatantly ignore it – so what, they're on holiday! If your road is truly MLFF you won't be able to stop them using it, so the next thing to do is make sure the actual road signage is clear:

- Tell them they are about to enter a toll road, and
- That they have to do something about it by making a call or going to a website.

It sounds obvious but some people still won't get it, and checking out the local toll roads won't be a high priority on the list of things to do for visitors to your part of the world.

Road names and numbers can be very confusing. One of the most complex has to be the I95[20] on the East coast of the USA. Yes it is the I95, but just about every section has another "local" name, and it is a combination of free and tolled roads, and those tolled sections are operated by a number of different organisations with non-interoperable tolling systems. I know that I would be hard pressed to remember the name of any road I've used, but I'll be talking about the "great time I had in New York and the drive to Boston" for years to come. So the second thing to get right with your website is to talk about the places your road can take you. By all means use your road name, but also name the towns and cities connected by it.

Figure 34 – Signage for toll roads in Victoria, Australia. The convention has become to use blue and gold colours for toll road signs.

If people make it on to your website you've won half the battle. You'll probably lose the other half if you have a button that says something like "Temporary Validations". What does that mean? Much better to say something like "Travel on NextLink". That assumes they know they travelled on NextLink, but given they're on the site we can assume they do. Once they click on that link you have a great opportunity to sell them that pass product and explain the virtues of other tolling products. A "toll product selector", a guide to which type of product is best for each type of user is a neat idea. These are some elements to consider in the **inform, educate, advise** section of your site:

- To answer the question – where can I go? Where did I go? Maps showing the towns linked by your road,
- To answer the question - how much do I have to pay? Closely linked to the maps, the interactive toll calculator,
- To answer the question – how do I pay? That toll product selector which should include any rules about the length of time after travel that a payment can be made, and then tell them what happens after that. And of course a transact component that actually lets them buy a temporary product of some kind to pay for their travel.
- Notifications about road works and road closures,
- A link to a real-time traffic monitoring service to show congestion on the road network,
- Services available if you break down on the toll road, and
- Links to sites that advertise events going on in the local area – very cute.

Do whatever you can to make sure that customers are using the most appropriate toll product for their circumstances so that you don't end up in some enforcement or debt collection regime. It makes for a much better experience with the customer and a lot less cost and aggravation for your business.

Inform, educate, advise for disgruntled

Disgruntled in this sense because they've travelled on your road without an arrangement to pay and you sent them that NATP Invoice demanding payment – and they are trying to comply with the order, but aren't thrilled about having to do it. It's important that the words on the piece of paper match the words on the website. If the piece of paper talks about a "NATP Notice" and the website refers to a "Toll Invoice" then people are going to get confused. That sounds obvious, but the only reason I mention it is that the people who look after your website aren't necessarily the same people that design and send out the pieces of paper.

The button next to the "Travel on NextLink" then becomes "Received a NATP Invoice". I'm using the word Received here rather than Pay because the customer might want to dispute the fact they owe you money. The person driving the car might have been the idiot son (who was told not to use the road) or Uncle Samba over from Germany (who they can't stand anyway). Clicking on that button therefore gives the customer two options:

- Pay the invoice based on the invoice number – which should be in big font at the top of the piece of paper, or
- Nominate another person, like Uncle Samba.

What you are allowed to do will depend on the laws applying in your jurisdiction. Make paying as simple as possible – a clean interface that takes a credit card number and provides a receipt. Only at the end of that transaction should you then consider going for the up-sell to a regular tolling product of some sort. One trick is to put a QR code on the piece of paper which takes the customer straight to the payment window with the NATP Invoice number and trip details pre-populated.

Allowing people to nominate their NATP Invoices is fair and reasonable – after all, they may not have been driving the car, but the process can become complicated. If the person wants to nominate the whole invoice, then all well and good. You should require that they have to provide a significant level of detail about the person who was actually driving the vehicle to add a certain robustness to the process. It starts getting complicated when there are three trips on the NATP Invoice, and they only want to nominate one of them to another person. How you deal with that scenario depends on your own internal business rules and the capabilities of your tolling system. The other complication with this scenario is that the person nominated might well turn round and deny that they were driving the vehicle at the time. Quickly you can end up disappearing down the rabbit hole of a third person being nominated or trying to resolve a dispute between a disgruntled father and the idiot son. You really have to work these scenarios through in the context of your own business.

Transact

Transact is where your tolling system website should start to save you money in terms of customers being able to do things for themselves, rather than calling your contact centre. We've already identified a few "interact" operations which it is to be noted, do not require a "log in" by the customer:

- Buy a temporary toll product such as a trip pass,
- On occasion view the status of a temporary toll product i.e. I bought a few trip passes last time, are any still valid for travel?
- Pay a NATP Invoice,
- Nominate another person having received a NATP Invoice.

The "log in" operations start with the creation of an account. An account is the portal which transforms an anonymous road user into a known customer. It's very important and should be the third button on the front of your site – "Open an Account" – and of course be linked to your "toll product selector" section. The account type (the toll product) and your own business rules will determine the information a customer will have to give you – but whatever that information is, forewarn them at the start of the process. If you don't there is a good chance they'll have to go off and rummage around in a box of files somewhere, not find what they're looking for, come back to the computer, decide it is all too hard and read the news instead. It's not difficult – at the top of the page just state you'll need to give us your name, e-mail address, home address, driver's licence number, details of your vehicles, your credit card number, proof of identity from three independent sources, surety based on your first born etc.. It goes without saying that the more information they need to provide, the greater the chance that the account opening process won't be completed in one go. Given that, the tolling system should provide a function that allows customers to recover semi-completed account applications.

It follows that the flow of the account opening process will be based around the data requirements of the toll product, but it can also be used to drive outcomes favourable to the road operator. Good examples are to default options to:

- Statements and invoices produced quarterly and delivered by e-mail – reduces costs associated with printing and sending paper. Paper could be an extra cost option.
- Automatic account top-ups based on a credit card – do you even want to offer alternatives?

Some accounts can be become active almost immediately based on a real-time validity check of a credit card number. Some, such as those for post-paid business accounts may take a little longer because there may be a business credit check involved. Whatever the situation, make it clear at the end of the account opening process what the customer is and is not able to do. For example, it may take three days to get their tags to them, but that shouldn't stop them using the road in the meantime – but your tolling system has to know that so for those three days it can waive the image processing fee.

Take a moment to think about how customers will log-in again once they have an account. For security and privacy reasons they will have to have a log-in ID and password of some sort. There are a number of options for log-in IDs:

- The account or customer number – but seriously, who remembers that?
- The e-mail address they gave you – that's always a good one,
- The licence plate of one of their vehicles – maybe, not a bad idea.

Or allow all three! Obviously then the website needs a "Log-in" button. Once an account is up and running, for your regulars, the set of interact functions includes:

Account maintenance – all the usual things around updating addresses, telephone numbers and passwords. Crucial to this section is payment methods. Customers will need to update credit card details or details around other payment methods. This section can also give options concerning contact channel preferences (e.g. SMS, e-mail) and statement and invoice preferences. Contact channel preferences are important because we want to warn customers about low account balances before accounts get suspended and everything heads off down the enforcement route. Important for businesses is the ability to give more than one person authority to manage an account, so this section should include functionality to specify those other people. This section is also where you might want to hide the "Close Account" button.

Payments – hopefully you have most of your customers on an automatic top-up arrangement, but for those who aren't, or where an auto top-up has failed, the ability to make a manual payment is crucial.

Account status, transaction and payment history – this is the real heart of the account. It should show clearly the account balance, the account status i.e. is everything OK, the transaction history and the payment history. Again if your tolling system is smart it will show transactions and payments as a continuous flow of activity with a running account balance. That way customers can see exactly what is going on. It's a neat trick if you can let customers download their transaction history directly as a CSV file or spreadsheet. This section should also contain links to previous statements and invoices stored on-line. Depending on how smart your roadside equipment is, you might also be able to indicate the status of a customer's tag. Some roadside equipment will send through a tag status message in situations where a tag battery appears to be low or tag reception is intermittent indicating that it might not be mounted correctly. This is only worth doing if you're sure the tag status information is correct and you can offer advice as to what to do about it.

Vehicles – updating vehicle details. This is important when people buy new vehicles or dispose of or sell a vehicle. As discussed previously, if your tolling system is smart enough, it should work out the class associated with the vehicle based on its licence plate and state of registration. This section should also let customers report that a vehicle has been stolen, often along with its tag, on the basis that they can provide a Police report number.

Tags – which includes ordering an extra tag, returning a tag or registering that a tag has been lost, stolen or destroyed – the "dog ate my tag" scenario. Often there are fees and charges associated with tag movements, so these need to be communicated to the customer. If a customer wants to return a tag, it's a nice gesture to send them out a shielded bag. After all, the mail truck may use your toll road to bring you the tag back.

In addition to the above, there are a couple of more specialist operations you may want to offer:

Nominations – much like the nominations associated toll invoices, you might want to allow customers to nominate trips on their account to other people – the scenario where Uncle Samba borrowed the car for a day without asking.

Toll invoice transfers – given that the interoperability system is not 100% perfect, on occasion a customer who has a valid account with one toll road operator may get a toll invoice from another toll operator. One function you might provide is the ability for that customer to apply the toll charges on that toll invoice directly to their account – on the understanding that you will make the other fees and charges go away because something stuffed up in the interoperability system.

Interact

Interact is simply giving a person, the Informers, a way of getting in touch with you. You can consider two distinct forms of interactions:

- Those that are "anonymous" – that can come from anybody using the website, and
- Those can come from a customer when they are logged in.

Depending on your business rules, and in some cases your KPI regime, you may want to use the tolling system to create a case around the communication, and then manage that case through to some sort of completion.

A feature which is becoming increasingly popular on websites is interactive chat. I'm sure you've been on a website where one of those little windows has popped up and asked you whether you need help. The technology behind this kind of system can be very clever – it can detect if people appear to be "dithering" i.e. uncertain as to their next move. I'm told that the great thing about web chat is that an experienced operator can successfully maintain more than one line of chat at a time, which is not really possible with normal telephone conversations. So web chat can be a good way of enhancing your customer's experience of your website and in the process reinforcing it as the best channel to use, while making better use of your contact centre staff. But all things in proportion. Some customers will find that web chat pop-up very annoying.

In summary, we've identified four buttons for your website:

- Travel on NextLink,
- Received a NATP Invoice,
- Open an account, and
- Log-in.

Figure 36 below shows the real Roam website from Transurban.

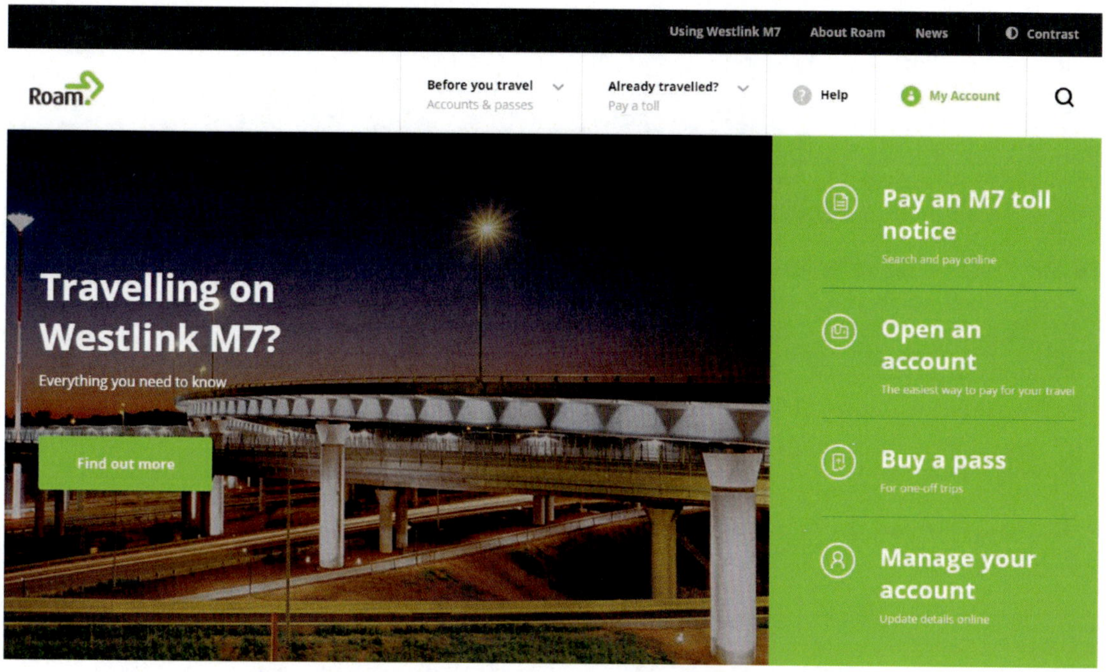

Figure 36 – the Roam website from Transurban (2017)

All the features we've just discussed are present on this site:

- *Travel on NextLink* is covered by the two buttons at the top – "Before you travel" which is all about toll products, and "Already travelled" which is about buying a pass up to three days after travelling.
- *Received a NATP invoice* is covered again under the "Already travelled" button at the top, but also by the big button on the right "Pay an M7 toll notice" – and it's *notice*, not *invoice* in this case.
- *Open an account* is clear, again a big button on the right hand side.
- *Log-in* is covered in two areas – the "My Account" button, top right, and the "Manage your account" button on the bottom right.

This site also provides a Help link and a search function. I've only shown the top half of the site. On the real site, scrolling down reveals further options, including a nifty FAQ feature designed, I'm guessing, to stop people calling the contact centre.

Other functions

In addition to all those functions needed to support customers, your tolling system has to be able to do so much more.

Customer Service Operators have to be able to do all of the above for customers, plus:

- Have access to sophisticated search functions so that they can find information quickly to help customers on the phone,

- They have to be able to adjust and fix things, so they need extra functions that allow them to manipulate data within the tolling system,
- Manage the workflow associated with cases.

In addition to that, the tolling system needs to support the following:

- User access roles, groups and security,
- User audit – keeping track of who is doing what,
- System audit – keeping track of what the system is actually doing with all those trips and payments,
- Financial reconciliation – a tolling system is a big money making machine and the Finance Department will want to be able to constantly reconcile the money collected from customers against the trips made, the fees and charges, interoperability interactions, what has ended up in the General Ledger and how much money there actually is in the bank account,
- Tag logistics – all the operations around ordering, issuing and retrieving tags,
- Interoperability – the daily management of data between all the toll roads within an interoperability group.

Figure 35 – Samantha – "Geee, customer service is just dreamy ..."

Enforcement Systems

Of all the enforcement systems currently in operation around the world, I firmly believe that the most exciting must be being chased by the Californian Highway Patrol down a HOV lane, your FasTrak Flex rammed into position 3, with a well-used blow up rubber doll at ya side. The only thing punctuating the wail of the police sirens is the roar from the big Jaguar V8. You turn to her "Honey, if we get out of this one without a traffic violation, boy are we going to make sweet music tonight". But you know she doesn't need words, no more empty promises, no more lies – just an air compressor and a bottle of canola oil …

Yes, the real problem with writing about enforcement systems is that everybody does it differently. There is no standard across states in a country, let alone across the world. But every operator of a multilane free-flow toll road knows why we have to have some kind of enforcement system. In my opinion MLFF toll roads work because:

- Most people have a certain respect for the rule of law,
- They recognise that the service provided by a toll road comes at a price – the service wouldn't exist otherwise,
- The prices charged for that service are reasonable and there are channels for recourse in the case of disputes,
- There is an alternative free route, albeit a more dangerous and congested one, and
- Most people want to do the right thing most of the time if they are treated in a decent way.

If you lose sight of those five basic things then you will be heading for trouble. The truth is that the worst nightmare for an MLFF toll road operator is a massive and sustained campaign of non-compliance. If a population turns against you nothing is going to save you – you'll have to throw up the boom gates again, and let's see how long those last. Fortunately the last riot I know of that involved Turnpikes was way back in the 1840s in Wales, the Rebecca Riots[21]. Those riots were more about unfair taxation in general, but the Turnpikes were a strong symbol of those taxes.

Most people will do the right thing most of the time. Enforcement is there to remind those that don't that their behaviour can't and won't be tolerated. Enforcement is a stick, but one that has to be used in a fair and measured way so that you don't end up staring at out of your tolling office window at pitchforks and burning torches.

The best I can do here is describe the system in Victoria, Australia, which is an interesting model to study because it has good and bad features. It all starts with a person driving on the road who has no valid arrangement to pay i.e. no tolling account, a tolling account that is suspended or no trip pass. After three days, if the account hasn't been reactivated (un-suspended) or an account hasn't been opened or a trip pass purchased the trip becomes a NATP trip. I'll talk about the suspended account scenario later. Let's keep it simple for now.

The NATP trip is identified by the licence plate string and registration details. If the state is Victoria, then the licence plate string is sent off to VicRoads who can look up the licence plate and return a registered address. This activity incurs the "VicRoads look-up fee". In the vast majority of cases VicRoads will return an address, but sometimes they can't. Without that address the enforcement process is scuppered and has to stop. That trip toll is lost. With an address the process continues with the first NATP Invoice. The first NATP Invoice may contain just one trip or several. There is the concept of an aggregation period for NATP trips which is a business rule governed by some legislation – for example, a company may decide to aggregate three days' worth of trips onto the one NATP Invoice.

The first NATP Invoice is a piece of paper which requires payment of three things:

- The trip toll(s),
- The VicRoads look-up fee,
- An administration fee to cover the cost of issuing the invoice,

and is sent to the person whose address was supplied by VicRoads. A first NATP Invoice can turn a $1 toll into a $15 bill. At this point four things can happen:

- The person can open the letter and pay the invoice – which is great. Hopefully you can catch them at that point and get them to open an account.
- Somebody writes "return to sender" on the letter and puts it back in the post. This is problematic. The person may genuinely no longer be at that address, and haven't informed VicRoads – or they might just be hiding. Either way, unless you can find better information about the person, again the enforcement process is scuppered.
- Somebody opens the letter and reads it, then works out that they weren't actually driving the car on that date. They nominate another person to receive the NATP Invoice. In this case, if the nomination is accepted, the process starts again but with this new person.
- Nothing.

If nothing happens, then after a couple of weeks you can issue a second NATP Invoice. This is pretty much the same as the first except that the fees go up. So now that $1 toll could be a $25 bill. The same four outcomes apply to second invoice.

If nothing happens again, then things get a bit more serious. The NATP Invoices having been ignored, the matter becomes a Government civic compliance issue. If you think about it, this is a little unusual. The Government doesn't step in if you don't pay your telephone bill, or miss an instalment on your credit card. Yet in Victoria they do get involved with non-payment of tolls. In a way it could be argued that it is traffic related in the same sense that speeding and red light tickets are traffic related. But at the same time it's the Government acting as a debt collector for private companies. It was a feature of the original deal to get CityLink built and is "business as usual" now.

The NATP Invoice now becomes a fine. The responsibility for further actions moves away from the toll road operator and to the State Government department responsible for these things – except not entirely. The law states that a person can only be fined for one trip per day, so if the original invoice had more than one trip per day recorded, the other trips cannot become the subject of the fine. They remain as debt for the toll operator and it's up to the operator to try and recover that through other means, like a professional debt collection agency.

The fine is a lot more money – typically around $150. That $1 unpaid toll is now becoming a real liability. If the first fine is paid, then the State keeps most of the money and the toll road operator gets the trip toll value and an administration fee. If the first fine isn't paid, then the fine amount keeps ratchetting up. It is now not uncommon to find people who owe $1000s and sometimes $10,000s in unpaid toll related fines[22]. This problematic for two reasons:

- Most people think it unfair that $1 of unpaid tolls can result in $1000s of fines. Often, when these matters do get to court, the court settles on a much smaller sum than that represented by the fines. In the meantime it can be very worrying for the person faced with having to pay the fines – even though they could have taken action earlier to prevent the situation occurring in the first place.
- The State is having to keep millions of dollars of unpaid fines on its books, and dealing with the fines clogs up the courts which should be focussing on more serious matters.

There is a case for looking again at this system and trying to come up with something more efficient and a little less dramatic.

Suspended accounts

A pre-paid account is suspended when the balance crashes through the low balance threshold, then continues on into negative territory and stays there for seven to ten days.

The rules around post-paid account suspensions are less clear cut. Most of these are operated by businesses and discussions around the payment of invoices usually ends up in some kind of financial negotiation.

Once an account is suspended, the account holder's arrangement to pay with the toll road operator is cancelled meaning:

- The tolling system no longer recognises the account as valid – and propagates that status to other toll road operators through the interoperability files,
- The tags associated with the account are put on the tag blacklist. This ensures that if that tag passes under a tolling gantry, the tag gives off the one plus three beeps signal – indicating a suspended account – and even though there is a tag in the vehicle, the roadside equipment will take and keep an image of the vehicle as evidence of travel for enforcement purposes.
- The licence plate strings associated with the account are taken off the whitelist.

If the account holder continues to use the road, or any road in the interoperability group, they will start to incur NATP Invoices. Customers with suspended accounts are different to people with no arrangement to pay because you know who the customer is and hopefully where they live. So those new NATP Invoices become part of their account. A smart tolling system will be able to accommodate and manage those invoices as part of the account structure. Given that you know who the customer is, hopefully you can communicate with them in good time to stop the situation getting any worse and recover the money owed.

Ombudsman

In Australia, if you end up in a serious dispute with a toll road company you have the option of referring the matter to the Tolling Customer Ombudsman[23]. The Ombudsman is there to take an independent and impartial view of a situation and make a finding as to how it best be resolved.

Finance

If, like me, you identify yourself as being an Ingenieur, you must approach the Finance Department as though you are a pilgrim in an unholy land. Most accountants look and sound like regular people but don't be fooled. No matter how valuable you are to an organisation, there will be an accountant who is viewing you as a Cost Centre that reduces the amount he or she can distribute to the shareholders (and their CFO's bonus for that matter). Maybe that is just my post-traumatic stress and paranoia talking? Who cares! In a business like a toll road, which is a huge money making machine, most decisions will get made based on the numbers in spreadsheets produced by some Svengali type figure who hides in an office at the back of the Finance Department and who reacts badly to sunlight.

But that said, while we are gainfully employed we do want to get paid and so it remains in our interests to ensure that the tolling system feeds the right kind of data into the corporate financial system to keep those accountants occupied and balanced. One thing I do know is that an unbalanced accountant is a dreadful thing. They will actually leave their office, come and find you and ask you *questions*. Believe me that is not something you want to experience on a regular basis.

Money is the life blood of every business. Very few people go into business for the love of it. They want to make money. But to make money usually requires that you have to spend money. The role of the accountant is to keep track of all this money to ensure that you know you are making more money than you spend. If you are then you're making a profit and the world will seem like a good place to be. If you are spending more than you make then you're making a loss and that is generally not a good thing. At the simplest level, accountants keep track of all the individual transactions that represent money in and out of a business so they can tell us if we are making or losing money. Before computers the records of all these transactions were written down on parchment using quill pens and book-keepers would labour away by candle light to keep everything on track. Now these things can be handled much more efficiently using sophisticated software applications.

These software applications are vital for businesses like toll roads. With hundreds of thousands of transactions being recorded every day we just couldn't do it any other way. The sheer number of transactions also means that we can't consider each one individually – we have to group transactions into financial types. Once grouped, the accountants can then use the data to produce their reports, and it's those reports that reveal the financial situation of the business. Crucially the transactions we see moving through our systems have to be reconciled with the real money we end up with in our bank accounts.

The same financial data can be used in a number of different ways. In business there are two basic types of accounting – financial and management. Financial accounting is about producing the reports needed to satisfy regulatory regimes such as the Tax Office and the Stock Exchange. Both have their own sets of reporting rules. Most Stock Exchanges for example have quite strict continuous disclosure rules, so if your reports are telling you things aren't going that well, you have to share that information with the Stock Exchange pretty quickly. Management accounting is more concerned with information that allows the senior management team to make informed business decisions such as the need to borrow more money, the ability to pay off debt, or that the funds are there to support reinvestment or a research and development project. It enables the monitoring of business expenses, explains profit margins and makes possible the forecasting of future financial results.

To explain how the tolling system has to provide its own financial data, I'm going to start at the end of the financial process, and finish at the beginning. That may sound counter-intuitive, but bear with me. When I talk about the end of the financial process, I'm referring to the creation of two specific reports – the Balance Sheet and the Profit and Loss Statement. Just about every business in the world produces a version of these reports at least once a year. If you work for a business that is listed on a stock exchange you should be able to download these reports as part of their Annual Report. I could at this point show you examples of real reports but I won't, not because the concept is difficult, but the particular terms used in these reports can be quite opaque and won't help us in our understanding. In a sense the Balance Sheet and the Profit and Loss Statement are the parents of all the other financial reports. They usually combine all the financial data accumulated over the previous year into one snapshot showing the financial health of the business.

To help us understand what is going on here, I'm going to show you the Balance Sheet and Profit and Loss Statement for Mr and Ms Devonish in figure 37. If you would like to look at real ones for a toll road, great examples can be found in the Annual Report of Transurban[24].

In the Balance Sheet we're listing everything the couple own (assets) and everything they owe (liabilities). The difference between the two is their capital (worth). They seem to be doing quite well in that regards. Similarly for the Profit and Loss Statement we're listing all the money coming in (revenue) and all the money they have to pay out (expenses). The difference is the profit they've made for the year, and again, they seem to be doing quite well. No sign of any children which makes a huge difference. For a normal household without very complex financial affairs, getting hold of the numbers in these two reports should be fairly straightforward. You can check your payslips to work out how much money you earned. You can look at your bank statement to determine the cost of your mortgage and so on. For a business like a toll road though the problem is more complicated. You can think of each line in those two reports as representing "accounts" in the company's accounting system. But what we're seeing here is a summary (one line) of data that is derived from many discrete sources of data. So in practice each line, each account, actually has sitting beneath it a whole series of sub-accounts which together go to a form a company's *Chart of Accounts*.

Mr and Mrs Devonish (2017)
Balance Sheet

You can think of each line here as an "account"

Assets		Liabilities	
Current Assets		**Current Liabilities**	
Cash at bank	2,500	Mortgage interest	350,000
Share portfolio	26,000	Vehicle lease	14,000
Jewelry	17,000	Credit Card	4,600
Non-current Assets		**Non-current Liabilities**	
Property	800,000	Mortgage principal	130,000
Furniture	37,000	Vehicle balloon	26,000
Vehicles	72,000		
Super Fund	650,000		
Assets total	**1,604,500**	**Liabilities total**	**524,600**

Assets – Liabilities = Capital → **Capital** **1,079,900**

Profit and Loss Statement

You can think of each line here as an "account"

Revenue		Expenses	
Normal activites		**Normal activities**	
Salary Mr Devonsih	113,000	Mortgage interest	19,650
Salary Ms Devonish	126,000	Utilities	12,000
Share income	3,000	Credit Card	5,000
Other income		Vehicles	23,200
Bequest Ms Ng	34,000	Household	72,000
		Travel	32,000
Revenue total	**276,000**	**Expenses total**	**163,850**

Revenue – Expenses = Profit → **Profit** **112,150**

Figure 37 – Balance Sheet and Profit and Loss Statement for Mr and Ms Devonish

These sub-accounts are used to show exactly where the data came from and in accounting terms how they should be treated. Take revenue for example. A toll road might wish to know how much revenue came from pre-paid tolling accounts, how much came from trip passes and how much they managed to claw back from NATP Invoices. The chart of accounts would be structured with a sub-account for each of these items, and crucially each sub-account is given a unique code to identify the source of the revenue. Figure 38 demonstrates this concept.

How complex your company's chart of accounts actually is depends entirely upon the rules governing your business and the kind of reports your senior management team want to see. The granularity of those sub-accounts will determine the extent to which you can finesse your financial reports. Also the chart of accounts will live in the corporate financial system and so this drives a crucial set of requirements for the tolling system. The tolling system has to be able to feed data into this chart of accounts and to do so it has to correctly classify and code all the transactions it processes.

NextLink Chart of Accounts

Revenue – account codes 4001 to 4999

Tolling Revenue – account codes 4001 to 4099

	Unbilled	Billed	Paid	Bad debt
Toll Exempt	4001	4002	4003	4004
Toll Pre-Paid Customer	4011	4012	4013	4014
Toll Post-Paid Customer	4021	4022	4023	4024
Toll Interoperable Customer	4031	4032	4033	4034
Toll NATP	4041	4042	4043	4044
Toll Trip Pass	4051	4052	4053	4054

Fee Revenue – account codes 4101 to 4199

Lots more categories follow to make up the Chart of Accounts

Figure 38 – Example of part of NextLink's Chart of Accounts

But note that the tolling system is not the only source of data for the chart of accounts. You wouldn't use the tolling system to pay an invoice for the office cleaner, or the garage that services the road's emergency response vehicles. In a tolling company the tolling system is a significant source of data for the financial system, but by no means the only source of data. To get a feel for how that all fits together we're now going to look at the process from the other end – the beginning. Figure 39 summarises the accounting process from the beginning – the creation of financial transactions – through to the end – the production of those key financial reports.

In the first instance all the company's financial transactions, including those created within the tolling system, are written into journals. In modern software applications you can think of these as files or database tables. Crucially journal entries must have a time date stamp, describe the nature of the transaction and its source, as well as the monetary value of course. Periodically journal entries are "posted" to accounts within the ledgers. There may be several ledgers dealing with specific types of transactions, but ultimately everything ends up in the General Ledger that holds the chart of accounts we discussed earlier. This General Ledger is the repository of the company's financial information, and the source of data for all the company's financial reports.

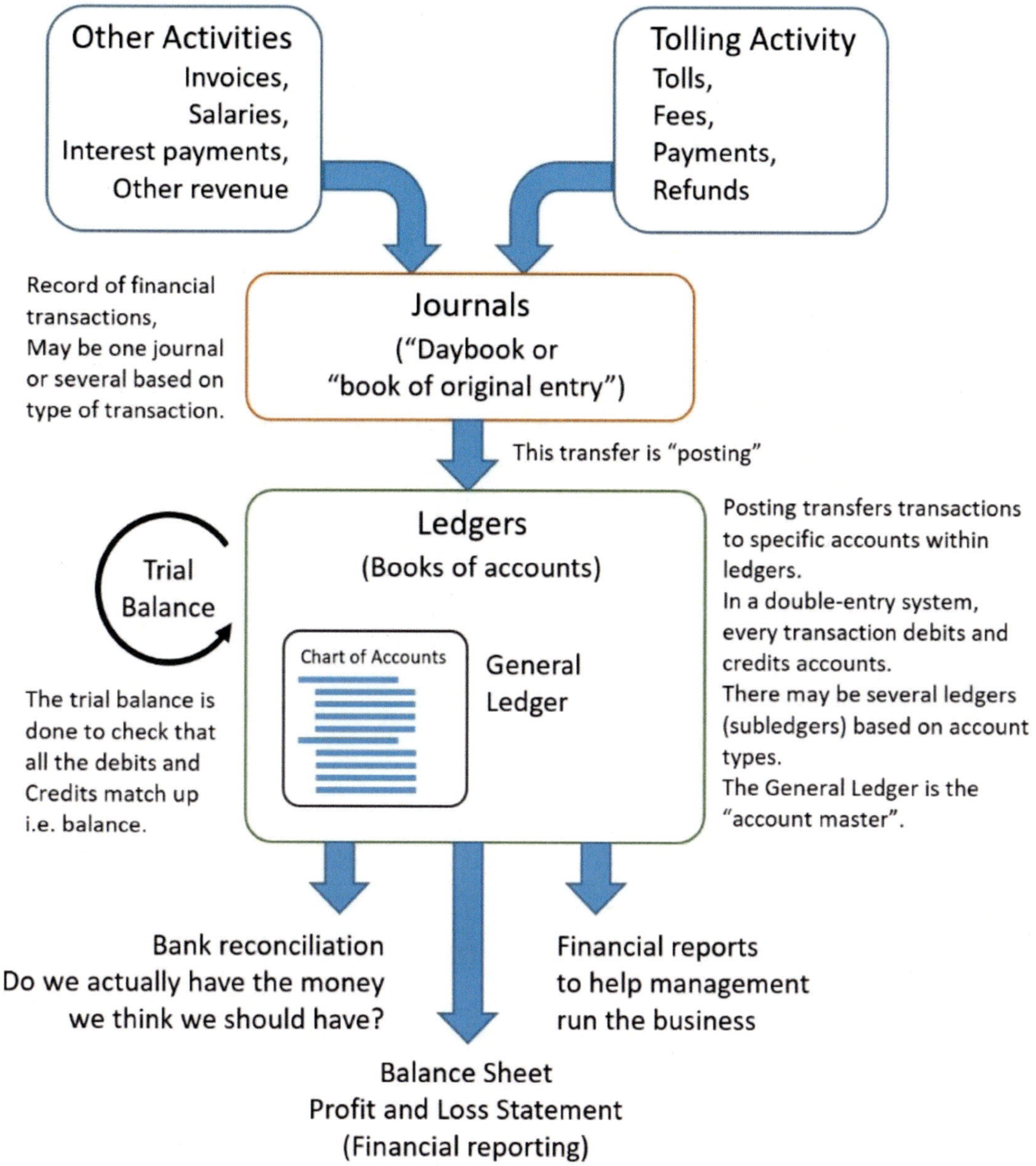

Figure 39 – The basic accounting process with journals and ledgers

Now just to confuse you when you thought you were on safe ground, the accountants throw in the idea of double-entry bookkeeping. This is based on the concept that every financial transaction has an impact on two of your accounts. Let me try and give you a couple of examples:

> The Customer Service Manager withdraws $200 from the company bank account to put into the customer service cash desk. This means we must:
>
> > Credit the bank account, and
> >
> > Debit the cash account.
>
> Mr Barnes pays his $56 post-paid account invoice. This means we must:
>
> > Debit the bank account, and
> >
> > Credit Mr Barnes tolling account.

The whole process behind a trial balance is to add up credit and debits and make sure the numbers you get at the end match i.e. the accounts balance. If they don't something has gone astray and accountants will spend as long as it takes rummaging through journals and ledgers to find the missing piece.

I'll be absolutely honest and say that this whole double-entry concept is confusing. As a concept it is centuries old. According to Wikipedia[25] the earliest accounting records that follow the modern double-entry system in Europe come from Amatino Manucci, who produced the Farolfi firm's ledger of 1299-1300 which employs full double-entry bookkeeping. It just shows you the pace of innovation in the accounting world. If information technology had followed a similar model we'd still be using the abacus. Granted it might be made of carbon fibre with a graphene coating for easy bead sliding, but it would still be an abacus. That said we're still using the wheel so if it works just go with it.

For the tolling system, the most important thing to consider is at what point do you want the tolling system to interface with the financial system? Do you want the tolling system to dump out a whole stream of transactions and let the financial system put them into the journals? Should the tolling system create its own journals, do its own posting and then drive data straight into the chart of accounts? If the later, you will need to sit down with the accountants in your company, understand the chart of accounts, and then decide, for each transaction in the tolling system, where the debits and credits have to fall.

It is my expectation that a tolling system would:

- Maintain its own set of journals,
- Regularly post journal entries to a subset of the chart of accounts (the bits relevant to tolling transactions),
- Be set-up correctly so that the debits and credits for every financial movement are recorded properly,
- Be able to transfer that data to the corporate financial system at least on a daily basis,
- Have the capacity, and that capacity proven, to correctly handle adjustments, refunds and cancellations within the chart of accounts.

Now if you're feeling a bit icky after all that it's nothing that a stiff gin and tonic and soak in the bath won't cure. And while you're there, I find it helps to hum this little ditty from Monty Python's "Crimson Permanent Assurance[26]".

It's fun to charter an accountant
And sail the wide accountancy,
To find, explore the funds offshore
And skirt the shoals of bankruptcy!

It can be manly in insurance.
We'll up your premium semi-annually.
It's all tax deductible.
We're fairly incorruptible,
We're sailing on the wide accountancy!

Part 2

A more detailed look at the technical architecture of modern tolling systems including Data Items.

Tolling System Projects

Figure 40 – A tolling system project kick off meeting

Welcome ladies and gentlemen to this our project kick-off meeting! Now, who can tell me what we're supposed to be building?
Um, well, a tolling system.
Great work John – off to a flying start. A tolling system. Now what sort of a thing is that?
What, you didn't read Rupert's book?
Detail John, just detail. Now, let's bring this up a level ...

Be under no illusions – building a tolling system is a major undertaking. It takes expertise, time, money, resources, patience, planning and a good deal of nerve to get this kind of project over the line in a satisfactory manner. Yes it is just another big software project, but one with a lot of moving parts, spurious data from numerous inputs and that has to deal with Physics impinging on the real world through the roadside equipment. To put this in perspective, on a typical project which includes roadside equipment, you can expect to generate in excess of 5,000 business requirements which can easily translate into over 10,000 detailed system requirements, and even then there is a good chance you'll miss defining something. That is quite a lot of data to manage right there. "But dude!" I hear you say, "What is it with all this requirements stuff? So yesterday! Let's break out the post-it notes, knock out a few user stories. We'll do agile man." It might work. Good luck with that one. Go for your life. Today, the reality is a project is most likely to take the form of a traditional requirements gathering and analysis phase followed by a software delivery process that is based on sprints or a series of releases that gradually builds functionality. That does make a lot of sense – it gives the team time and opportunity to adjust requirements and functionality during the project, rather than have a nightmare panic scenario at the very end when you realise you wanted an elephant and you're getting a giraffe.

It sounds clichéd, but when thinking about getting a big project up one of the most important things you have to understand is your own corporate culture and the thinking of senior executives – especially if you are on the hook to deliver anything. In fact don't get yourself on the hook for *anything* until you do know what they are thinking. I was on a project working with a very competent local software house. We were in the specification phase of the project and from where I was sitting it looked to be going well. The CIO at the time then dismissed that software house on the basis that, and I quote "they aren't tier 1 enough". What that should tell you is nothing you could have done would have ever made a difference. This CIO and his ego wanted to play with the big boys. The end result wasn't as important as who he was seen to be dealing with. To be fair, those tier 1 software houses are very good at massaging the egos of C-level executives. They have teams of "relationship managers" whose role in life is to smooch senior people, and they carry a small arsenal with them in terms of tickets to Wimbledon, paddock days at the Formula 1, a Grand Final box and special lunches in the vineyards. All the things that C-level executives have naturally come to expect. Small software houses and some specialist tolling system providers can't match that level of largesse and actually have to rely on doing a good job to win business – not that the tier 1 boys and girls don't. This is the *realpolitik* of working in organisations. So before you take responsibility for a project or any part of it, try and find out:

- What is the real agenda behind this new project? Is it genuinely just a new system? Is it a stalking horse for the outsourcing of IT in your organisation? Is the company lining itself up for a sale or a take-over of another company?
- Is there an agenda with regards to who should do the work? Is there a "preferred" supplier, or will there be a true tender process?
- Who in the senior management team supports the project and who is less than enthusiastic? If you put your neck out on the line, is there anybody there with any real power to back you up?
- Is your company's board going to have visibility of project progress? Board scrutiny puts extra pressure on everybody and can lead to altered states of decision making.
- What are the expectations with regards to budget and timescale, and what are the parameters to be used in determining the business case, one of the most critical being the pay-back period? With what you know before you even start, will the business case ever get up? Do you have a hope of meeting expectations?

Some organisations will take the view that you are an employee and should carry out assignments as they are given to you. All these other considerations are not really relevant. If we say we're doing the project, you're doing the project. Yes, up to a point. Remember this is your career, your life, and you do have some say in the matter. Big projects can burn people up very quickly. Be comfortable with the situation before you dive in. On the other hand, your unique set of skills might make you the only person in the company who could pull this off. Sometimes it is a case of "Who Dares Wins[27]".

You've agreed to sign up to the deal. In my experience, and it's the same for every large project, to give yourself the maximum chance of success, get hold of the best people you can to form your core project team. By best I mean that they:

- Are subject matter experts – they really know what these systems are supposed to do and how they work, but are still open to innovation and finding better ways of doing things,
- Have a great work ethic but do know when to call it quits i.e. they can self-manage their workload and the stress they're experiencing. They'll tell you when they need to go and lie in a darkened room,
- They "get" each other and respect the way other people work. But they're not shy in telling people when they think the wheels are about to fall off,
- They enjoy project work and are committed to the journey – but it helps to add financial incentives along the way,
- They have skills that boost their performance – simple things like they can write their own SQL queries to troubleshoot problems, rather than shout for an analyst to help them. They know their way round Linux and understand the technology in a web stack – that kind of thing.
- They think about things from a technical point of view but in an instant can switch to the user view i.e. they test their work against the needs of the project's ultimate customers.

Get a team of people like that around you and you're off to a great start. Put a load of strangers in a room and shout Charge! – they'll all run off in different directions.

I'm not going to turn this section into a treatise on Project Management. There are hundreds of good books out there already on how to manage projects. But what I do want to do is spend time talking about something I call Project Design. Project Design is analogous to project planning, but I like to think it's more than that because it includes Solution Design. It's not just about the Gantt chart, but rather the *whole shape* of the project. It is an iterative process, to determine the best way to structure a project to achieve the required outcome. Defining a project means identifying and defining the form of project variables – each variable has to be resolved before the project can take "shape". Figure 41 identifies these variable.

Iteration comes about because as you get close to defining one variable, you have to check the effect its form is having on the other variables. For example, you may be quite clear that you want a new tolling back office. You can buy one from supplier A or supplier B. Supplier A's solution is more complete so should take less time to implement. However it is more expensive and means that the company has to adopt some of the "out of the box" processes which means more training. Supplier B's solution needs more work but we get a greater say in the final product. It's cheaper but the project will run longer. All these variables push and pull against each other to give you a shape for the project. This idea is summarised in figure 42.

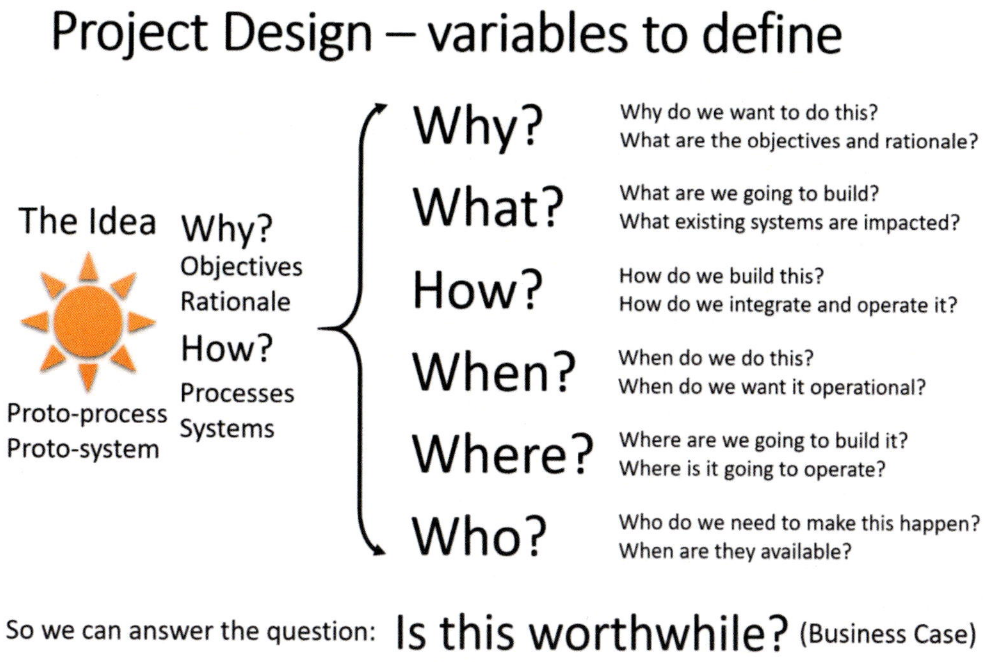

Figure 41 – Project Design variables

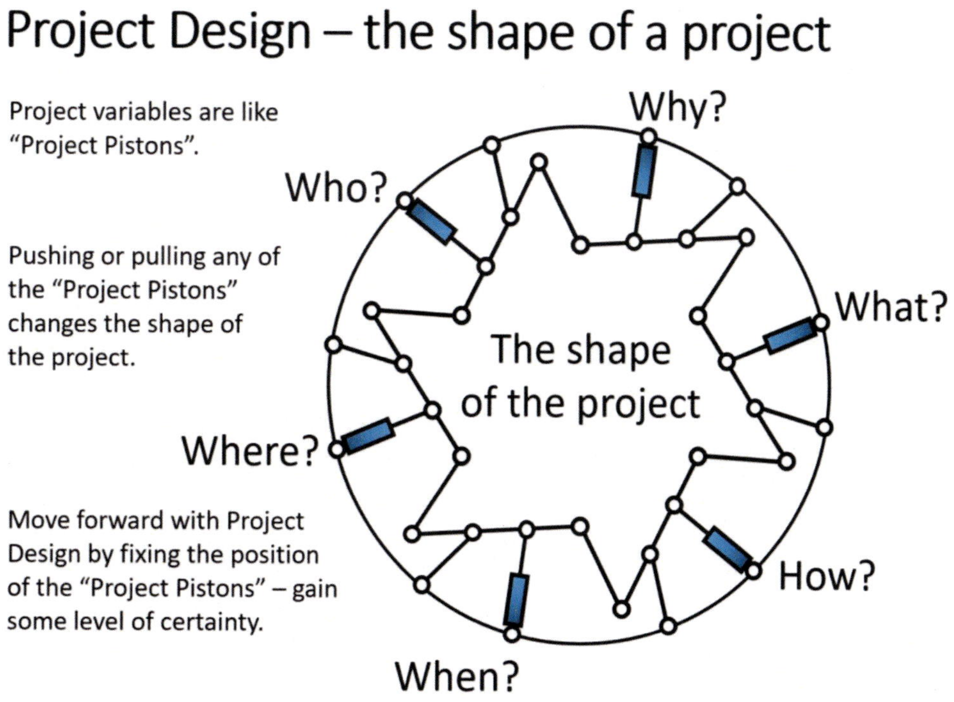

Figure 42 – Project Design, the shape of a project

Project Design is hard work. It's a combination of thinking, estimating, designing, brainstorming, more thinking and talking to people across the industry. You have to write requirements, design briefs, numerous plans, and if you're going to test the market, Expression of Interest (EOI) and Request for Proposal (RFP) documents for suppliers, as shown in figure 43.

There is no guarantee that the Project Design process will result in a viable project. Ultimately the Business Case might show that the project isn't worth pursuing. But much better to find that out now than six months and hundreds of thousands of dollars into the project. The aim of Project Design however is to give yourself the best chance of designing something – shaping something – that is viable, and proving it through a Project Management Plan (what you're going to build, when and how) and that Business Case (how it benefits the company).

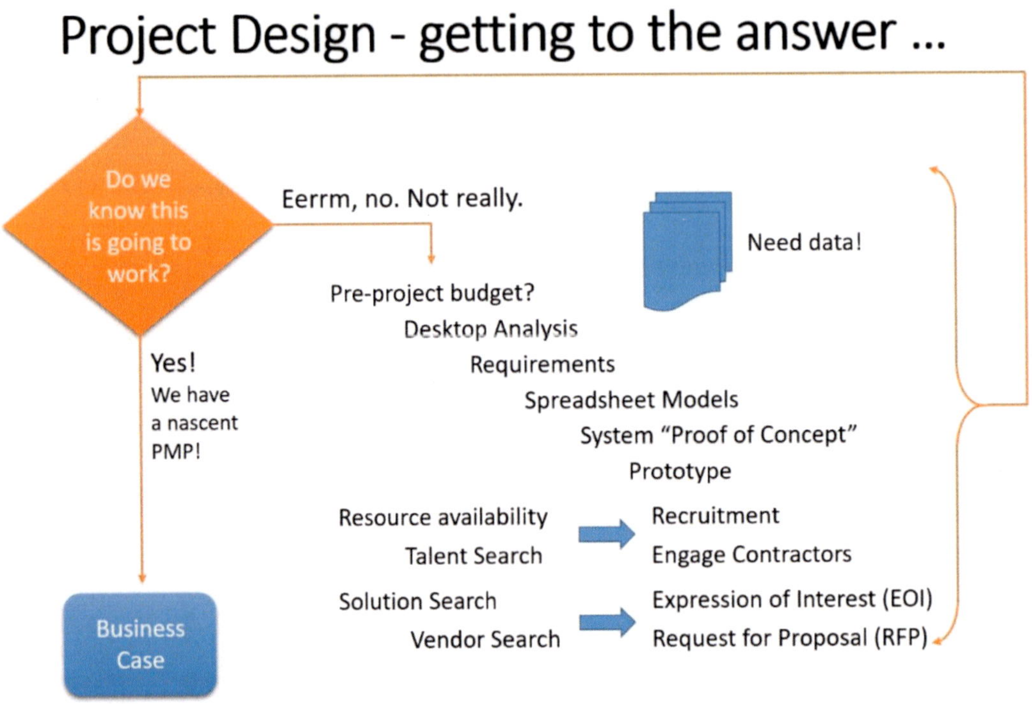

Figure 43 – Project Design, getting to the answer

Think on this – the size and shape of the Space Shuttle's solid fuel booster rockets were determined, to an extent, by the width of a horse's arse. The rockets were moved by rail which included going through some tunnels. The width of the rail tracks, and the tunnels, when they were built, were traditionally based on the width of a horse drawn carriage. Good Project Design uses that kind of information before you realise you've built something that can't be moved.

When designing a project, one very important consideration is the full lifecycle cost of the system. The project might be the exciting bit, but for the owners of the road that is only an enabling act for the real business. They want years of efficient operations, at low cost, so that they can maximise the returns they get from tolls. This "total cost of ownership" has to be taken into account as part of the Project

Design and used to make those "buy or build" and "support internally – outsource" decisions. Some toll roads may want to do everything themselves and retain a tight level of control over their systems. Others will want to run their systems and support teams as lean as possible and rely on third party support contracts. Everybody wants to see value from the money spent.

With tolling systems there are technical options that can alter the shape of your project. But the specialised nature of the tolling business also means that for some components there are a very limited number of suppliers. With reference back to figure 2, a good example of that is the Vehicle Detection equipment. This is an amalgam of complex electronics and software that has been developed and enhanced over many years by a handful of suppliers around the world. You would have to be very brave indeed if you intended to build your equipment, rather than buy from an established supplier. So in terms of your project, the Vehicle Detection component would probably come from a simple competitive tender between those suppliers. Later in this part of the book I describe that Vehicle Detection equipment in some detail. It's the way we've done things for some time. But every industry would now appear to be susceptible to disruption, and Vehicle Detection is not exempt. I said you would you have to be brave to build your own, but if your new model is truly disruptive and just as effective, it might be the best thing you could do.

Looking again at figure 2, components such as Trip Reconstruction, Trip Rating and Interoperability need careful consideration. There are suppliers in the market now who can sell you these components "off the shelf" but because every toll road is different in terms of topology and toll and fee structures, you still have to do some customisation to suit your circumstances. The choice then becomes:

- Create your own "skunk works" and build your own system or get a software house to build it for you. In my experience toll road operators tend to shy away from this one for good reasons. They understand that their core competency is toll road operations, not necessarily the specification and management of large software projects. The benefit to this approach is that, in theory at least, you do get exactly what you want and end up owning the source code. You buy the right to be the master of your own destiny.
- Deal with a specialist tolling supplier, pay for the "off the shelf" component and the cost of the customisation. Rely on that supplier to do the project managing. You trust in their competence to do work in this area.

Which of those makes sense will depend entirely upon your own company circumstances.

The Account Management, Billing and Invoicing component is where it gets really interesting. There are many really good "off the shelf" account management, billing and invoicing systems out there but none that I know of which have simple tolling "plug-ins". What this means, if you want to use one for tolling, is a long and complex process to build customisations. As soon as you do that you're looking at spending a lot of money – for a long time. Some things to consider with this approach are:

- The up-front cost of the licence fees for the product, and then the on-going maintenance and support fees which can be as high as 22% of the up-front fees payable every year.

- The need to have your own team to do nothing more than apply and test the regular core product upgrades and patches you have to install to keep your support agreement valid. This is rarely about adding new valuable functionality – this is just about keeping baselines current. You can think of it as "work required to stand still".
- The cost of the consultants, the product specialists you will need to hire to do all those customisations. If you've ever used a big software consulting firm you will know just how eye-wateringly expensive those guys can be.
- Your team needs to be trained in the core product so that they understand what the product specialists are saying, designing and planning to do.
- The complexity of the monster you end up creating. Sure it works to support your business now, but with all those customisations how easy, quick and expensive is the system to adapt to make the best of new business opportunities and technology? What is coming next after we've all got bored of our smartphones?
- You never really "own" your system and you never have complete control over it. That may or not be a problem for you if it's delivering the functionality you need.

All that said, this is a very valid approach. There are many tolling systems around the world operating successfully using this model. But it comes with a cost base that can be significant, and that cost is money taken from your toll revenue which then can't be used for distributions – which is one thing toll road owners are very interested in. What are the alternatives? Well you can:

- Go down the "skunk works" or software house route as described before.
- Deal with a specialist tolling supplier. Now in the world there are companies who do have products specifically designed for this tolling account management task. Dealing with them means you end up in a situation which is sort of halfway between the big customised off-the-shelf solution and the skunk works.

There is no definitive answer to this question. It really depends on your needs as tolling operator, who is available in your market that you trust, who can help you achieve the desired outcome, and who will be around for the long term to provide you with support. Not forgetting of course that whatever the answer is it has to fit within a budget.

With all these different components coming from potentially different suppliers, who is going to take responsibility for the systems integration task? Are you going to take that on, or commission somebody else to do it? Whoever does it, that systems integration task represents another team of people in their own right and, from a contractual point of view, requires that you write very clear rules about who bears responsibility for fixing things when they don't work.

Finally we come to data migration. If you're building a new system for a road that hasn't opened yet this is obviously less of a problem i.e. there isn't much data to migrate. But don't be too complacent. The company may want to start opening customer accounts and issuing tags before the road opens and awkwardly, before the tolling system is ready to be commissioned. You might find yourself having to put together a very basic CRM system to service that need and then migrate the data from that system to the tolling system at road opening.

If you're not a greenfield site and already have many years of tolling data in your current system, then you should approach the migration of data from the old system to the new as a major project in its own right. The data migration project team will need its own Project Manager. You will need to invest in people who are experts in migrating data, and give them the best Extract, Transform, Load (ETL) tools which are by no means cheap. To cap it off they will also need their own IT infrastructure environments to do their work – at least two in addition to all those environments you are building for the new system. Then you'll have to convince the people who work with the current system (the one you're going to get rid of) that the data migration project is a great opportunity. You need their knowledge of the existing system to help with that ETL process. As for budget, allow around 25% of the cost of the main project – and be prepared to spend a little more.

Simple really. With a good Project Manager on the job what could possibly go wrong?

Data and Operations

Figure 44 – A modern tolling system control room (NOT)

It would be fabulous if tolling systems came with great big control rooms, loads of flashing lights, men in white lab coats all controlled by a sinister looking Chief Scientist armed with a clipboard. The reality unfortunately, is much less dramatic. The operation and use of a tolling system is done through ordinary looking GUIs running on PCs in ordinary looking offices. If you're lucky you may spot the odd large screen TV with real-time transaction figures displayed against gantries in a groovy geo-location type display – but don't hold your breath.

That said, to keep a tolling system operational a lot of behind the scenes activity has to occur. This section looks briefly at what that work entails and how it should influence the design of the tolling system itself.

To talk about data and operations in the context of a tolling system requires us to be clear as to the assumptions we're making of that tolling system architecture. Those assumptions are based on the tolling system model presented previously in the Tolling System Overview section, namely that:

- There is equipment out at the roadside that is responsible for the detection and classification of vehicles – which produces the "roadside data",
- There is a big, fast network that gets the roadside data back to the tolling system,
- That the tolling system is a number of computer applications running on servers,
- Those servers may be physical or virtual, based at the tolling operations centre or somewhere off in the cloud,
- Customer Service Operators and Human Image Processors are interacting with the tolling system through GUIs,
- The public is interacting with the tolling system through a website site, mobile application and possibly an IVR channel,
- All sorts of other businesses are interacting with the tolling system through on-line or batch file interfaces,
- You use a lot of electricity and without it you're stuffed,
- You use internet connections and without them things get very difficult,
- Most of the people who work in your organisation are quite rational and sane, but you're really not sure about Zandra ...

Really important data

If you work in the software industry it is always really embarrassing to lose data. It's embarrassing enough to have data stolen by those evil hackers from Buwapbackistax, but just to lose data, especially on a Friday afternoon, after a good lunch – well that is not only bad for your indigestion but simply unforgiveable.

There is no point me trying to explain to you how to set up a data recovery plan and, if at this point you're wondering what a data recovery plan actually is, then please do get professional help. No, the reason why I can't help you is whatever technology you are currently employing in your tolling system will naturally lend itself to a particular industry solution. So cheerfully phone your local technology sales rep and enjoy the moment while he/she scrambles for a calculator (they do still exist) to work out how much commission they can make from the deal.

Before we go there though, think about the data you actually need to protect and under what circumstances. To my mind the worst kind of scenario is one where, for a period of time, all operations appear normal – and then suddenly a fault becomes apparent. GUIs freeze, systems become unresponsive and you have to call a halt to all normal tolling operations. You send the team in to investigate and the news comes back that there is corruption in the database but – it happened two hours ago and nobody noticed. You have to restore back to a point before the point of corruption, to the nearest back-up you have. What data are you going lose? How much is that going to cost?

At this point the data recovery solution salesperson on the other end of the phone is telling you that that scenario is impossible because of their double vectored scaled helix technology that provides instant snap-back recovery which can be activated from a mobile phone app while you holiday in

Scandinavia. No – all you want to do right now is pump that person full of lead using a very viable Walther PPK Short – but you won't because that sort of behaviour is illegal and very anti-social.

So when designing your tolling system think about the following:

- No matter what planet you are from you need to take regular back-ups of your tolling system's databases – and equally important you have to be able to restore a back-up so that you can recover the data it contains.
- Roadside data is gold – it is the money. If you lose this data you actually lose real money and there is no way you can recover it. Do spend money on protecting that data. This means, out at the roadside:
    - Having uninterruptible and back-up power supplies,
    - Having dual independent grid power feeds,
    - Having the latest RAID storage devices,
    - NOT deleting data once it's been sent to the tolling back office, but keep it hanging around for several days before deleting it.

  That said, with the best will in the world there will be times when you do lose data. Roadside equipment does fail occasionally, and like all equipment exposed to the elements needs periodic cleaning, maintenance and calibration.
- Customer and CSO interaction data is very significant. If you reverted to a system back-up which was several hours old, do you have any way of recreating those interactions? And yes you can try phoning everybody up and asking them if they can remember what they did – good luck with that one. If you don't have any way of recreating those interactions then seriously think about developing one. Often the simplest method is to make sure the system generates really good interaction log files – and then keep those log files safe and away from anything else (like the database server) for a number of days.
- Business to business on-line transactions need looking after in the same way as customer interactions.
- Ironically batch files, the latest thing from the 1970s, are the most reliable in this scenario – just so long as you don't delete your batch files as soon as you process them.

You've restored your database and corrected the corruption – then what? Well, your tolling system has to be designed so that it can reconnect to the roadside and pick up the data it has missed, and replay interaction log files to recreate all those interactions that were lost, and reprocess your batch files – and crucially to be smart enough to recognise and ignore transactions it has already seen before so you don't get duplicates.

The Salesperson from MegaCorp (Value Invoicing isn't just a word) will tell you that with their double vectored scaled helix technology that provides instant snap-back recovery, such nonsense as replaying logs really isn't necessary. They may be telling the truth. When designing data recovery solutions, what you have to figure out is the balance between the following:

- Are the vendors telling the truth?

- How would you know if they weren't telling the truth?
- How much is it going to cost you whether it's the truth or not?
- Can MegaCorp's solution really do everything you want? How do we test it?

Thinking about all this really hurts but it can be source of much professional embarrassment when things go wrong, so persevere. The best solution to this problem is one that you understand, you have the budget for and you have confidence that it really works because you've tried it – more than once. That last point is really important and everybody in the industry knows it – recovery systems are only any good if you can successfully recover.

Environments galore

To make your tolling system work you obviously need a production tolling system environment – where environment is that whole collection of servers, networks and interfaces that make up the tolling system. Almost certainly though that is not going to be enough. You will also need:

A **Quality Assurance** (QA) environment: This is so you can test things before they make it into production. There will be a lot of things to test – new pieces of functionality, changes to interfaces and new interfaces, new releases of software to your class libraries, operating systems and virtual machines.

A **Training** environment: With the best will in the world your contact centre will experience staff churn. If you're lucky it might be as low as 15% per annum. If you're unlucky, or just bad at running a contact centre, it could be 30% or more. Whatever the situation, you will have to train new people in how to use your system all the time. You could use your QA environment, but that will only infuriate your testing professionals who have spent weeks getting data ready to test out very specific scenarios. Best not to do that because new operators, by definition, will always do weird and seemingly impossible things and mess up the test data.

A **Project** environment: The need for this really depends on the amount of change you are putting through your tolling system. If you plan on developing several large releases to the tolling system over an extended period of time, then a Project environment is a really good idea. Yes, the Accountants will say "Just use QA!", but QA's primary purpose is to get the Production system out of trouble. Imagine your Production system is on version 2.03 of HyperToll software. You have taken the Accountants' advice and are using the QA environment to develop a big new release. QA is loaded with version 2.1 of HyperToll and you are half way through a very complex series of tests when suddenly Production develops a problem that needs a very hot fix and fast. Now you have to revert QA to version 2.03, do a data refresh from Production and then start looking for the fix. That adds time and a lot of stress to an already trying situation.

A **Development** environment: The need for this really depends on the extent to which you make changes to your own source code. If your tolling system is a creature of your own invention, and your development team is in-house, then a Development environment is essential. Similarly if you have bought a third party product but can create or change functionality using modules or custom programs then you will need a Development environment. Your developers need a space to develop. If however your tolling system source code is in the hands of a third party, then the responsibility should rest with them to maintain the Development environment as part of their support contract. A halfway house, if your supplier exhibits some dodgy tendencies, is to maintain a Development environment with your source code in a kind of pseudo Escrow on your site. That way, if they do go bust, or mad, or to Peru to find themselves, at least you know where everything is.

The environments should be identical in some respects. They should be running on the same hardware, with the same versions of firmware, virtual machine and operating system software – except that testing new versions of those things is all part of the job. However they do not need to be specified to cope with the same levels of performance. Ideally the QA environment should be the same as production – so that you can test functionality AND performance. The Project and Training environments do not need to carry that same level of grunt. Also it is very important to think about interfaces for training and testing purposes.

One of the most important interfaces is to the roadside equipment, but only your Production environment is actually connected to that equipment. For the others you need a "Roadside Simulator" – a software application that can generate realistic roadside transactions and images so that you can feed them into your other environments. If you are really clever you'll find a way of duplicating real roadside data and use that – without messing up the Production environment.

Batch file interfaces are easy. Given that you don't have privacy issues around the real data in batch files, you can just use your Production batch files for the other environments. Generally batch files, even with dummy data, are relatively easy to fabricate.

On-line interfaces with business partners can be more problematic. Your best business partners will have test interfaces you can use, but a lot won't. This is where you need to box clever and develop interface simulators. It may sound like a phaff, but it will pay dividends in the long run. To be honest, if you are using mechanisms like web services, then developing simulators is not that big a deal. If you are struggling in this area head on down to the programming course of your local Technical College, find a hungry looking Geek, buy him or her a pizza and explain the problem. It may cost you a few more pizzas, and a subscription to Disney+, but you'll probably get a worthwhile outcome.

Outages and performance

"*Gentlemen* (said he not noticing that half the room was female) *I want this operation to run 24 by* 7 – *no exceptions! The traffic never stops on our road, so neither shall the tolling!*" thus speaks the new CEO of DriveHard who recently joined the organisation from a paint logistics company. This is a man who knows how trucks on tarmac really work!

But hang on. Before you go and phone the Salesperson from MegaCorp (Value Invoicing isn't just a word) – who, by the way, is still gutted you didn't buy their double vectored scaled helix technology that provides instant snap-back recovery – and try and buy their PowerThrust High Availability solution (MegaCorp is always UP!) – think again about what you really need. Modern high availability systems are very good, but they are also expensive and they add complexity to both your system configuration and the way you have to operate and maintain it. The anecdotal evidence is that it is not uncommon for the high availability system, whatever it may be, to be the source of more problems than it solves. "When you're clustered, you're always flustered". Seriously, I didn't make that up. Or maybe I did. Whatever, the chances are, if you really think about it you can tolerate a number of system outages without any real detriment to the business – with the one exception being the roadside. Roadside data is the gold of the tolling industry – protect that at all cost costs. I might have mentioned that before.

So let's not get MegaCorp excited just yet. The truth is we will always need outages of some sort, even if your super high availability solution is in the cloud. At some point there will be one idiot with a tractor and a hydraulic auger digging up your broadband connection – "Yeah, just got to install this new guard rail fencing. Ealth an' Safety – you know". In reality outages are going to be about much more mundane things such as security patches to your virtual machines, operating systems or applications. So this leads to consideration of the quality of the architecture of your tolling system.

Is your tolling system one big thing? To patch the database does the whole thing have to be off the air for a number of hours? Or is it a highly cohesive, loosely coupled system of discrete components that means Trip Reconstruction continues while Account Maintenance is being, well, maintained? Referring right back to figure 2, in your tolling system is each one of those boxes a discrete system or are they effectively all part of one large system? There is no right or wrong answer to this. It comes down to how you want to manage your system. Ultimately I think it is about how you can manage your recovery from outages.

You will have outages but the roadside will continue to collect that valuable roadside transaction data. When the tolling system comes back, you are then faced with the prospect of having to process the backlog and process the usual roadside transactions. So, as with image processing, your tolling system has to have the capacity to process far more than just a usual day's worth of transactions. Typically it has to be capable of handling double a usual day, in a day, so that it can recover from those outages.

But making the system a number of discrete highly cohesive and loosely coupled systems reduces that recovery burden. If you've been patching the Account Management, Billing and Invoicing component with Trip Reconstruction and Interoperability still working, then the recovery load will be reduced – because Interoperability will have dealt with a large proportion of the trips. Similarly can you keep the web site open while you're patching Trip Reconstruction? Something to consider when you get into the tolling system's detailed IT architecture.

Other things to do with data

Tolling systems connected to busy roads generate a lot of data – potentially millions of transactions and many thousands of images each day. Over time that begins to add up. You can avoid embarrassing questions simply by buying more disk space on a regular basis so it never really becomes an issue. However, even the best database systems tend to struggle when tables get to be more than a few hundred million rows long. The most sensible way to deal with this is to develop a data archiving strategy. Having a strategy is a career enhancing position, even if that strategy is a few squiggles on the back of a beer mat – just so long as you don't show people the beer mat when they ask.

There are three components to an archiving strategy:

- Leave in the Production system only that data which is needed for day to day operations – including responding to customer queries. Customers around tax return filing time possess a great ability to lose all the communications you have previously sent them. They call up and ask if you could send them copies of their statements for the last five years. Sure! But apart from those statements, and invoices, do you need to keep data in the tolling system older than a year? It's something you'll need to work out for your business. Regular archiving of data from the Production system keeps it neat and trim and humming along in a predictable way.
- Genuinely throw away old data you don't need. There is a great temptation to "keep everything" simply because it's relatively easy to do so. But only do that if you're storing that data somewhere and in a manner that allows you to reuse it. Which leads to the third component:
- Keep all the useful data, log files and roadside images in the context of a reporting and data mining system – sometimes referred to as a "Big Data" system. Then you can say to the CEO of DriveHard things like "We did a strategic study based on the ROI of an investment in MegaCorp's PowerThrust High Availability solution versus Randjit's Big Data "Data Everywhere" solution. The Ranjit system allows us to monetise our data assets in ways we hadn't previously thought possible, and you get a cool dashboard on your phone." That dashboard nails the deal. For once he has something to show his new CEO friends down at the country club. So long as that thing keeps working, and what is being displayed is simple enough to understand, he probably won't bother you again.

So archiving is a really good idea. Having a neat reporting and data mining system is another really good idea. Once you start seriously trying to understand what your customers are doing on your road through deep data analysis, you will be amazed. Their behaviour will not be straightforward at all. Now there is a whole new world of opportunity – artificial intelligence (AI) and machine learning. Get your AI system set up right and soon it will be predicting what your customers will do before they do it! Either that or it will take over the organisation and enslave you. Go for your life.

But there is more you need to do with your data. To keep those other environments worth using, on a regular basis you will need to refresh their databases with up to date data from the Production system. This requires another mechanism to transfer that data. You could pull out a Production back-up and simply restore – but approach with caution. The Production database backup will contain tables of data that tell the system it is the Production environment – and everything that goes with that. So do your restore, but don't overwrite the data that tells QA it's the QA environment and so on. Could be very embarrassing to fire up QA only to find that it is now competing with the real Production for IP addresses, interfaces and B2B passwords.

Figure 45 below is an attempt to pull all these ideas together in to one diagram.

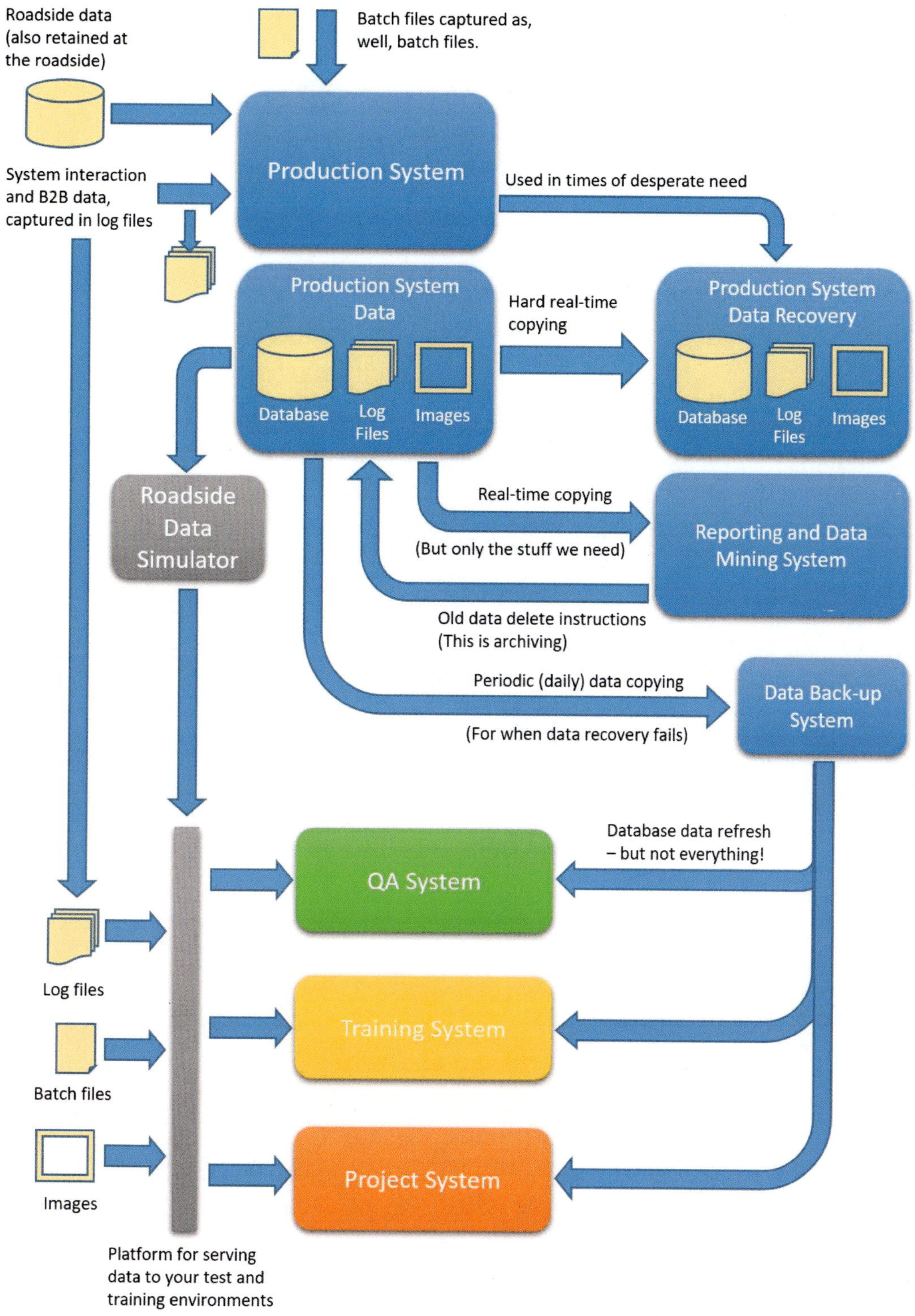

Figure 45 – Moving data around tolling system environments

People and office ethical dilemmas

At the start of this piece I mentioned Zandra. Well here's the thing. Zandra is a very capable member of the IT team and the one who does the most to ensure all the system data is securely backed up. She also has runes for summoning dragons tattooed along her inner thighs and books the small meeting room for fifteen minutes every day, leaving it with just a hint of the odour of saltpetre. So what is the problem here? Is it:

- She has dragon summoning tattoos?
- She wears skirts so short you can clearly see those tattoos?
- She wears skirts that short AND you keep on looking and wondering about her inner diameter slope?
- You have a sudden urge to sign up to that tattooing and body piercing course on offer at the local bikie gang club house – "Lurn now and do us a favor later!"
- You've started dreaming about dragons with milky white thighs that breath saltpetre fire – and you like it.
- Obviously tattoos and short skirts affect her ability to manage IT systems.
- Why are we even talking about this – is it because Zandra is a woman and you're a sexist pig?

All those statements in some way are very wrong but I did want to highlight the fact that the tolling system business, much like IT in general, is very blokey and we have to be very aware of that. You really have to pay attention to that equality and diversity training you sit through every year. It is very important. But I'm not about to start lecturing you on IT system security and sexism in the workplace. There are many people much better qualified to do that, and who enjoy it. I do have emotional intelligence though. I know this because I went on a course and they gave me a certificate of attendance at the end and everything. In short you have to rely on people to do business critical activities, so my suggestion would be to:

- Trust them,
- Value the work they do and give them honest feedback (bearing in mind your own numerous failings and idiosyncrasies) which means,
- Engaging with people on a daily basis, and that means talking to them and trying to get a sense of how they are feeling – yes, seriously, and
- Putting simple controls in place so that if they (or yourself for that matter) do go completely open loop one day, the organisation isn't stuffed as a result.

You'll know when Zandra has succeeded. They'll be a big hole where the small meeting room used to be and a saltpetre haze trail climbing up to the clouds.

Data Items

In the following sections I'm going to introduce the concept of data items. Because different tolling systems work in different ways, it's not possible to describe the "one industry standard way" of doing things. However, at a high level, tolling systems do share common data items, and it's around these data items that I'll base an explanation as to how tolling systems work.

When I describe a data item all I'm trying to do is lay down a blueprint or template for what an instance or object of that data item might look like. I'm thinking in terms of the classic Java Data Access Object. The actual implementation of these items, especially the links (active processes) between them, is quite another matter and will be driven by your or your supplier's software design gurus. Through my blog on tollingbook.com I've provided some more detail around the form of these links.

There are two very important data sets – the topology of the road itself and everything that goes into defining your toll products. These could be data items in their own right, or you might prefer to set them up as reference data in another structure. Your road topology may change over time but for the most part it will remain static. For toll products though you will want to increase your prices as often as you are allowed. Make sure whatever structure you do use to represent this data allows you to "effective date" prices increases and other variable changes. By that I mean you can specify a date time from which a new toll price or fee becomes applicable. That way you won't be sitting up at midnight on toll price increase day hoping you're typing in the right numbers when you'd much rather be in bed. Also the old toll products have to remain available. You may get trips coming through from image processing that are several days old and have to be rated against the old prices, not the new ones.

If you have a very dynamic pricing structure, for example when you're using pricing to try and control traffic flow along a road, that requires quite a different system. Pricing of that sort has to be the output of a sophisticated algorithm that is running 24 by 7 and taking into account traffic flows and to an extent an understanding of customer behaviour. Unfortunately a look at that algorithm is outside the scope of this book.

Detection Systems

The detection systems at the roadside are there to detect and measure who uses our road and when. Without reliable detection systems, and the enforcement processes they enable, we'd still be pulling up at the barriers and tossing coins into the bucket. And if you are still having to pull up and deal with change, respectfully suggest to whoever runs the roads in your country that they get with the times.

Figure 46 – A classic example of neo-brutalist gantry design from the Spanish School (2006, SICE on EastLink)

Figure 46 reminds us of the "front and rear" gantry configuration. In this case the front gantry for lanes in both directions of travel spans the whole road. The rear gantries are separate installations.

In Australia it would be fair to say that the Austrian company Kapsch rules the roost when it comes to roadside equipment. Their detection systems are operating on just about every Australian toll road with a few exceptions. But around the world there are many different manufacturers and detection system configurations. SICE, who are a major player in the Australian market thanks to their back office systems, also have a roadside equipment offering as shown in figure 53. The basic detection sequence for a two gantry configuration is as follows.

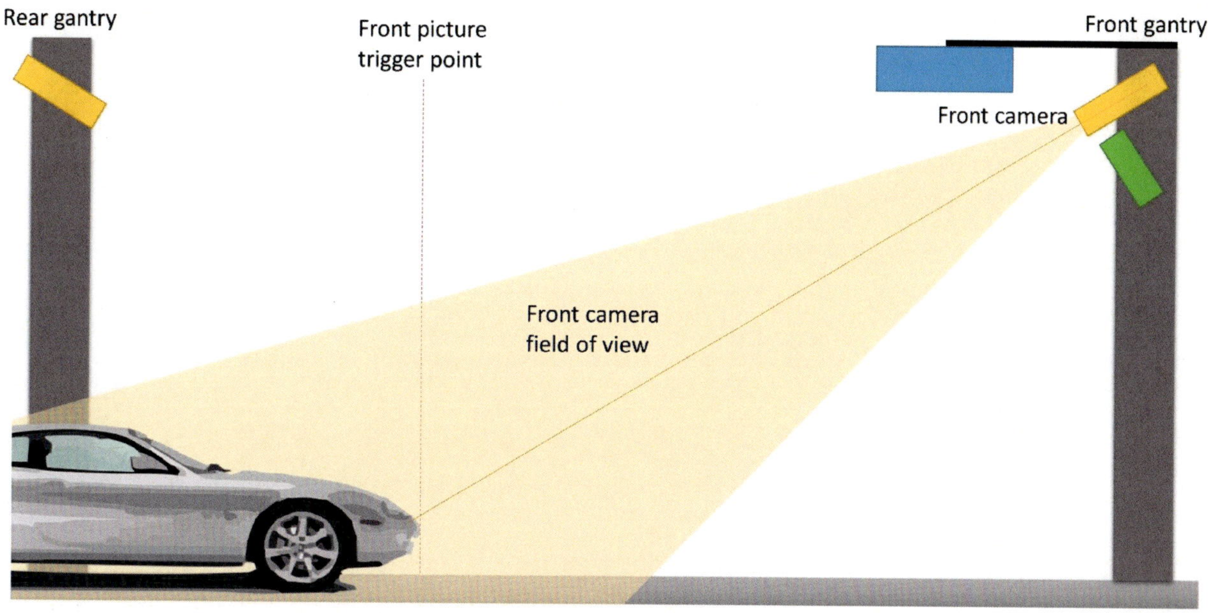

Figure 47 – The vehicle enters the tolling gantry and reaches the front image trigger point

In figure 47 a vehicle enters the space between the front and rear gantries and reaches the "front picture trigger point". This is the position of the vehicle best suited to take an image of its front licence plate. The cameras can be triggered to take the picture of the vehicle at that point by a number of means:

- Some cameras are now smart enough to be self-triggering i.e. they have their own vehicle detection system built in based on processing the video stream from their sensor,
- The Kapsch system triggers its cameras in a similar way, but the image processing is done by the Vehicle Detection and Classification (VDC) system, which sits high above the road between the gantries on its arm.
- Laser curtain – essentially LIDAR (which means Laser Imaging, Detection and Ranging, depending on who you talk to).

In figure 48 the vehicle moves on into the space between the front and rear gantries. It enters the tag communication zone, and if it is carrying a tag then a transaction should be recorded. It is also firmly in the field of view of the vehicle scanning device. In the Kapsch world this is their VDC – a clever video based system that makes use of stereoscopic cameras to not only track the position of the vehicle, but also to gauge its dimensions. Alternatives include a "double headed" LIDAR system. Regardless of the technology, the aim is to produce data on the size and position of the vehicle that can be linked to the images taken of the vehicle.

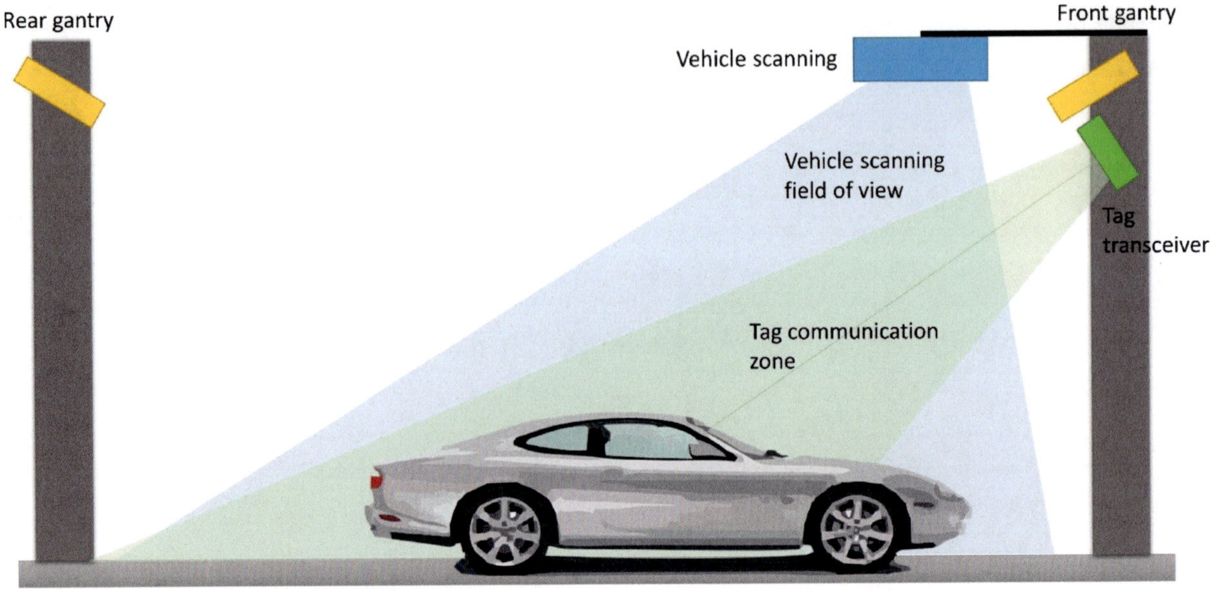

Figure 48 – The vehicle is between the front and rear gantries

In figure 49 the vehicle moves forward towards the front gantry and reaches the optimum position for the rear facing camera to take an image of the rear of the vehicle and its licence plate – the "rear picture trigger point". Options for triggering the rear camera are the same as those for the front camera.

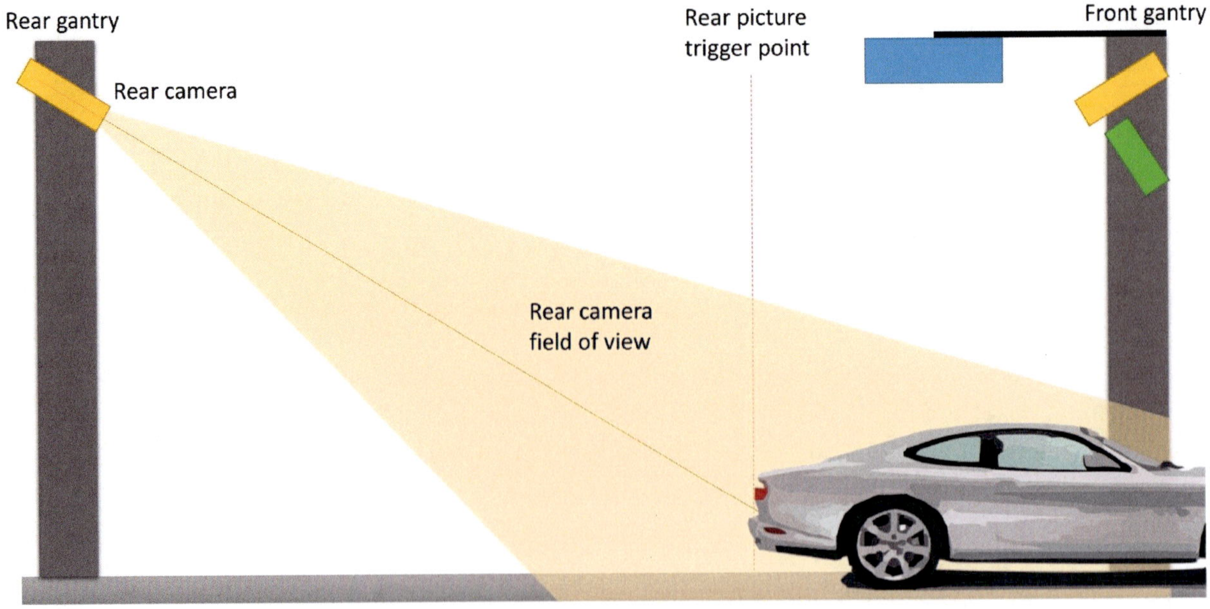

Figure 49 – The vehicle passes through the front gantry

Single gantries

The two gantry model has been around for a long time and is proven to work well. But it is possible to squeeze all the roadside equipment on to a single gantry and have it perform the same range of functions. Figure 50 shows the basic configuration for a single gantry system. The designers make these things look a lot neater than my representation.

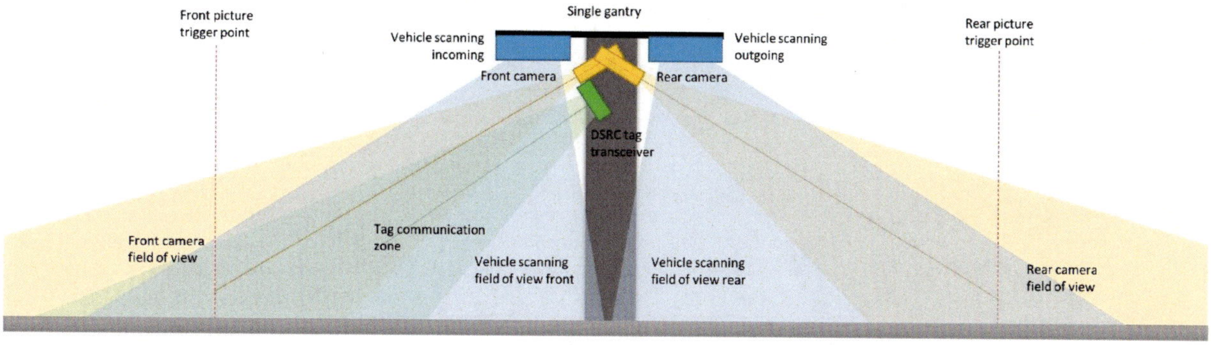

Figure 50 – Single gantry configuration.

Possibly the biggest complication with this arrangement is the vehicle scanning component. Depending on the scanning equipment, and the design of the gantry, it may turn out that you need twice as many vehicle scanning devices because now we have effectively created two areas of road that need monitoring – and that will almost certainly be the case if the vehicle scanning equipment is used to trigger the cameras. So the money you save in only having the one physical gantry structure may be eaten up in the addition equipment costs needed for the single gantry.

Tag Detection

As we've discussed previously, most toll roads around the world do make use of some form of tag, be it a little RFID sticker tag, or the more sophisticated DSRC tag. In Australia, as the vehicle equipped with the tag passes under the tolling gantry it comes within range of the tag transceiver and all being well the transceiver initiates the communications protocol as outlined in AS 4962(INT)-2001 "Electronic toll collection - Transaction specification for Australian interoperability on the DSRC link". Others standards will apply depending on which country you are in.

Built into this protocol is a level of security. This is to stop people setting up on the side of the road and "reading your tag", then going off and cloning it so you end up paying for all their trips. Security takes the form of encryption of the messages between tag and reader. One of the tasks associated with setting up a tag from a new operator is to ensure that their security "keys" for un-encrypting messages are stored within your roadside equipment so that their tags can be read.

This communication can also include those instructions for the tag to "beep". The number of beeps is dependent on the status of the account with which the tag is associated, and is data passed to the roadside equipment from the tolling back office. Figure 51 shows the super colourful TRP4010 tag and TRX-1320 transceiver from Kapsch.

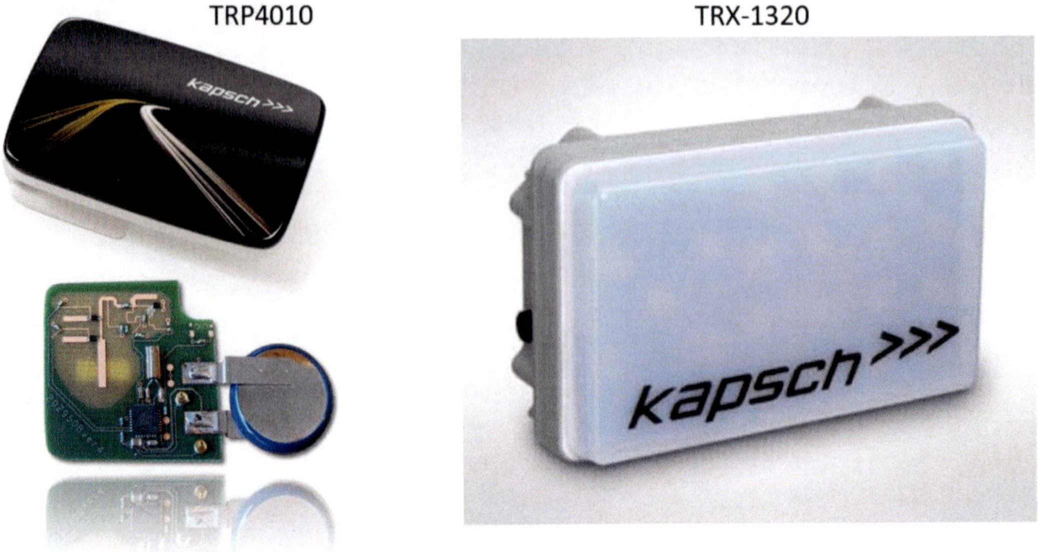

Figure 51 – No more dull fawn tags with Kapsch! Now the TRP4010 with added graphics.

These tag passages are very reliable. With correctly fitted tags it is possible to get accurate reading rates in the order of 99.9% of all tag transactions. That accuracy is important – it's the data associated with those passages that you're after.

Data Item 1 shows the minimum amount of data needed from a tag passage.

Typically tag passages contain a lot more data. This can include security information, a status on tag battery life, whether the roadside thinks the tag is in the tag holder correctly and the settings of any tag switches (FasTrak Flex). It's up to your tolling system as to whether that kind of data is of use.

Also in the case of #8 it makes sense that a Tag Passage should be associated with a Vehicle Passage. After all, if a tag is not in a vehicle how on earth is it travelling down your road? Unless it's that idiot Barney again and his "tag on a pole" trick. There will also be situations where a vehicle is carrying more than one tag and several Tag Passages will be associated with the same Vehicle Passage.

Data Item 1 – Tag Passage		
ID	**Name**	**Description**
1	Tag Passage ID	The unique identification number of the passage itself assigned by the roadside equipment.
2	Tag Broadcast ID	The identification number of the tag. When combined with the tag issuer and country IDs this should be a globally unique number.
3	Tag Issuer ID	A unique number (for a given country) assigned to the organisation that issues (owns) the tag for interoperability purposes (Concession ID).
4	Country ID	A globally unique number assigned to the country in which the tag issuing organisation resides.
5	Tag class	The vehicle class assigned to the tag. Usually tags are assigned to customers on the basis of the vehicle class into which they will be fitted.
6	Date-Time Stamp	The date and time (to milliseconds) that the passage was recorded.
7	Toll Point ID	Details as to exactly where the transaction occurred. Ideally this would go as far as to identify the transceiver that recorded the passage. As a minimum it must include the toll point and the direction of travel.
8	Vehicle passage ID	The vehicle passage associated with the tag passage.
9	Action List	Whether the passage is associated with a vehicle on the action list.
10	Date-Time Stamp data received by back office	The date and time (to milliseconds) that the tag passage was received by the back office (Trip Reconstruction).

Data Item 1 – Tag Passage.

Vehicle Scanning

Figure 52 – A parade of Kapsch VDCs on their "arms".

Vehicle scanning is a serious and complex business. What we're asking the roadside to do is individually identify every vehicle passing under our gantries – vehicles travelling at different speeds and not necessarily sticking to their lanes. When they're going at speed it is tricky enough, but what about when there is slow moving or stationary traffic under your gantry? How does the equipment cope with that?

Figure 53 – SICK LIDARS on a SICE gantry.

You have to imagine a two dimensional space – the width is defined by the width of your road including any running lanes at the extreme left or right. The length is usually at least as long as the space between your gantries but ultimately depends on the capabilities of your vehicle scanning equipment. The vehicle scanner has to identify every vehicle that enters this space and keep tracking it, quite independently of any other vehicles, until it leaves the space. In effect it has to draw a box around the vehicle and maintain a record of that box's X and Y coordinates. This activity becomes particularly important if your scanning equipment is also triggering your cameras. When that vehicle hits the best points for front and rear images, then the cameras have to be fired.

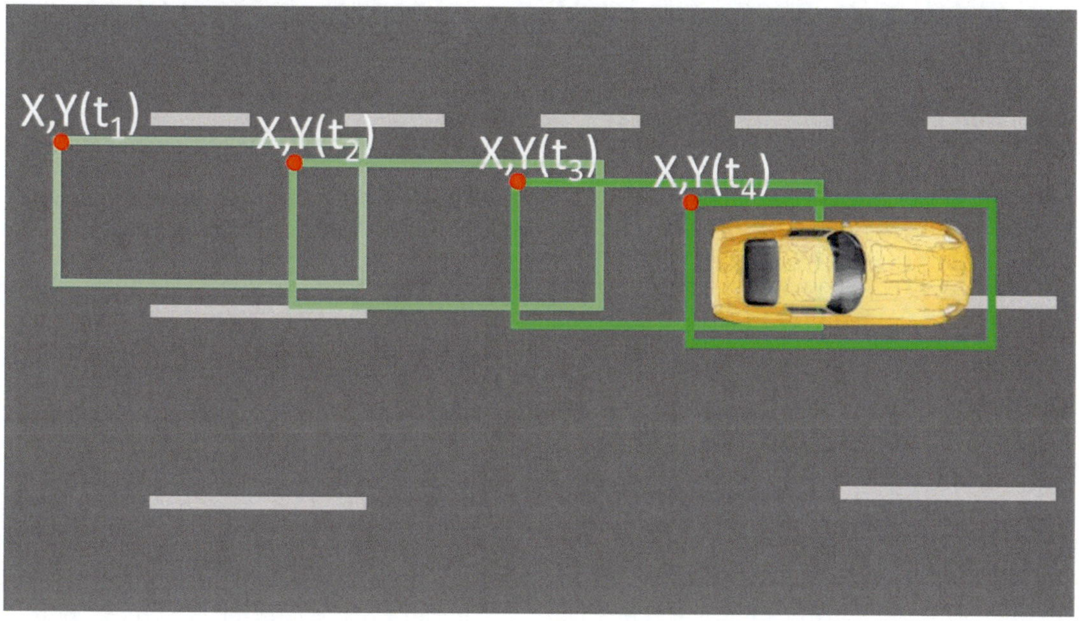

Figure 54 – Representation of a scanning system tracking a vehicle as it moves through the detection area.

You'll notice in figure 54 that the view from the vehicle scanning sensor is not limited to one lane. It covers more than two. If you have one sensor per lane these views will overlap and that is exactly what you want. The trick is that the sensors do not work in isolation. Behind the sensors, and taking their data is a coordination computer which stitches all the views together to form a master view, and then crucially keeps track of all the individual vehicles within that master view. In this way the system as a whole can relate the movements of one specific vehicle to a known camera trigger event to a uniquely identifiable set of images. It also means there is redundancy in the system if a sensor fails.

And there is more! The vehicle scanning equipment is also working out the dimensions of the vehicle and in some cases even count the number of axles. This is all to do with determining vehicle class. As we've discussed previously, getting vehicle class correct is not simple and very much depends on the rules of your concession deed, but the scanning equipment, at the very least, should be able to determine basic vehicle dimensions.

The Kapsch equipment is able to do this because each VDC uses that clever stereoscopic camera trick. Two cameras, offset from each other, but taking pictures of the same thing can be used to create a three dimensional image of an object – an old technique from photo-reconnaissance. The Kapsch VDCs use this trick to generate three dimensional volumetric data on every vehicle they sense as represented in figure 55 below.

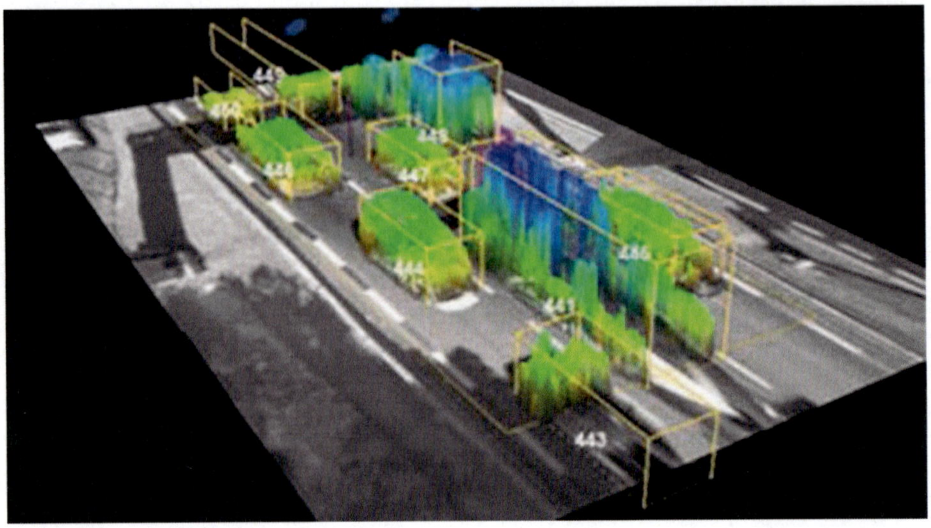

Figure 55 – Kapsch VDC sensor three dimensional view.

The LIDAR uses a different technique. A spinning LIDAR can create a two dimensional image of an object in the plane of the laser. As an object moves through that plane so it can capture "slices" of the object to build up a three dimensional image. If you combine two LIDARs, offset from each so that you guarantee to capture the entire volume of the object in different axes of motion, so you can build a complete three dimensional picture of that object. This is represented in figure 56.

But for accurate tolling we need the licence plate string, and that is where the front and rear images play a vital role.

Image Processing

Triggered by whatever means, our cameras have taken images of the front and rear of a vehicle. We now need to extract the licence plate strings from those images. Figure 57 is a representation of a roadside image of the rear of a vehicle.

It is a grey scale image. Often these roadside cameras operate in the infrared range of the spectrum. Infrared can be better at seeing through weather such as rain and fog. They can give a better performance at night, and at night the infrared illuminators do not light up the whole neighbourhood making your tolling gantry less obtrusive to those living nearby. But you can pick cameras to suit your needs and regulations. Full colour are readily available.

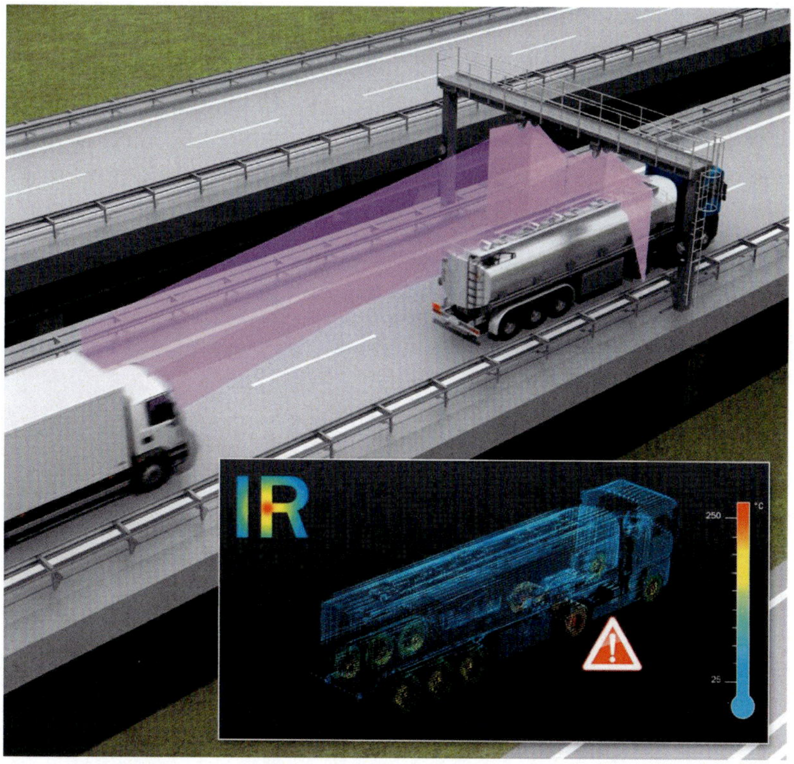

Figure 56 – SICK LIDAR sensor three dimensional view.

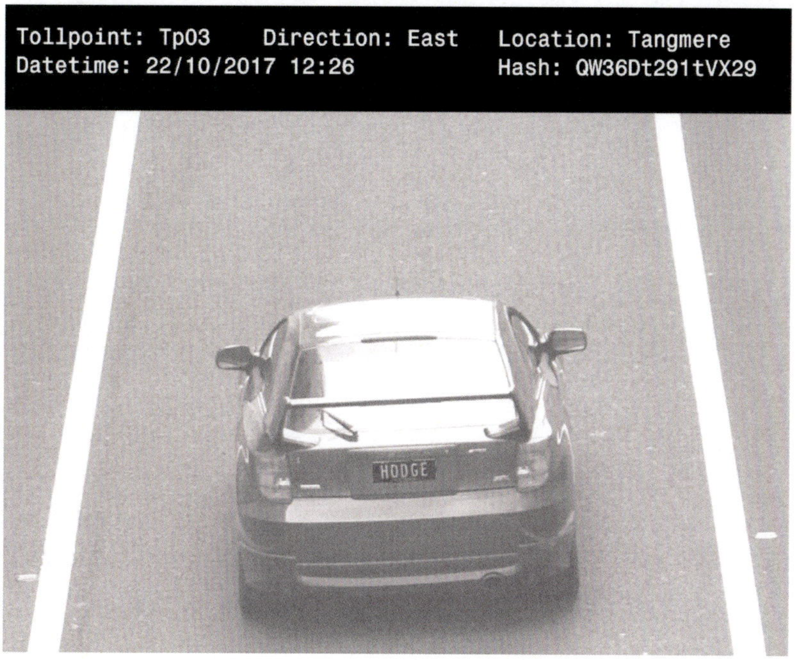

Figure 57 – Representation of a roadside camera image of the rear of a vehicle.

It has a black stripe along the top with data written in to it. Whether you have this depends on your supplier, but it is a useful feature. Once the camera has taken the image it runs a hash type function over the image. It then appends a black stripe to the top (or bottom) of the image and in that stripe writes the basic details of when and where the image was taken, and the hash function value. That complete image is sent to the back office. The hash function is part of the process to prove that the image has not been tampered with, if it ever gets used in court as evidence of travel. If you strip away the black stripe, and run the hash function over the image again, you should get the same hash function value out. If you don't, then something well dodgy is happening in your tolling system.

There are four things you can do with an image from the roadside cameras:

- Use optical character recognition (OCR) to derive a licence plate string and state or country of registration,
- Use another type of image processing function to derive a "signature" for the licence plate,
- Use a machine learning framework to identify the make and model of the vehicle in the image to define vehicle class, and
- In a similar way, use another type of image processing function to derive a "signature" for the whole vehicle.

Of these, usually only the OCR function is provided by the roadside equipment. A further OCR read and the other functions would be provided by a central image processing system.

When you feed an image into an OCR engine, the first thing it has to do is locate the licence plate. That is more complicated than it sounds. Granted that in most images the licence plate is roughly in the same place, but in quite a few it isn't, and vehicles often have other signs attached to their bodywork. If your OCR engine keeps on returning licence plates with the readings "TOYOTA", "AMBULANCE" or "HEAVY GOODS" you might want to contact your supplier.

Some roadside cameras will try and do more than just find the licence plate – they will actually cut out a plate image for you. This is valuable if the plate image is kept in a format which retains all of its data.

A digital camera can take a "raw" image which is basically every reading you get from every pixel on the sensor of the camera. With modern cameras these images are fantastic in the level of detail and quality of image they can produce. The problem is the image is huge in terms of megabytes. If your roadside cameras were delivering raw images to you, and you had a busy road, you would be forever buying more disk space, or filling up the cloud. So images tend to get converted to jpegs, a very clever compression algorithm that can reduce the storage size of your image to a tenth of its raw equivalent while still maintaining a really good looking image. The rub is that OCR engines rely on the differences between pixels values to do things like edge detection. With a jpeg image some of that clear differentiation between pixel values is lost as the compression algorithm "smears" together pixels with roughly the same values.

A clever camera will deliver a plate image to you in raw form, while delivering the full image in a compressed jpeg form. The plate images in raw form are usually only a few hundred pixels wide, so not huge in terms of size, but the extra data they carry can improve the accuracy of your OCR read. The roadside equipment has already given us an OCR reading. We can use the plate image to do the second OCR reading in the back office.

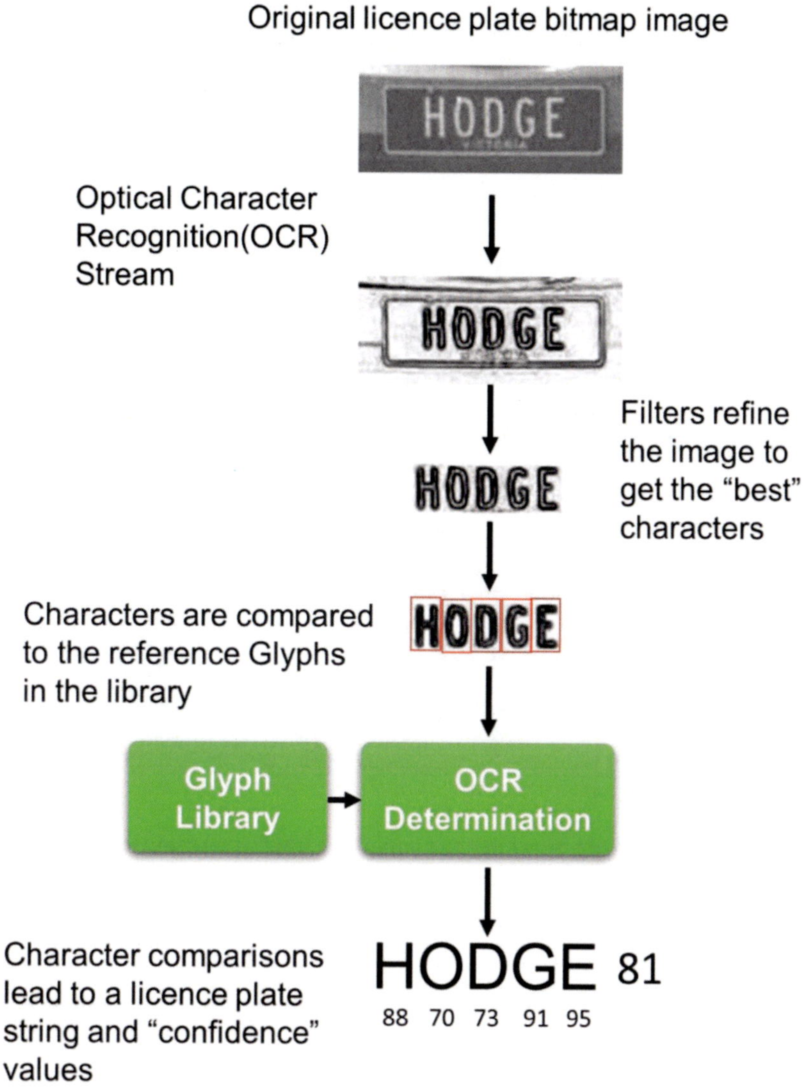

Figure 58 – The OCR process.

In figure 58, as humans, we can clearly see that the licence plate is HODGE. To achieve the same thing our silicon friends need cunning algorithms. The basic principle is for the algorithm to compare the value of a pixel in an image against all those around it. Where pixel value differences exceed a certain threshold, the algorithm assumes it has detected an edge – hopefully the edge of a character. The OCR engine may have several filters which seek to refine and define these edges till it can extract a character. The OCR engine needs something against which to compare the read characters. These reference characters, glyphs, are stored in a library within the engine. The engine hunts around for a glyph that best matches the read character and so arrives at a result. The degree to which a read character matches a glyph is indicated by the confidence level the engine assigns to that character. Confidence levels can be useful, but you need to understand how they work. The OCR engine puts all the read characters together and produces a licence plate string. It also combines all the character confidence levels into one overall confidence for that licence plate string. Different OCR manufacturers have different ways of determining and combining confidence levels.

You might also hear manufacturers talk about "training" their OCR engine. Exactly what this means will depend on the manufacturer, but one important part is tuning the engine to get the glyph comparison function as accurate as possible. Licence plate issuing authorities can help in this regard by picking very clear and unambiguous fonts for the licence plate characters. It does help if O and 0 are quite distinguishable from each other and don't look like Q. Similarly for I and 1, S and 5, and G and 6 and so on.

At this point you should be wondering why this confidence level thing is important, and that is a very good question to ask. The answer is that we want:

- Our systems to be able to read licence plates automatically so that we don't have to have armies of people manually looking at roadside images, and
- A result we can trust – so that we don't end up tolling incorrectly.

We just can't trust the OCR engines explicitly because they do get it wrong. So we need a mechanism to determine when we can trust an OCR result – this is where the confidence level comes in. The key point here is that confidence is not the same as accuracy. An OCR reading can be 100% confident and 100% wrong in terms of the licence plate string it delivers. If you're building a new tolling system with new OCR engines you should consider performing the "Grand Experiment".

The Grand Experiment is to take a lot of images, a couple of hundred thousand real images from the roadside, and shove them through the OCR engine recording the licence plate string and associated confidence. Then take those same images and have them all manually reviewed by real people, again recording the licence string. Now compare the two sets of licence plate string data and identify all those that are different, and review all those images again. Who got it right – the human or the machine? In this way you can correlate confidence against accuracy (or correctness of licence plate string). You can then plot confidence level against accuracy as shown in figure 59.

If you end up with a graph that looks like figure 59 basically you're screwed. It demonstrates that there is next to no correlation between confidence and accuracy, so you might as well give up on the idea of using confidence right now. This would be an unusual outcome – OCR engines are getting better and better all the time. The kind of result you want to see is in figure 60.

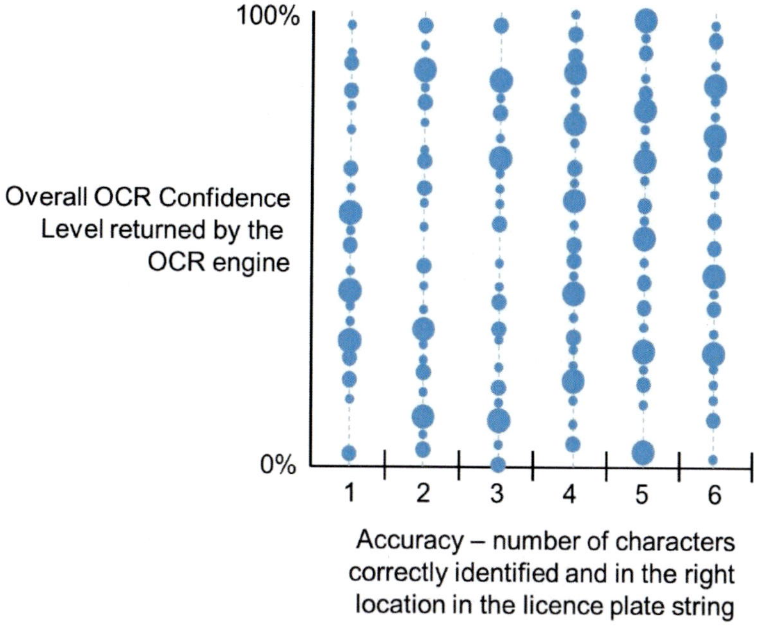

Figure 59 – OCR confidence versus accuracy.

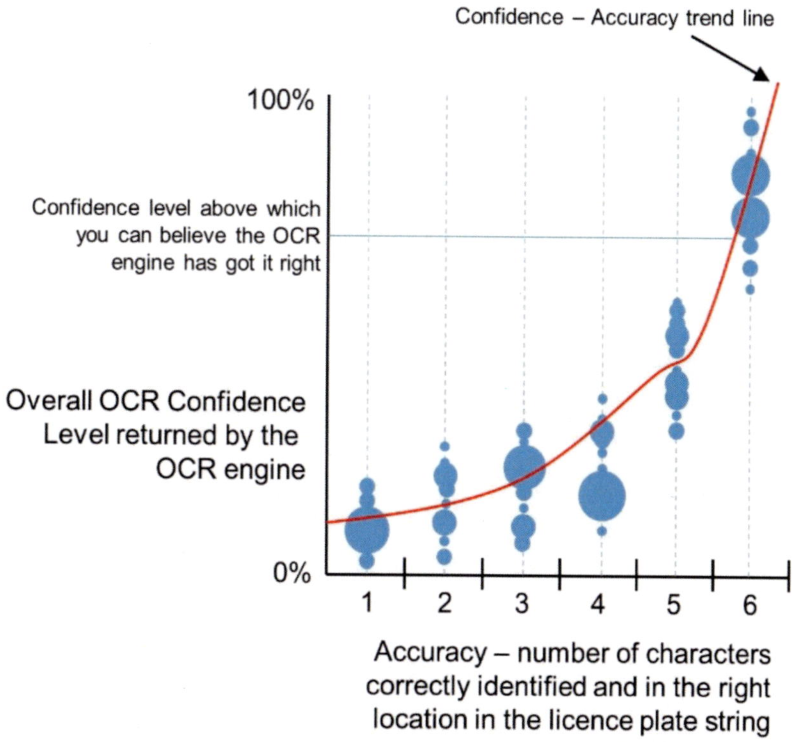

Figure 60 – OCR confidence versus accuracy – good result.

Figure 60 is clearly showing that there is a correlation between confidence and accuracy, and it is strong enough to enable us to be able to draw a trend line. I will point out that figure 60 probably isn't strictly representative when it comes to the sample sizes depicted on the graph i.e. a lot more of your samples should be squished into the right hand side if the OCR is working well. Using the trend line it now becomes possible to pick a confidence level above which we can start to believe the OCR licence plate string. In the back office we will use confidence level and business rules to get the best automatic read of licence plates possible with the highest level of accuracy.

But there is one further danger lurking in the data, and that is the "false confirmed result" we discussed earlier. To get a sense of how big a problem this might be, go back to the Grand Experiment data, and sample some of those images where the humans and machines agreed on the licence plate string. On this second review, how many incorrect strings did you find? Hopefully the numbers are tiny, fractions of a percent, but these false confirmed results exist and weave their way through the system causing some trouble down the processing chain.

I mentioned previously that New Zealand can claim to have some of the highest OCR performance results because they have very clean and clear licence plate designs. As soon as you offer people weird colour combinations and fancy plate pictures you are going to be making it more difficult for the OCR engine to do its job. Faced with pink characters on a pale blue background incorporating a sunset over the Golden Gate Bridge I think I would struggle to read the licence plate accurately. Some plates are really dirty, bent, obscured or missing. Unfortunately the OCR engine return of "NO READ" will always be a feature of this operation. And just for fun see if you can buy a licence plate with the characters "NO READ". What does your system make of that?

Being where it is, I'm guessing that it is rare to see a car in New Zealand that doesn't carry a New Zealand issued licence plate. This is not the case in Australia where each of the states and territories issue their own plates. In Europe it's a similar situation with vehicles registered in different countries able to move freely across borders. As well as the licence plate string, ideally you want your OCR engine to be able to tell you where the vehicle was registered. How well the system can do this is driven to an extent by licence plate design. The plate itself may have specific characters or markings that the OCR engine can identify – glyphs don't have to be just letters and numbers. It could be character syntax – the arrangement of characters and letters in the licence plate string, and the number of characters in the string. It could even be as subtle as different character fonts. In Australia getting hold of the state of registration is important because the states and territories have issued plates with identical licence plate strings. The state then becomes essential to differentiate between two plates with the same string.

Pulling all that together, Data Item 2 shows the minimum amount of data needed from a vehicle passage.

With reference to Data Item 2, you will probably be interested in Trailer Detected #12 only if you're allowed to charge extra for that trailer. Otherwise it can help to explain a very long vehicle, Vehicle Length #10, which in every other respect looks like a car. Closely associated with the Vehicle Passage, our last data item from the roadside equipment is the Image Package.

Data Item 2 – Vehicle Passage		
ID	**Name**	**Description**
1	Passage ID	The unique identification number of the passage itself assigned by the roadside equipment.
2	Front Licence Plate String	The string containing the characters of the front licence plate as read by the OCR.
3	Front Licence Plate Read Confidence	The confidence value associated with the OCR read of the front licence plate.
4	Rear Licence Plate String	The string containing the characters of the rear licence plate as read by the OCR.
5	Rear Licence Plate Read Confidence	The confidence value associated with the OCR read of the rear licence plate.
6	State/Country of Registration	The State or Country of registration as determined by the OCR engine.
7	Position	An indication as to where the vehicle was detected within the context of the front and rear gantries.
8	Vehicle Height	The measured height of the vehicle.
9	Vehicle Width	The measured width of the vehicle.
10	Vehicle Length	The measured length of the vehicle.
11	Assigned Vehicle Class	Based on the height, width and length measurements, the class assigned to the vehicle by the roadside.
12	Trailer Detected	The roadside equipment detected that the vehicle was towing a trailer.
13	Vehicle Speed	An indication of the vehicle speed as detected within the context of the front and rear gantries.
14	Date-Time Stamp	The date and time (to milliseconds) that the passage was recorded at the roadside.
15	Toll Point ID	Details as to exactly where the transaction occurred. Ideally this would go as far as to identify the detection asset that recorded the passage. As a minimum it must include the toll point and the direction of travel.
16	Image Package ID	The image package associated with the vehicle passage.
17	Date-Time Stamp data received by back office	The date and time (to milliseconds) that the vehicle passage was received by the back office (Trip Reconstruction).

Data Item 2 – Vehicle Passage.

Data Item 3 – Image Package		
ID	**Name**	**Description**
1	Package ID	The unique identification number of the package itself assigned by the roadside equipment.
2	Front Image ID	The unique identification number of the front image assigned by the roadside equipment.
3	Front Image Hash Value	The value produced by the hash function when it is run across the image.
4	Front Image Hash Key	A key which indicates which hash function or version of a function is being used to generate the hash value.
5	Front Image Camera ID	A unique number which identifies the camera taking the front image.
6	Front Date-Time Stamp	The date and time (to milliseconds) that the front image was taken.
7	Rear Image ID	The unique identification number of the rear image assigned by the roadside equipment.
8	Rear Image Hash Value	The value produced by the hash function when it is run across the image.
9	Rear Image Hash Key	A key which indicates which hash function or version of a function is being used to generate the hash value.
10	Rear Image Camera ID	A unique number which identifies the camera taking the rear image.
11	Rear Date-Time Stamp	The date and time (to milliseconds) that the rear image was taken.
12	Date-Time Stamp data received by back office	The date and time (to milliseconds) that the image package was received by the back office.

Data Item 3 – Image Package.

The roadside equipment may bundle the images and the data in the Image Package data item into one discrete file before sending the whole thing to the back office.

That was exhausting! All that for three data items.

Yes Darling, but they probably are the three most important data items. They represent the money.

Vehicles, Tags and Interoperability Partners

Now that we have the three data items from the roadside that let us toll, it would be natural to want to rush into the whole trip reconstruction and rating thing. But before we do it is important to think about vehicles and tags.

For tolling purposes what defines or identifies a vehicle? Most people would answer the licence plate string and the state or country of registration. You have to have that so you can identify the owner of the vehicle and charge them the toll. And I would agree, but I want to be a bit more pedantic about things because identifying a vehicle using the licence plate doesn't sit well with my purist object-orientated brain.

Yes, for all practical purposes the licence plate does identify the vehicle, but licence plates can get stolen, moved, re-assigned, and destroyed. So in that sense they are distinct and separate from the vehicle itself. The thing that uniquely identifies the vehicle is that Vehicle Identification Number (VIN). But you can't read VINs using the roadside equipment, so we have to rely on licence plates – and there is the rub.

Following our model in figure 2, I believe vehicle details should live in the Vehicle Database component, but that is really up to your tolling system designer. Let's define some more data items starting with the Vehicle Type – Data Item 4.

You're free to play any number of tunes with the Vehicle Type data item. Its purpose in life is to give you the data you need to identify any given vehicle's class. For example, Toyota has been manufacturing a car called the Corolla since 1966. There are now eleven generations of Corolla. You could use the Series #5 and the Start #15 and End Year of manufacture #16 to identify those eleven generations. On the other hand you might not worry because no matter what generation it is, for your road a Toyota Corolla is never going to be anything other than a car. But there are examples in Victoria, Australia, where the changes made to a vehicle type has resulted in the vehicle classification moving from Car to Light Commercial Vehicle. You might decide that trying to get a reference picture for every vehicle type is "gilding the lily", but again these can be useful for training your image processing operators. Vehicle Identification Numbers #17 are surprisingly complex. There is an ISO standard for them and to get a feel for how they work I recommend you look at the page on Wikipedia[28]. As we've seen, VINs have two parts – the first part does identify a vehicle type, and the second part seeks to identify a unique vehicle. So that first part is of value to us in this vehicle type table.

As I mentioned previously, you can populate your Vehicle Type data items using a commercially available data package. Whatever you do though, the tolling system has to allow you to manually add vehicle types, for the simple reason that somebody, somewhere will have privately imported a Trabant and will be searching for a Tatra from the Czech Republic – and there is a good chance they won't appear in anybody's data package.

Data Item 4 – Vehicle Type		
ID	**Name**	**Description**
1	Vehicle Type ID	The unique identification number of the vehicle type.
2	Make	The name of the manufacturer of the vehicle – the "badge" name.
3	Model	The model name assigned to the vehicle.
4	Body Style	A reference to the particular body style of the vehicle e.g. hatchback, saloon, wagon, coupe.
5	Series	Any other identifier given to the vehicle by the manufacturer.
6	Weight	The weight of the vehicle when unloaded.
7	Vehicle Height	The manufacturer's declared height of the vehicle.
8	Vehicle Width	The manufacturer's declared width of the vehicle.
9	Vehicle Length	The manufacturer's declared length of the vehicle.
10	Assigned Vehicle Class	Based on the rules pertaining to your concession deed, the class assigned to the vehicle type.
11	Number of Seats	The seating capacity of the vehicle.
12	Load Carrying Capability	In the case of trucks, the weight of the load that can be carried.
13	Axles	The number of axles the vehicle has.
14	Metallic Windscreen	Whether the factory delivered car was fitted with a metallic windscreen.
15	Start Year of Manufacture	The year that this vehicle type was first released.
16	End Year of Manufacture	The year that this vehicle became no longer for sale.
17	Short VIN	The first characters of the VIN that identifies this vehicle type.
18	Reference Picture URL	The URL of reference pictures for the vehicle type.

Data Item 4 – Vehicle Type.

Data Item 5 – Licence Plate		
ID	**Name**	**Description**
1	Licence Plate ID	The unique identification number of the licence plate assigned by the tolling system.
2	Licence Plate String	The character and number string of the licence plate.
3	Register	The authority that issues and controls this licence plate.
4	Type	The plate type.
5	Decoration	The decoration visible on the plate.
6	Reference Picture URL	The URL of reference pictures for the licence plate as captured by the roadside equipment.
7	Signature URL	The URL of signature strings for the licence plate as captured by the central OCR system.

Data Item 5 – Licence Plate.

Introducing the Licence Plate, Data Item 5. That Type #4 - in Victoria, Australia, VicRoads runs the licence register. They are happy to sell you plates of different types such as "Heritage", "Custom" and "Slim Line". Similarly with Decoration #5, if you so choose you can have a pink plate with black letters, or a plate with a love heart. The Reference Picture URL #6 is a link to real sample images of this plate captured on a vehicle by the roadside equipment. As for Signature URL #7, we'll discuss the idea of signatures later.

To be honest, to toll successfully, you only really need the first three lines in this data item. But as your tolling operation matures, and you look for ways to squeeze closed the little bits of toll revenue that leak around the edges, the other lines may become of use.

As shown in Data Item 6, the definition of a Vehicle becomes simple affair. A Vehicle has a Vehicle Type ID #2 that references all the make and model information. It has a Licence Plate ID #3. Ordinarily the class of this vehicle could be taken straight from the Vehicle Type data item, and in the vast majority of cases would be. However, people are allowed to modify vehicles, and in some cases those modifications can change the vehicle class. For example, in Australia you can buy a small bus. If you whip out a few seats that bus goes from being a Heavy Commercial Vehicle to being a Car – huge difference in the tolls you have to pay.

Data Item 6 – Vehicle		
ID	**Name**	**Description**
1	Vehicle ID	The unique identification number of the vehicle.
2	Vehicle Type ID	A reference to the unique identification number of the vehicle type.
3	Licence Plate ID	A reference to the unique identification number of the licence plate being carried by the vehicle.
4	VIN	The full vehicle identification number.
5	MAC Address	The unique identifier assigned to the SIM card carried by the vehicle.
6	Vehicle Class	The actual tolling class assigned to this vehicle.
7	Colour	The colour of the vehicle.
8	Modifications	Details of any modifications made to this specific vehicle that may have caused its vehicle class to change.

Data Item 6 – Vehicle.

I am being very presumptuous in giving my data item a MAC Address line #5 – or maybe not. I don't think it will be long before most new cars come with the ability to communicate into a mobile network, for all sorts of reasons including live traffic updates, technical problem troubleshooting and to call for help in emergencies. This holds out the possibility that we could use that communications capability to toll and be done with our DSRC tags for good. But at the moment it is very much a work in progress.

You can get vehicle details from several sources:

- Your own customers when they register for a tolling account or buy a pass product,
- From your interoperability partners,
- From your local vehicle registration authority.

Critically the tolling system has to be able to operate with different levels of detail. In the case of a pass product the only information you may have is a licence plate number, a state of registration, a vehicle class provided by the customer and a credit card number. For one of your own customers you may have the full suite of information populated in your data items. If you can negotiate a deal with your local vehicle registration authority and buy from them a full list of every registered vehicle in your state or country, complete with vehicle make, model and VIN then you will be in a very good place when it comes to understanding who is using your road.

Data Item 7 – Tag		
ID	**Name**	**Description**
1	Tag ID	The unique identification number of the tag assigned by the tolling system.
2	Tag Broadcast ID	The unique identification number of the tag which it broadcasts to the roadside. It is a combination of the tag's own serial number, the number of the tag issuer and the Country ID.
3	Tag Serial Number	The serial number of the tag.
4	Tag Issuer ID	The unique identifier assigned to the issuer of the tag for interoperability purposes (Concession ID).
5	Country ID	A globally unique number assigned to the country in which the tag issuing organisation resides.
6	Tag Class	The tolling class assigned to this tag.
7	Manufacturer	Identifies the manufacturer of the tag.
8	Manufacturer Serial Number	The serial number assigned to the tag by the manufacturer.
9	Battery Insertion Date	The date the battery was inserted into the tag.
10	Activation Date	The date the tag was registered as in active use.
11	Usage Monitor	An indication as how much the tag has been used.

Data Item 7 – Tag.

Most DSRC tags do have a battery which has a long but finite life. Some tag manufacturers try and indicate the extent to which a tag has been used through the Usage Monitor #11. In my experience this data is quite tricky to interpret but if you can it is intended to help you predict when tags will start to fail and so need replacing – to avoid that "mass extinction event".

Populating Tag data in the tolling system would come from the tag logistics function and be based on tags delivered by your supplier and issued to your customers.

Finally on to the Interoperability Partner data item. An Interoperability Partner is any Tag Issuer with whom you have an interoperable agreement. They will have a unique Tag Issuer ID (Concession ID) #3 which identifies their tags when you see those tags travelling on your road. For those tags to work on your road you will need to install Tag Keys #10 in your roadside equipment to decode the messages. You need to know their Bank Account Details #6 so that you can pay the tolls of your customers travelling on their road, less the roaming fees determined by the Roaming Agreement Fee Schedule #8. Account ID #11 is the mechanism used to manage what you send to them.

Data Item 8 – Interoperability Partner		
ID	**Name**	**Description**
1	Issuer ID	The unique identification number assigned to this Issuer by the tolling system.
2	Issuer Name	The business name given to the Issuer.
3	Tag Issuer ID	The unique identifier assigned to the issuer of the tag for interoperability purposes (Concession ID).
4	Country ID	A globally unique number assigned to the country in which the tag issuing organisation resides.
5	Issuer Contact Details	The contact details including address, telephone numbers and e-mails of the Issuer.
6	Issuer Bank Account Details	The details of the Issuer's bank account to facilitate interoperability payments.
7	Roaming Agreement URL	A link to the signed roaming agreement currently active with the Issuer.
8	Roaming Agreement Fee Schedule	Details of the roaming fees applied by the Issuer.
9	Tag Type	Details of the tag types distributed by this Issuer.
10	Tag Keys	The electronic keys used at the roadside to decode the messages from the tags provided by this Issuer.
11	Account ID	This Partner's account ID within the tolling system.

Data Item 8 – Interoperability Partner.

Business rules

At this point we should have a think about some of the business rules we might apply to these data items.

Once defined, should we allow a Vehicle Type to change? Well strictly speaking I don't think so. So long as you got the data correct when you created it, a Vehicle Type is what it is and shouldn't change. The only thing you should be adding is the End Year of Manufacture #16.

For a Licence Plate the Licence Plate String #2 and Register #3 should never change because they identify that plate. If they do, then logically we have defined a new plate with a new Licence Plate ID #1. The rest of the lines in that data item may change. I have a licence plate that has had two changes of Type #4 and Decoration #5, and been registered against two different vehicles. When they do change we should save the old data in a history table with a time-date stamp marking the change event.

For a vehicle its Vehicle Type should never change, but modifications and subsequent changes to class should be updated in the Vehicle Class #6 and Modifications #8 lines. A VIN #4 should never change. The Licence Plate ID #3 and Colour #7 can of course change, and it is too early to know what to do with MAC Address #5. As before, when there are changes we should save the old data in a history table with a time-date stamp marking the change event.

For a Tag the only thing that should be changing is the Usage Monitor #11 if you decide to keep track of that data. The Tag data item represents the tip of an iceberg. As I alluded to in the Toll Products section, a lot of work is needed to manage tags. This data item would be used in conjunction with other data structures which, as a bare minimum, gives each tag a status along the lines of "in the warehouse", "ready for issue", "active", "lost" and so on, all part of the tag logistics function.

As an aside, back in 2013, Holman Benitez and I presented a paper at the Intelligent Transport Systems (ITS) Summit in Australia. In this paper are state transition diagrams for tolling accounts, vehicles, licence plates and tags. I drove myself to distraction in drawing them and probably confused most of the people in the room when I presented them, the point being that each diagram is complicated enough in its own right, but when you combine them together, as every tolling system has to do, the situation becomes positively byzantine. For completeness I've included the four diagrams in Appendix B. Take a moment and see if they make sense to you.

Trip Reconstruction and Rating

The roadside equipment needs to be sending Tag passages, Vehicle passages and Image Packages to the back office all the time, 24 by 7. Again with reference to figure 2, all this roadside data arrives at the Trip Reconstruction process. The roadside equipment impinges on the real world using physics and although very reliable cannot be guaranteed to deliver all the data all of the time. The first job of the Trip Reconstruction process is to check that the data received is sufficient. These checks include, but are not limited to:

- Passage and Package IDs are correctly formed, follow a logical sequence and are not duplicated (unless the back office is requesting the data be sent again).
- Date-time stamps are correctly formed and within acceptable time limits. There may be a delay in sending data to the back office, but you should be suspicious if the roadside starts sending data time-stamped from a year ago.
- For tag passages, the Tag Broadcast ID is correctly formed, and the Tag Issuer ID is one that is recognised as being in the current interoperability group i.e. there is a known Interoperability Partner.
- For vehicle passages a detection has been made and there is at least one image available in addition to any OCR readings.

If any of those checks fail then unfortunately it means you lose the message and the money – you end up with a "tolling loss". But don't ignore these losses as a bit of analysis might reveal a problem with a tag or the roadside equipment that needs fixing. If you encounter a tag with an unknown Tag Issuer ID then you should get very interested. That might indicate fraudulent activity.

Once the basic checks have been passed Trip Reconstruction seeks to form passages into transactions that can then be used to form trips. I'm following the Class Model I described earlier where, regardless of the presence of a tag, we're seeking to get a good licence plate read from every tag-vehicle passage pair, and we've got a central OCR system to help us. A good question at this point is "If you're going to do that, why bother with tags at all?" The answer lies in the way the Australian concession deeds are written and the way interoperability works.

Australian concession deeds typically require that operators offer customers a "free" tolling product, one that does not in the normal course of events attract account keeping fees and charges. That usually means a tag account, and from the word go tag accounts were the focus of interoperability arrangements. Operators can and do offer video based accounts but they attract the image matching or processing fee. As an operator you could say to all your customers you no longer need to use your tag, and we'll waive the image processing fee. But unless you could convince all the other Australian operators to do the same thing, you would end up paying the image processing fees your customers incur on other toll roads which puts the business case for doing away with tags on shaky ground. So for the time being we'll stick with the tags – which are very good – and use image processing to check that we're not losing revenue through vehicle class problems. In short this means another discussion around the processing of images.

OCR, Confidence Levels and Business Rules

We have vehicle passages coming in from the roadside. They contain licence plate reads and confidence levels. We need a set of business rules, table 20, to determine if we are ready to trust those reads as accurate enough for the purposes of tolling.

Do we have a front and rear licence plate string?

- **No:** Is the confidence level associated with the licence plate string we do have above a [*parameter 1*] value?
  - **No:** Send the images to the central OCR system and let it have a go.
  - **Yes:** Is this a licence plate we see on a regular basis? At this point we do a search of our vehicle database.
    - **No:** We haven't seen that licence plate before. OK, send the images to the central OCR system and let it have a go.
    - **Yes:** Let's trust the system. Assume that licence plate is correct.
- **Yes:** We do have a front and rear licence plate read.

  Is the confidence level associated with either the front or rear licence plate read above a [*parameter 2*] value?
  - **No:** Send the images to the central OCR system and let it have a go.
  - **Yes:** Does the front licence plate string match the rear licence plate string?
    - **No:** Send the images to the central OCR system and let it have a go.
    - **Yes:** Is this a licence plate we see on a regular basis? At this point we do a search of our vehicle database.
      - **No:** We haven't seen that licence plate before. OK, does the licence text pass the basic syntax rules i.e. maximum number of characters etc.?
        - **No:** Send the images to the central OCR system and let it have a go.
        - **Yes:** Let's trust the system. Assume that licence plate is correct.
      - **Yes:** Let's trust the system. Assume that licence plate is correct.

Table 20 – Basic roadside licence plate read matching rules (ref. figure 27)

With a limited data set, there are only so many rules you can conjure up that are worthwhile, but that said, there are endless tunes you can play with this kind of logic. You have the two parameter values to tweak. You may trust front licence plate reads more than those from the rear and might weight their OCR confidence values accordingly. You may involve vehicle class in the logic to identify motorcycles as a special case. It's a set of rules that you tune till you get the highest proportion of "Yes, let's trust the system" for the lowest number of those nasty "false confirmed results". Let's leave the Yes path on hold for the moment and look at what we do with the Nos.

The No vehicle passages and their images get sent off to the Central OCR System. This can have a number of functions and really depends on what you buy from your supplier. At the heart of it is another OCR engine but crucially one from a different OEM supplier to that of the roadside equipment. If it is the same engine as the roadside you'll end up with the same results and will have gained little. The basic principle of this central processing stream is the same as that shown in figure 58.

Some manufacturers go further and can do clever things with the plate image. Kapsch has a system which is a good example of this technology. The OCR read is one form of image processing. But there is more information to be had from the pixels in that plate image – a type of electronic signature. Figure 61 shows the basic principle.

A filter is run over the plate image which produces "points of interest". Those points of interest can be combined into a signature for that plate image. The exact nature of the filter will almost certainly remain the intellectual property of your supplier. The most important thing is that it produces very similar signatures under different lighting and weather conditions. That signature then becomes a second, quite independent way of matching a licence plate – but it means you have to store up a reference library of plate images and signatures in your vehicle database for comparison purposes. It is this reference library that I am referring to in Data Item 5 – Licence Plates with the line Signature URL #7.

So after all that hopefully now we have:

- Licence plate strings and confidence values from the roadside,
- Licence plate strings and confidence values from the Central OCR System, and
- Matching information from the licence plate signature.

To make use of all that data we need to reform the rules in table 20 with the same aim as before: to get the highest proportion of "Yes, let's trust the system" for the lowest number of those nasty "false confirmed results". But if after working through all those rules the system still can't automatically confirm a licence plate string there is one last line of defence, the Human Image Processor.

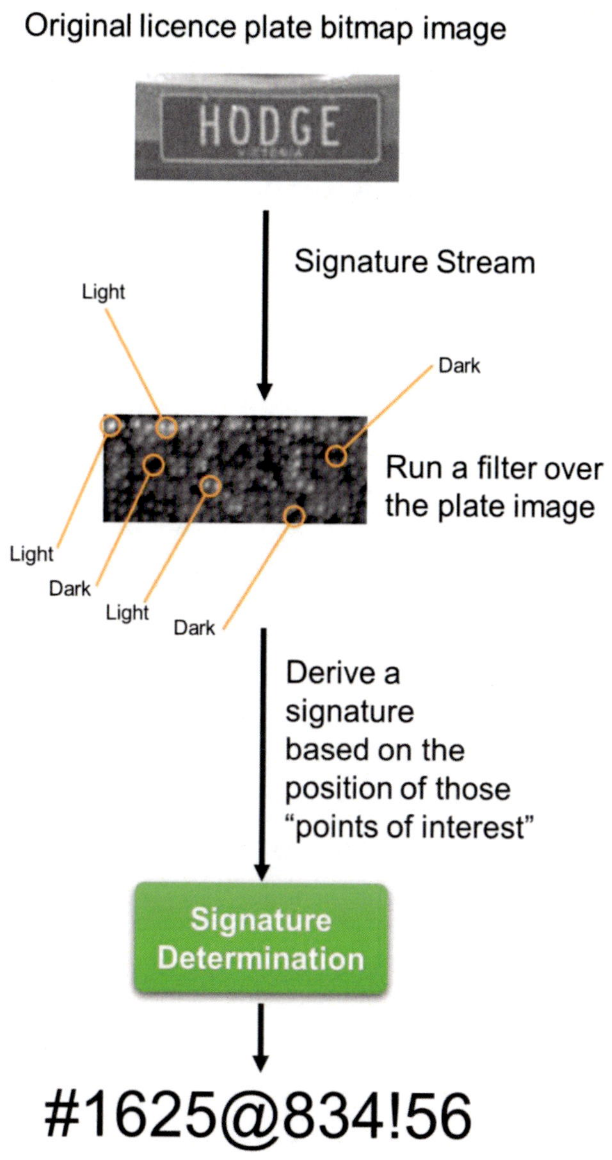

Figure 61 – The image processing signature process

Depending on how your system's action lists are set up, some images will get sent to a Human Image Processor directly. It will depend on your business rules, but reasons include:

- The roadside measured the dimensions of the vehicle and the inferred vehicle class from those dimensions doesn't match the tag or vehicle class recorded in the system (obvious class mismatch).
- We found a licence plate that we have no record of.

- The licence plate string matches closely a licence plate that for some reason often results in a false confirmed result. For example there might be two plates, **O MY** and **0 MY** out in circulation that keep on getting confused.
- A licence plate belonging to a serial toll dodger and the operator wants to monitor his or her activity closely.
- The local law enforcement agencies have asked for a particular vehicle to be watched. Whether you are allowed to do this will depend on your local privacy laws.

There is now the potential for another reason to call on the Image Processors enabled by the latest developments in machine learning software. Technologies such as Google's TensorFlow are holding out the possibility of being able to analyse a vehicle image such as figure 57 and with training identify the make and model. That make and model can be compared against the make and model of the vehicle associated with the licence plate and if there is a difference, the images sent to a Human Image Processor for analysis. This kind of process would help to stop those situations where licence plates have changed vehicle and the operator hasn't been told. This can be a legitimate change of registration details, but also may be a situation involving stolen licence plates. In recent years in Australia many licence plates have been stolen to facilitate "drive aways" from petrol stations and other criminal acts. In such a situation the chances are you will lose the tolling revenue, but spotting the problem early may well save on a heap of rework down the processing chain.

Human Image Processing

Human Image Processors have to work fast. They are given quite strict average handling time (AHT) targets. It is very important therefore to give them a graphical user interface that is highly intuitive and fast to use. I'm not going to show you a picture of a real GUI because they remain the intellectual property of the operator or supplier, but I can talk about some of things that I think are important when you are specifying one of these systems. The GUI should:

- When available be capable of showing both the front and rear images of the vehicle on the screen at the same time,
- Zoom the images to the point where the whole vehicle is still visible, with the extra space around the vehicle cropped out - this means that the licence plate is made bigger on the screen but still is presented in the context of the vehicle, which is helpful for determining vehicle class,
- Display under the relevant image the licence plate text strings and state or country of registration from the roadside and Central OCR systems when available – and one click allows the operator to populate the "final" licence plate and state reading,
- Pre-populate the vehicle class, based on the best available information in the vehicle database for the licence plate string and registration,
- Have controls to manipulate the images such as zoom, brightness and contrast – bearing in mind that the only thing being altered is the presentation on the GUI. The actual image has to remain unaltered. Remember that image hash value?
- Give the Image Processor the option of using the mouse or shortcut keys – different people like working in different ways,

- Display supporting data from the vehicle database – reference images and other data where appropriate,
- Alert the Image Processor if the vehicle is on the action list for some reason, and what they should check for,
- Make the editing and confirmation of the "final" licence plate, state or country of registration and vehicle class as simple as possible,
- Allow the Image Processor to pass a vehicle on to a supervisor if they are unsure about some aspect,
- Allow the Image Processor to declare a Vehicle Passage a tolling loss if there really is no chance of getting a licence plate read from the images,
- Be fast. The loading of new images once a vehicle has been confirmed should appear to be instantaneous.

You can see from that list that getting the Image Processing GUI right is a complex user experience design challenge. If you don't get it right your Image Processors will get fed up and leave and then probably sue you for repetitive strain injury.

Tolling Losses

With the best will in the world there will always be tolling losses. A small number of licence plates will be impossible to read or simply missing. One of the most frustrating aspects in this area are people who seem to be deliberately obscuring their licence plates. It is illegal but trivial in the overall scheme of criminal acts so it is hard to get law enforcement agencies to take it seriously. In Australia two of the biggest problems we see are the "mini bull bar" and the tray.

The mini bull bar is a small piece of tubular stainless steel that is fixed to the front of a vehicle just above the licence plate. It is intended to be a mounting point for extra lights but a consequence is that it perfectly obscures the front licence plate when viewed from a roadside camera on a gantry. Ironically the Victorian Police use them on their vehicles to hold some of their flashy pursuit lights. The tray is the tray on the back of a Ute. Sometimes the licence plate is mounted well under the tray so that the tray itself obscures the plate.

One potential solution to this problem is the low level camera. This idea is simply an extra camera fitted to one of the gantry columns at a height of about a meter off the ground and looking across the lanes of traffic. It is a video camera rather than one that takes still images and has to be time synchronised to the gantry time. It can see under the mini bull bars and trays and capture those obscured licence plates. There are several issues with this idea but the biggest that I have come across is that the business case doesn't stack up. Yes there is money to be had in stopping those tolling losses but to date it hasn't justified the extra expense of the roadside equipment – which can be quite significant.

Another feature of that 2013 Intelligent Transport Systems (ITS) Summit paper was an idea by Holman Benitez to actually enable trip reconstruction on tolling loss Vehicle Passages. Much as you can get a signature of a licence plate, you can get a signature of a whole vehicle and match them to form a trip –

given that you have one good licence plate string from a low level camera. Holman worked out that if you only have a couple of low level cameras at your busiest gantries, and can match a low level camera image to one of the tolling loss images from the gantry camera, you could identify the vehicle and charge it the toll for the whole trip. Figure 62 shows this concept.

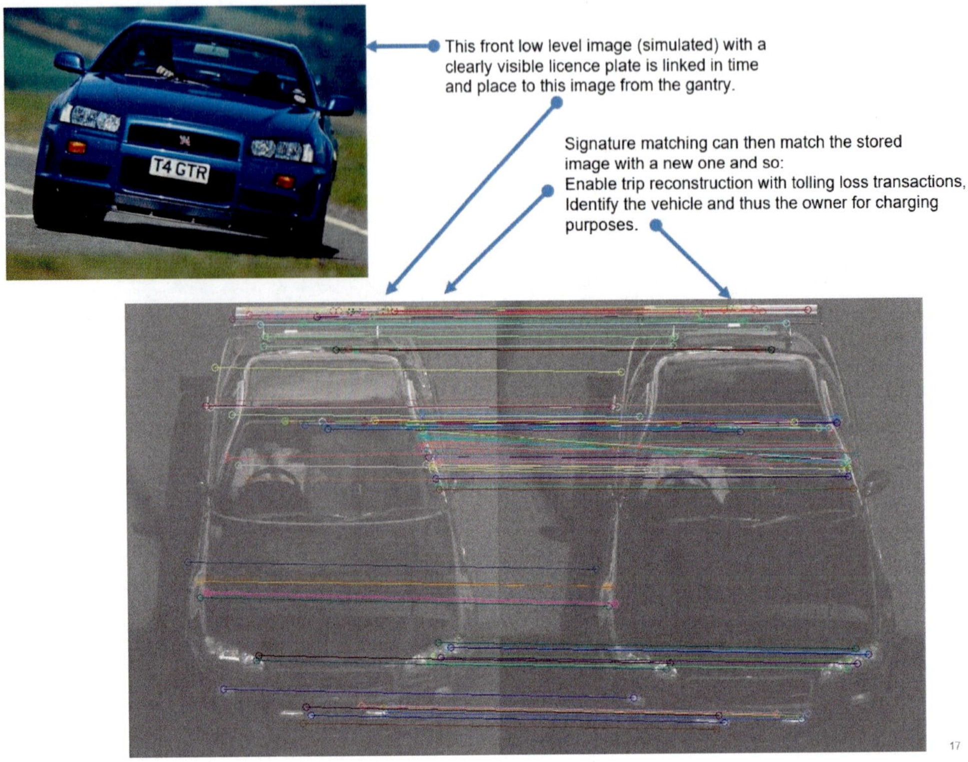

Figure 62 – Taking a signature of the whole vehicle to enable the charging of tolls against "tolling loss" trips. Note the vehicles in the greyscale images have no visible licence plate.

Unfortunately we didn't have the time to pursue this clever idea further, but it might be something for the future. It all comes down to that business case.

At some point in this process you have to apply your business rule for charging the Image Processing Fee. It's really up to you and the rules in your concession deed as to when and why you do it but usually it's just for those vehicles not carrying a tag. You might want to get a bit creative and include those vehicles where the tag class doesn't match the actual vehicle class.

You know, we've been banging on about roadside this and image process that and we haven't even formed a trip yet!

Patience Darling, that is coming in the next bit.

Transactions

You only need trip reconstruction if you need trips and usually you only need trips if you've got more than one gantry and you're going to give your customers some kind of trip cap or trip related discount. If you're not doing that then you can skip the whole bothersome business of creating trips and charge your customers simple transactions, which is what we look at next – the Transaction data item.

Transactions are formed by the Trip Reconstruction component from the data in the Tag and Vehicle Passages after all the image processing we've just discussed. It seeks to represent the "best" data set we can achieve with the data made available to us from the roadside. Every transaction will be unique and will vary in the data it holds. If you have a good level of tag penetration then hopefully most of your transactions will contain all the lines of data. Obviously if the vehicle wasn't carrying a tag, then only those lines relating to the Vehicle Passage will be present. Similarly you will get transactions formed from only tag data – so called "isolated tags". Vehicle detection and scanning equipment and cameras have to be taken out of service from time to time for cleaning and maintenance resulting in no recorded Vehicle Passages. What about the scenario where you get more than one tag associated with a Vehicle Passage? You need to develop some business rules for that scenario. Business rules could be along the following lines:

- If you have a smart tolling system that lets you identify which tag is most often seen in a particular vehicle you might pick that tag and create a separate transaction for the other tag.
- You might pick the tag that belongs to one of your customers and create a separate transaction for the other tag which belongs to an operator in the interoperability group.
- You might base the decision on the status of the Arrangement to Pay (of which more later).
- You might defer your decision till you've seen what the Trip Reconstruction algorithm does with the transaction i.e. that second tag may only appear once amongst a number of otherwise matching transactions.

Whichever way you play it, your business rules should be based on recovering the maximum amount of revenue from your transactions in the easiest way possible.

Data Item 9 – Transaction		
ID	**Name**	**Description**
1	Transaction ID	The unique identification number of the transaction itself assigned by the Trip Reconstruction component.
2	Tag Broadcast ID	The identification number of the tag. When combined with the tag issuer and country IDs this should be a globally unique number.
3	Tag Issuer ID	A unique number (for a given country) assigned to the organisation that issues (owns) the tag for interoperability purposes (Concession ID).
4	Country ID	A globally unique number assigned to the country in which the tag issuing organisation resides.
5	Tag ID	The unique identification number of the tag assigned by the tolling system.
6	Licence Plate String	The string containing the characters of the final licence plate.
7	State/Country of Registration	The final State or Country of registration.
8	Vehicle Class	The final class assigned to the vehicle.
9	Trailer Detected	The roadside equipment detected that the vehicle was towing a trailer.
10	Vehicle ID	The unique identification number of the Vehicle assigned by the tolling system.
11	Date-Time Stamp	The date and time (to milliseconds) that the transaction data was recorded at the roadside (based on Vehicle Passage if available).
12	Toll Point ID	Details as to exactly where the transaction occurred. As a minimum it must include the toll point and the direction of travel.
13	Tag Passage ID	The Tag Passage used to construct this transaction.
14	Vehicle Passage ID	The Vehicle Passage used to construct this transaction.
15	Image Processing Fee	Applied or not.
16	Transaction Date-Time Stamp	The date and time (to milliseconds) that the transaction was created.

Data Item 9 – Transaction.

Trip Reconstruction

Trip Reconstruction needs a few things:

- An understanding of the topology of the road i.e. where gantries are in relation to each other, including whether the road is open or closed,
- The business rules as to what constitutes a trip, and
- A sense of time.

We've discussed these concepts before in previous sections. In this section we'll bring all these ideas together and show you what trip reconstruction means in practise. For an open road, let's remind ourselves of the EastLink trip rules from their website:

> An EastLink 'trip' is defined as travel on EastLink in one direction only. You may leave and re-join EastLink in the same trip, provided you keep going in the same direction, don't repeat any section, and complete your trip within 60 minutes. A return journey constitutes two EastLink trips.

By comparison, Westlink M7 in Sydney, Australia, which is closed, isn't quite so specific. On the Roam website they just refer to tolls being charged based on entry and exit points, which makes sense for a closed road, but make no mention if there is a time limit for a trip.

Time is important in a couple of ways. Obviously the time of the transaction as measured at the roadside is vital to order transactions in the correct way for a particular vehicle. But equally important is a sense of the time difference between transactions. A car travelling at 100km/hr covers 1 km in 36 seconds. If you record a transaction at the start of your road for a vehicle and then think you see the same vehicle 20 seconds later at the other end of the road – 20 kms away – you should suspect that something is not quite right. The Trip Reconstruction component should have "time bounding" rules built into its logic.

Another time aspect which is important is when to consider a trip complete. With the closed road it is relatively safe to conclude that a trip is complete when you have an entry and an exit transaction – although that isn't always the case as we'll see later. But how long do you wait if no exit transaction turns up? Or even weirder, if you have an exit transaction but no entry? You'll have to decide on a business rule so that you can close the trip and move it on to Trip Rating and ultimately somebody's account. With the open road you are never quite sure whether a trip has ended at any given time so again you need a business rule to close the trip after an appropriate amount of time.

Unless you are turning on your tolling system for the very first time, you will always have data in different states of processing:

- New transactions sitting in a transactions table waiting to be examined,
- Trips which are "in progress" – they haven't met the business rule yet to be considered "closed",
- "Closed" trips which can be sent off to Interoperability for processing,

- Trips which are having to be re-formed. For a variety of reasons both "in progress" and "closed" trips sometimes need to be adjusted, and
- A "bucket of bits" or transactions to re-process – transactions that don't seem to fit anywhere just at the moment.

You can think of trip reconstruction as a big search problem. You have a substantial database table (or equivalent) into which are being tipped transactions. The system has to look at each transaction and try and match them up based on the information presented. For the closed road the basic algorithm looks something like table 21.

Let's have a look at how this should work in practice. Figure 63 represents a simple trip on a closed toll road.

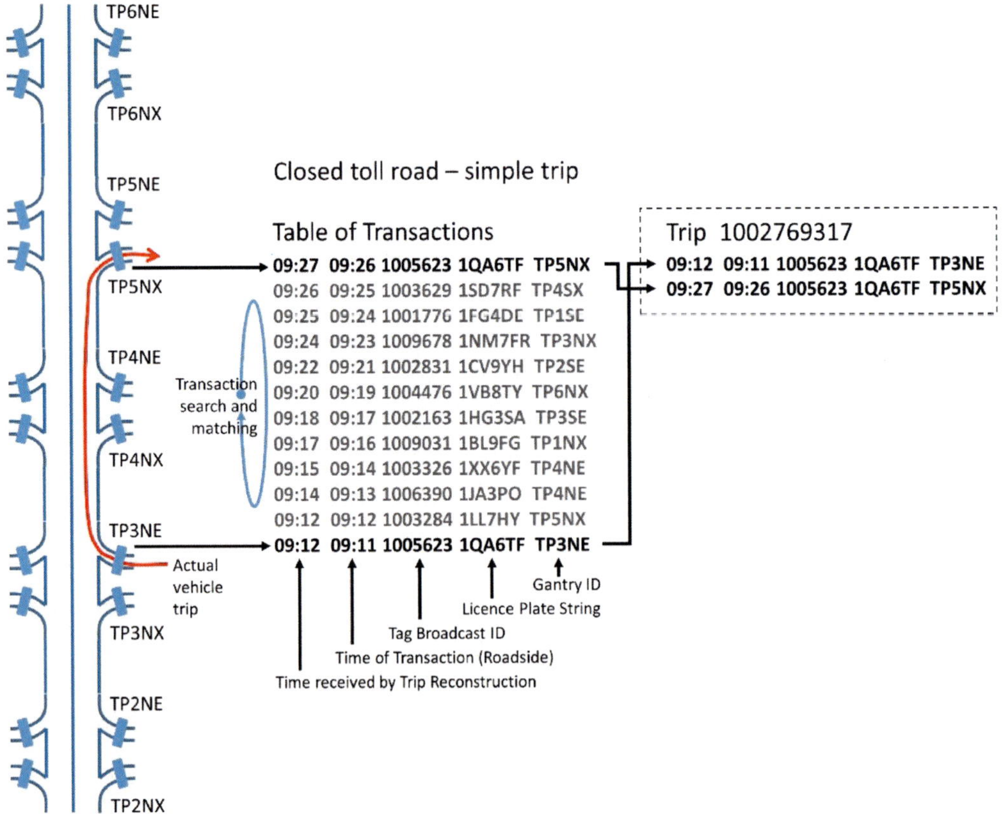

Figure 63 – Closed toll road, simple trip.

With reference to figure 63, a vehicle enters the road at TP3NE and travels north, leaving the road at TP5NX. All the transactions from the road are coming into the transaction table. When trip reconstruction finds that first TP3NE transaction it realises it's an entry transaction and so creates an "in progress" trip. When it gets to the TP5NX transaction it recognises it is an exit transaction and so uses the Tag Broadcast ID and licence plate string to search for a suitable entry transaction which it finds. The trip is formed, and in this case is quite correct.

For each available transaction: For a given [Tag Broadcast ID] OR [if no Tag Broadcast ID then licence plate string and registration]:

Is the transaction from an entry gantry?

Yes: create a new "in progress" trip using the transaction. Pick up the next transaction and start again.

No: {Assume the transaction has to be from an exit gantry} Search all the "in progress" trips for the same [Tag Broadcast ID] OR [if no Tag Broadcast ID then licence plate string and registration]. For each one found check:

The exit gantry is "further down the road" than the entry gantry i.e. works for the road topology,

Check that the time difference between the entry and exit transactions fits within the "time bounding" rules given the length of the trip.

For a [Tag Broadcast ID], if available check that the licence plate string and registration for the entry and exit transaction match,

Was there one good match?

Yes: Assign the transaction to the trip. Mark the trip "closed". Pick up the next transaction and start again.

No: Was there more than one match?

Yes: Look again at the time bounding rules. Find the "best fit" in terms of trip time. Assign the transaction to the trip. Mark the trip "closed". Put the others in the "bucket of bits" for now. Pick up the next transaction.

No: The transaction didn't match any "in progress" trips. Put it in the "bucket of bits" for now. Pick up the next transaction and start again.

The following rules are there to clean up and re-form trips.

Periodically determined by [*Time Parameter 1*]:

For every "in progress" trip with just an entry gantry transaction older than [*Time Parameter 1*] follow the matching rules above but include the "bucket of bits" and "closed" trips:

If a good match is found in the "bucket of bits" create a "closed" trip.

If a better match can be found based on the time bounding rules for an exit transaction in a "closed" trip, create a new "closed" trip by pinching the exit transaction. Mark the other (original) trip as "in progress" and create a negative value "adjustment trip" to effectively cancel it if it has gone to Trip Rating.

Periodically determined by [*Time Parameter 2*]:

For every "in progress" trip with just an entry gantry transaction older than [*Time Parameter 2*] mark the trip as "closed".

{Assume the "bucket of bits" will be exit transactions} For every transaction in the "bucket of bits" older than [*Time Parameter 2*] create a "closed" trip from the transaction.

Periodically determined by [*Time Parameter 3*]:

Move "closed" trips older than [Time Parameter 3] on to Trip Rating.

Table 21 – Basic closed road trip reconstruction rules

Figure 64 represents a slightly more complex scenario.

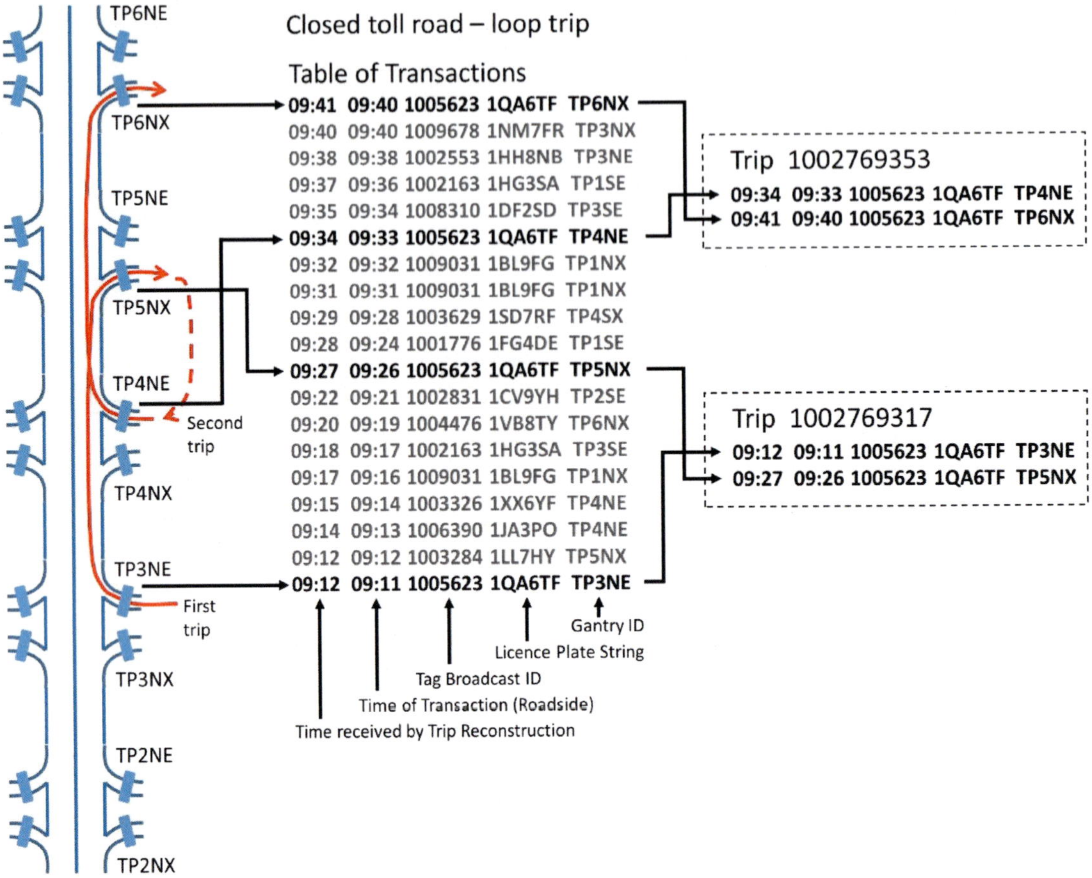

Figure 64 – Closed toll road, looping trips.

In figure 64 a vehicle joins the road at TP3NE travels north and exits at TP5NX. It then loops back, doing its own thing, and re-joins the road at TP4NE. It travels north again and leaves at TP6NX. We can see that everything is coming in to the table of transactions in an orderly fashion so trip reconstruction should not have a problem putting the TP3NE-TP5NX and TP4NE-TP6NX trips together. The outcome which is *not* desired in this case would be one big trip TP3NE-TP6NX and then two “orphan” trips, TP4NE and TP5NX.

In figure 65 the vehicle enters at TP3NE travels north and exits at TP4NX. It does its own thing for a while then re-enters the toll road at TP4NE and travels north again leaving the road at TP6NX. In this case however toll point 4 (TP4) is not having a good day and isn’t talking to anybody, so doesn’t send over the data for several hours. Sitting happily in the transactions table are TP3NE and TP6NX. Given that the vehicle didn’t spend a lot of time off the road, Trip Reconstruction happily puts TP3NE and TP6NX together as a trip.

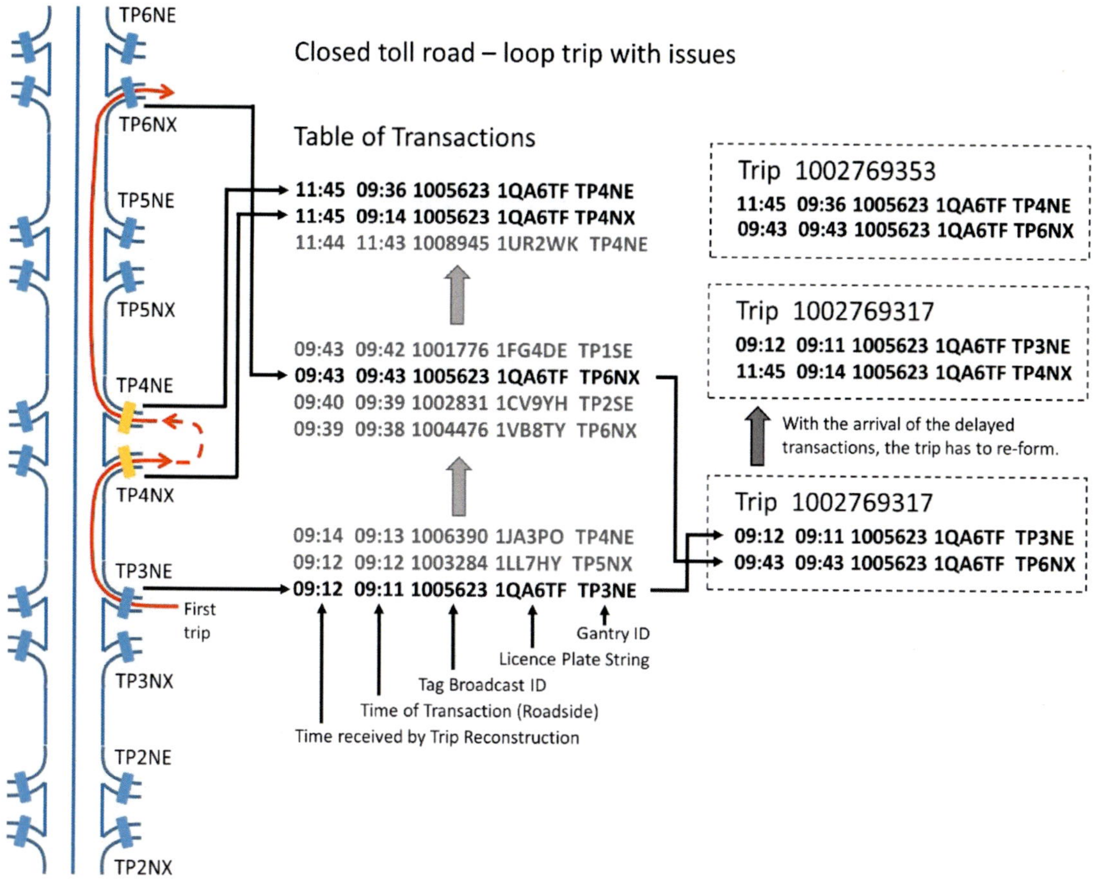

Figure 65 – Closed toll road, looping trips with problems.

TP4 comes good and fires off its data. Suddenly the TP4NX and TP4NE transactions appear. TP4NE gets turned into an "in progress" trip. TP4NX doesn't seem to fit anywhere for the time being and ends up in the "bucket of bits". Then the periodic process kicks in. The TP4NE "in progress" trip has a look at the other trips and decides that the TP6NX transaction is actually a better fit for itself than TP3NE, so it pinches the transaction, leaving TP3NE on its own as an "in progress" trip. Finally that same process allows the TP3NE trip to search the "bucket of bits" where it finds the TP4NX transaction and so can complete its trip.

For the open road the basic algorithm looks something like table 22:

For each available transaction: For a given [Tag Broadcast ID] OR [if no Tag Broadcast ID then licence plate string and registration]:

Search all the "in progress" trips first, for the same [Tag Broadcast ID] OR [if no Tag Broadcast ID then licence plate string and registration]. For each one found check:

The gantry of the transaction is "further down the road" than the last gantry allocated to the trip i.e. works for the road topology,

Check that the time difference between the transactions fits within the "time bounding" rules given the length of the trip.

For a [Tag Broadcast ID], if available check that the licence plate string and registration for the new transaction and the transactions already in the trip match,

Was there one good match?

Yes: Assign the transaction to the trip. Pick up the next transaction and start again.

No: Was there more than one match?

Yes: Look again at the time bounding rules. Find the "best fit" in terms of trip time. Assign the transaction to the trip. Pick up the next transaction.

No: The transaction didn't fit any "in progress" trips as formed. Does the transaction look like it is a "better" fit for a "closed" trip based on the time bounding rules?

Yes: Remove the transactions currently assigned to the trip that come after this transaction (in the time and topology sense) and put them back in the transaction pile for reprocessing. Add this new transaction and if "closed" mark the trip as "in progress". Create a negative value "adjustment trip" to effectively cancel the original trip if it has gone to Trip Rating

No: Use the transaction to form a new "in progress" trip.

The following rules are there to clean up and re-form trips.

Periodically determined by [*Time Parameter 1*]:

For every "in progress" trip older than [*Time Parameter 1*] mark the trip as "closed".

Periodically determined by [*Time Parameter 2*]:

Move "closed" trips older than [Time Parameter 2] on to Trip Rating.

Table 22 – Basic open road trip reconstruction rules

The open toll road algorithm has similar concepts and a few subtle differences. Here are some examples as to how that works, starting with figure 66, a simple trip.

The vehicle enters the road and passes under three gantries, TP3N, TP4N and TP5N. Each gantry passage creates a transaction which ends up in the transactions table. The first transaction, TP3N, can't be matched to any existing trip so is turned into a new "in progress" trip. The TP4N and TP5N transactions are added to this trip being a good match. After a period of time the trip is marked "closed" and moved to Trip Rating.

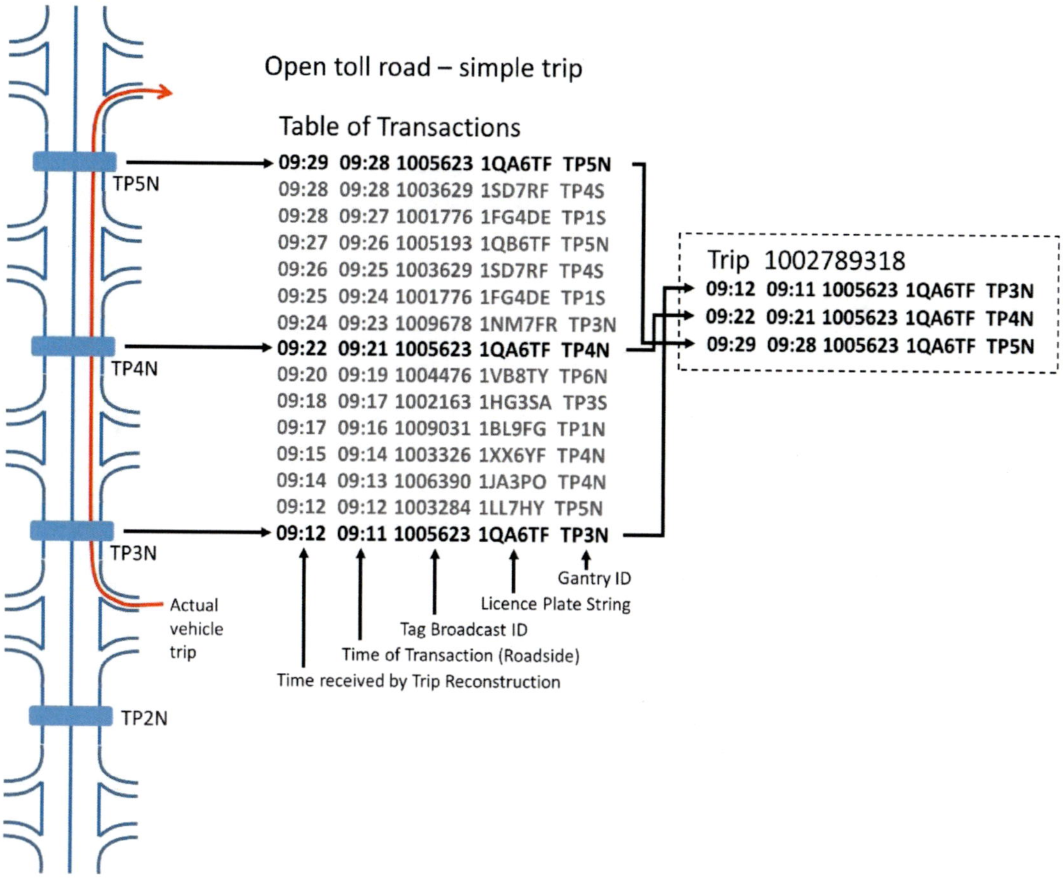

Figure 66 – Open toll road, simple trip.

Figure 67 demonstrates the effect of having to have a time limit on open road trips. A vehicle enters the toll road and passes under TP2N and TP3N. Transactions end up in the transactions table. The vehicle leaves the road, does what it needs to do and about three quarters of an hour later re-joins the road and passes under TP4N and TP5N. Those transactions end up in the transactions table. Trip reconstruction meanwhile is doing its thing. It forms TP2N into an "in progress trip and then adds TP3N. TP4N arrives and that gets added too. TP5N however isn't. Its roadside time is more than one hour later than the roadside time of TP2N, so under the business rules it becomes its own trip.

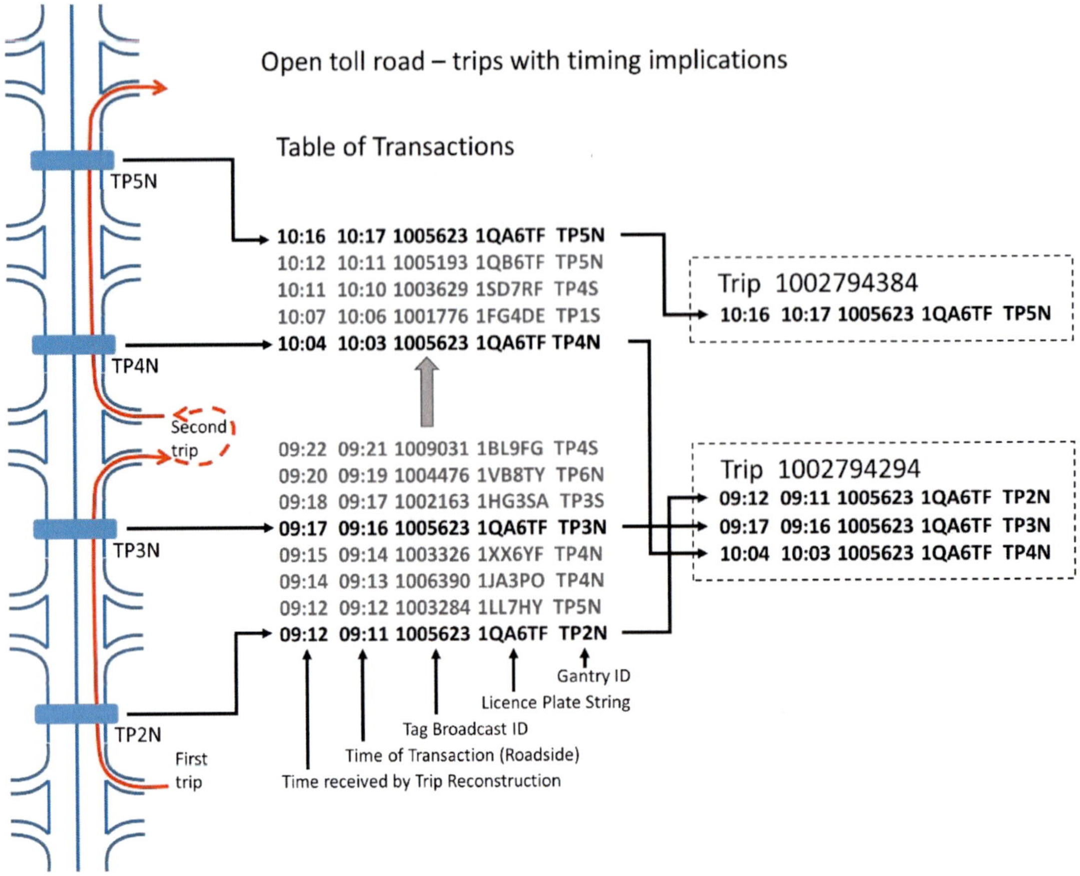

Figure 67 – Open toll road, timing implications on trip.

Figure 68 demonstrates the effect of having timing issues with transactions on open road trips. In this scenario the vehicle joins the toll road and passes under TP3N and TP4N, then leaves the road. The transaction for TP3N is created and is put in the transactions table. The transaction for TP4N is delayed. For some reason the tag didn't register and the vehicle passage ended up with a Human Image Processor. Meanwhile the vehicle re-joins the toll road, passes under TP4N again and TP5N and then leaves the road. Trip Reconstruction has three transactions which it is quite happy to put into a trip – TP3N, the second TP4N and TP5N. Then the first TP4N transaction arrives in the transactions table. With our current logic, trip reconstruction should recognise that the first TP4N transaction is a better fit for the TP3N transaction and consequently add it to the trip and release the second TP4N and TP5N transactions back for processing again – which in turn should form their own correct trip.

If you think through the possible scenarios for transaction and trip combinations, and the things that can happen, you will find there are tens if not hundreds of possible combinations. When building a Trip Reconstruction component all of these have to be tested to ensure it is doing the best it can for you and your customers. If it is any consolation, no matter how much you test, something weird and unforeseen will happen which produces that "impossible" trip.

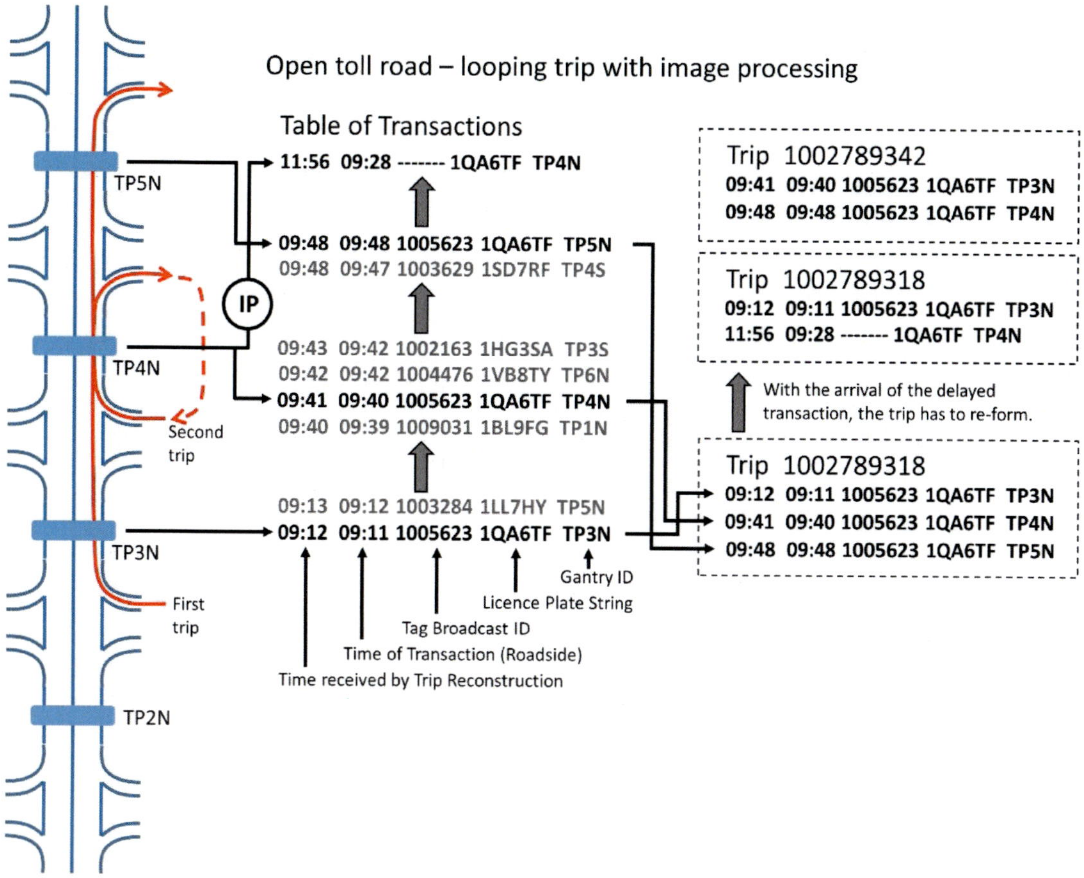

Figure 68 – Open toll road, transaction timing implications on a trip.

I am not claiming for a minute that my trip construction rules in tables 21 and 22 are definitive. Like the Pirate Code, at best they are a set of guidelines. There are Search Algorithm Wizards out there who will be able to do a much better job. I hope what I have been able to demonstrate is that while the basic search algorithm is quite straightforward, the trip re-forming logic requires real intellectual firepower to get right. Anyway, we get finally to the Trip data item.

Data Item 10 – Trip		
ID	**Name**	**Description**
1	Trip ID	The unique identification number of the trip itself assigned by the Trip Reconstruction component.
2	Trip Date-Time Stamp	The date and time (to milliseconds) the Trip was first created.
3	Cancelled Trip ID	If this trip has been created to cancel a previous trip this references the Trip ID of the cancelled trip.
4	Trip Status	"In progress" or "Closed"
5	Closed Date-Time Stamp	The date and time (to milliseconds) the Trip was marked as "Closed".
6	Adjusted Status	"Not adjusted" or "Has been adjusted"
7	Adjusted Date-Time Stamp	The date and time (to milliseconds) the Trip was adjusted.
8	Trip Rating Date-Time Stamp	The date and time (to milliseconds) the Trip was received by Trip Rating.
9	Tag Broadcast ID	The identification number of the tag making the trip. When combined with the tag issuer and country IDs this should be a globally unique number.
10	Tag Issuer ID	A unique number (for a given country) assigned to the organisation that issues (owns) the tag for interoperability purposes (Concession ID).
11	Country ID	A globally unique number assigned to the country in which the tag issuing organisation resides.
12	Tag ID	The unique identification number of the tag assigned by the tolling system.
13	Licence Plate String	The string containing the characters of the licence plate of the vehicle making the trip.
14	State/Country of Registration	The final State or Country of registration.
15	Vehicle Class	The final class assigned to the vehicle.
16	Trailer Detected	The roadside equipment detected that the vehicle was towing a trailer.
17	Vehicle ID	The unique identification number of the vehicle assigned by the tolling system.
18	Trip First Toll Point ID	The identification number of the first Toll Point ID of the trip.

19	Date-Time Stamp	The date and time (to milliseconds) of the first transaction recorded at the roadside.
20	Trip Last Toll Point ID	The identification number of the last Toll Point ID of the trip.
21	Date-Time Stamp	The date and time (to milliseconds) of the last transaction recorded at the roadside.
22	Trip Summary	A summary of the Toll Point IDs that form the trip.
23	Trip Type	"Home Customer", "Interoperable Customer", "Exempt Vehicle", "NATP Customer" (No Arrangement To Pay), "Tolling Loss". Includes Toll Product for "Home Customer".
24	Base Trip Toll	The base toll applied to the trip.
25	Trip Discount	Any discount applied to the Base Trip Toll on account of things such as the Trip Cap and time of day/day of week discounts.
26	Image Processing Fee	Value of the Image Processing Fee applied if applicable.
27	Rating Date-Time Stamp	The date and time (to milliseconds) that the trip was rated.

Data Item 10 – Trip.

The majority of the lines in this data item should be filled with data by this stage of the processing chain. Some however won't be. Lines #24 to #27 have to wait till we get to Trip Rating, and #23 Trip Type can only be determined as part of the Interoperability process. It makes good sense if we adjust a trip, to keep a history record of the original trip for reference purposes.

One implementation issue to consider is how to associate Transactions to Trips. You could have a Trip ID field in the Transaction data item. You could have a separate structure that makes that link, but obviously it has to be made.

A note on vehicle class

The final vehicle class applied to the trip should be a straightforward affair. If you're getting good licence plates reads you simply look up the class via the Vehicle data item and apply it. If it's a vehicle you've never seen before, then hopefully a Human Image Processor has determined the class correctly. If you're stuck with just tag information then the only thing you can do is go with the Tag class. Significant differences between the Tag class and the class inferred from the roadside dimensions should have already been dealt with by the Human Image Processors.

You may have noticed that I did not try and use vehicle class in my trip reconstruction algorithms for the simple reason that I believe it confuses an already complicated situation. Tag and licence plate strings combined with state or country of registration are the correct identifiers to use for trip reconstruction. However, the world is never that simple and there may be situations where vehicle class becomes important. In Victoria, Australia, for example there are a few licence plates that share the same string and state of registration – the only difference being that one is stuck on a motorcycle and the other same plate is stuck on a car. So just be aware, depending on your own circumstances, that it may be necessary to drag vehicle class into the trip reconstruction arena.

A note on tag vehicle associations

My tolling system architecture relies on having the tag and licence plate data where ever possible. If however you are not collecting the licence plate data all the time, you still need a mechanism to try and match Vehicle Passages to Tag Passages in cases where the tag didn't work correctly. In Australia this is where the F32 interoperability file comes in. That file contains all the tags and vehicles associated to accounts. The idea is that you can match a Vehicle Passage to a tag based trip if the vehicle is on the same account as the tag. This does work, but you have to be really careful with those time bounding rules to ensure the Vehicle Passage is a genuine fit. Further, once you have added one Vehicle Passage with a given licence plate, you can't then go off and add a second Vehicle Passage with a different licence plate string just because it also happens to be on the account.

Background processing with trip reconstruction

I'm a great believer in using data to gain insights as to what is going on inside a tolling system, or any system for that matter. This implies running a few extra processes "off to the side" of the main tolling processing stream. These can be part of the tolling system or your external data analysis tool. The extent to which you do this depends entirely on the value you think they bring to your operation. The sorts of things I'm thinking about are:

- Using the timing information associated with transactions to calculate real-time traffic speeds between gantries – to show just how the traffic is flowing on the road,
- Using transaction and trip data to plot the way your road is being used at different times of the day for different days of the week – to spot potential congestion hotspots before they happen and help with the planning of traffic management systems and road upgrades. Also to get a sense of the most popular journey start and end points of your customers.
- Using transactions to estimate toll revenue by gantry in real time – to give the accountants a lovely warm fuzzy feeling inside,
- Keeping track of the association between tags and the vehicles that are carrying them – to get a sense of how many tags get moved between vehicles,
- Identifying your most frequent road users, and those tags and licence plates that you infrequently see – you might find you have tags out there that are just never used.

It's great to use some or all of this data to create a display in the office that shows the road working; that it is a living thing that people rely on every day. I'm sure it helps keep people focussed.

Trip Rating

For trip rating, we need a couple of very significant data items, namely "Arrangement to Pay" (ATP) for Tags and Licence Plates. The Arrangement to Pay data items identify a few important things:

- The tolling account for a particular tag or licence plate,
- Which operator owns the tolling account for a particular tag or licence plate,
- The tolling product which is to be applied for that account,
- The status of the account i.e. whether it is active or suspended, and
- The complete absence of an Arrangement to Pay for a licence plate implies that this is a No Arrangement to Pay (NATP) trip.

The Licence Plate Arrangement to Pay is as follows:

Data Item 11 – Licence Plate Arrangement to Pay		
ID	**Name**	**Description**
1	Arrangement to Pay ID	The unique identification number of the Arrangement to Pay assigned by the tolling system.
2	Tag Issuer ID	The unique identifier assigned to this Interoperability Partner. This issuer owns the account associated with this licence plate.
3	Account ID	The account number to which this licence plate belongs.
4	Tolling Product ID	The tolling product to be used to rate trips made by the vehicle carrying this licence plate.
5	Vehicle ID	The unique identification number of the vehicle assigned by the tolling system.
6	Licence Plate Text	The character and number string that forms the text of the licence plate.
7	Register	The authority that issues and controls this licence plate.
8	ATP Status	Account Arrangement to Pay Status – "Active", "Suspended", "Closed".
9	ATP Status Date-Time Stamp	The date and time (to milliseconds) that the ATP Status was changed to the current value.

Data Item 11 – Licence Plate Arrangement to Pay.

And for the tag:

Data Item 12 – Tag Arrangement to Pay		
ID	**Name**	**Description**
1	Arrangement to Pay ID	The unique identification number of the Arrangement to Pay assigned by the tolling system.
2	Tag Issuer ID	The unique identifier assigned to this Interoperability Partner. This issuer owns the account associated with this tag.
3	Account ID	The account number to which this tag belongs.
4	Tolling Product ID	The tolling product to be used to rate trips made by the vehicle carrying this tag.
5	Tag Broadcast ID	The unique identification number of the tag which it broadcasts to the roadside. It is a combination of the tag's own serial number, the number of the tag issuer and the Country ID.
6	Tag Serial Number	The serial number of the tag.
7	Country ID	A globally unique number assigned to the country in which the tag issuing organisation resides.
8	Tag ID	The unique identification number of the tag assigned by the tolling system.
9	ATP Status	Account Arrangement to Pay Status – "Active", "Suspended", "Closed".
10	ATP Status Date-Time Stamp	The date and time (to milliseconds) that the ATP Status was changed to the current value.

Data Item 12 – Tag Arrangement to Pay.

You will notice that in both these data items I have made reference to a Tolling Product ID. We made reference to this briefly before in the Data Items section. However you structure your tolling product data, an Arrangement to Pay data item has to have some link to that data so that Trip Rating can determine the correct toll.

For your own customers the Account ID comes from your own Account Management component. For customers of an Interoperability Partner, the Account ID comes from the partner e.g. via the F32 file.

The other Arrangement to Pay data comes from several sources:

- The status of your own customers' tags and licence plates will come from your own Account Management component based on account status,
- The status of Interoperable customer tags and licence plates (and thus accounts) will come from your Interoperability Partners through daily batch files (F15, F21) or some on-line web service as described previously,

- Exempt vehicle status will probably be by arrangement between your organisation and the State's Emergency Services organisations and public transport companies,
- Any other special arrangements, by definition, have to be specially arranged.

Arrangement to Pay business rules

You have a trip with a good tag and licence plate string. You check the Arrangement to Pay for both. Both belong to the same active account. Pick up the toll schedule applicable for the tolling product associated with that account, work out the toll price and any discounts, then apply to the Trip data item. Simples!

You have a trip with a good tag and licence plate string. You check the Arrangement to Pay for both. The tag and the licence plate belong to two different accounts and both accounts are active. Hmm, that's interesting. Has somebody lent their tag to a friend? You decide to toll the account associated with the tag. Pick up the toll schedule applicable for the tolling product associated with that account, work out the toll price and any discounts, then apply to the Trip data item.

You have a trip with a good tag and licence plate string. You check the Arrangement to Pay for both. The tag and the licence plate belong to two different accounts and in this case the tag is on a suspended account while the licence plate is on an active account. Experience tells you it is always better to charge an active account, rather than get into the enforcement process. You decide to toll the account associated with the licence plate. Pick up the toll schedule applicable for the tolling product associated with that account, work out the toll price and any discounts, then apply to the Trip data item.

In those cases where you just have a tag or a licence plate you are restricted to checking the one relevant Arrangement to Pay. Hopefully its good and you can rate the trip. If there are no valid Arrangements to Pay then the trip becomes a NATP trip and you have to use your NATP toll schedule to rate the trip. That trip, for the time being at least, is heading off down the enforcement path. The exception to this belong to tag trips where you may not have an existing Tag data item but the tag does come with a valid Tag Issuer ID from one of your Interoperability Partners. You would rate that as a normal interoperable trip and create a new Tag data item on the side.

For those exempt trips, they get rated but the tolling product is an Exempt one. Similarly you may have a special Taxi product.

Interoperability

With reference all the way back to figure 6, one of the most significant functions performed by Interoperability is trip sorting – working out which operators manage the accounts of customers and then on a regular basis bundling those trips up and sending them off. Trip sorting takes all the trips from Trip Rating and those sent to you by Interoperability Partners. Each one gets checked against the relevant Arrangement to Pay and is sorted accordingly into five main categories:

- Trips for our customers to go onto our customer accounts,
- NATP trips which will head off down the enforcement process,
- Exempt vehicle trips,
- Trips for customers belonging to our Interoperable Partners, each trip being assigned to a Partner account,
- Disputed trips. To be dealt with based on your own business rules.

To make this work requires one existing and one new data item – the Interoperability Partner (Data Item 8) and the Interoperability Invoice. Imagine all our trips are sitting in a big database table. The Interoperability Partner data item gives us an account number to assign to all those trips belonging to a particular Interoperability Partner. The Interoperability Invoice then lets us bill that Partner on a daily basis for those trips, less any roaming fees. This is what it looks like:

Data Item 13 – Interoperability Invoice

ID	Name	Description
1	Interoperability Invoice ID	The unique identification number assigned to this Interoperability Invoice by the tolling system.
2	Issuer ID	The unique identification number assigned to this Issuer by the tolling system.
3	Issuer Name	The business name given to the Issuer.
4	Tag Issuer ID	The unique identifier assigned to the issuer of the tag for interoperability purposes (Concession ID).
5	Country ID	A globally unique number assigned to the country in which the tag issuing organisation resides.
6	Account ID	This Partner's account ID within the tolling system.
7	Issuer Contact Details	The contact details including address, telephone numbers and e-mails of the Issuer.
8	Invoice Start Date Time	The start date and time of the invoice. Trips made after this date time will be included in the invoice up to the end date time.

9	Invoice End Date Time	The end date and time of the invoice. Trips made after the start date time will be included in the invoice up to this date time.
10	Value Tag Trips	The financial value of all the tag trips in the invoice.
11	Value Video Trips	The financial value of all the video trips in the invoice.
12	Adjustments	You may make adjustments to the invoice to compensate for trips that are in dispute or changes carried over from the last invoice.
13	Image Processing Fees	The financial value of all the image processing fees applied to trips.
14	Other Fees	The financial value of any other fees applied to trips.
15	Roaming Fees	The amount deducted to cover the cost of Roaming Fees (account keeping fee).
16	Taxes	The value of any taxes applied – things like Goods and Services Tax (GST), Value Added Tax (VAT) or Sales Tax.
17	Total Invoice Value	The final total of the invoice.
18	Status	"Paid" or "Not Paid".

Data Item 13 – Interoperability Invoice.

What you actually need from an Interoperability Invoice will depend on your interoperability agreement and on the financial and tax laws of your country. But the idea is that interoperability trips for a given period of time get allocated to an invoice, and are marked using the Interoperability Invoice ID. The invoice is sent to the Interoperability Partner. Once the money is paid, all those trips can be marked as paid. Remember that on the other side of the fence you will be receiving these invoices on a daily basis too, for trips your customers are making on other roads. So the production and paying of invoices is a constant, and very important stream of activity. If you are the second or third toll road to open in your interoperability group in a given city, chances are most of the tolling accounts of your customers are owned by other operators and therefore most of your revenue is going to come through these invoices.

We can treat our Exempt trips as belonging to a strange Interoperability Partner – one that uses our road but never pays for it. Exempt trips usually represent a loss in financial terms.

Having sorted out our interoperable and exempt trips we are left with the trips belonging to our customers and those annoying NATP trips, and so to our Account Management, Billing and Invoicing component.

A note about finance

As soon as you rate and sort trips the Finance department get very interested. Suddenly they have a financial item to measure, report on and keep track of through their chart of accounts and General

Ledger. So be very mindful of the reports they are running. Basically make sure that what they think they are reporting on is actually correct – essentially make sure they understand the database schema and test the SQL in their report queries. We spend weeks, months, testing the tolling system functionality. Who spends time actually testing a report? Yet so many decisions are taken based on these things.

Also be very mindful about rounding errors which seem to be a constant source of aggravation. If you are creating an invoice and apply tax to every line item and then sum for a total at the end, you will get a different result to summing everything first and then applying tax. These differences are usually very small but very annoying. So develop one rounding algorithm and apply it consistently across the whole system – or forego floating point numbers and stick with integers, but even that doesn't work all the time.

Account Management, Billing and Invoicing

Because account management is a ubiquitous activity I'm not going to spend time explaining the whole process. Rather, in this section, I will focus on those aspects which make tolling a bit different. That said where do we start? With accounts and people of course!

In this tolling system architecture I'm making the statement that the account is the principal way we manage operations to ensure we get paid for the trips on the road. I'm also assuming that the person or entity opening the account is entering into a contract with the toll road operator. In most cases the relationships are quite straightforward – one individual opens the account and takes legal responsibility for any financial liabilities incurred by the account. That one individual is clearly the "Account Owner". They may authorise a partner to access the account and manage it on their behalf. This person is clearly not the "account owner" but is somebody we want to know about and be able to track their actions. Let's call him or her an "Authorised Agent". Finally we might allow a business or organisation to be the "Account Owner" and enter into the contract with us. We can't talk directly to a business, only to the business' Authorised Agents so again they take on a high degree of significance. At this point we need a design decision – do we have three distinct data items: an Account Owner (a person), an Account Owner (a business) and an Authorised Agent (a person), or do we just use one for all three types. In practical terms you can probably get away with one data item but I like to separate people from organisations. The main reason for this is that when people call or interact with us via the web, there has to be an identification and validation process. A business doesn't need that information.

Thus the intent with the Person data item is to ensure we can identify the Person correctly when they contact us and we have the information we need to contact them. I've taken the decision here not to include any credit card or banking information in this data item. With regulations like the Payment Card Industry (PCI) rules you have to be very careful about how you store that information so it is probably best kept secure and quite separate. The link between a Person and a Payment Method is made via the Account data item.

Data Item 14 – Person		
ID	**Name**	**Description**
1	Person ID	The unique identification number assigned to this Person by the tolling system.
2	Preferred Name	The name this Person usually uses to identify themselves.
3	Full Name	The full name of this Person.
4	Language	They prefer to speak in this language.
5	Sex	"Male Mr", "Female Ms", "Fluid Mx".
6	Date of Birth	The date of birth of this Person.
7	Drivers Licence Number	Which should be unique for a State or Country.
8	Home Postal Address	The address at which this Person currently resides.
9	Alternative Address	An alternative address such as a Post Office Box. They may prefer to receive mail at this address.
10	E-Mail Address	This Person's e-mail address.
11	Telephone Number	Preferably the number of their personal mobile phone that is capable of receiving SMS messages, and running your tolling app.
12	Preferred Communication Channels	Describes how the Person prefers to receive communications from you be it by regular mail, e-mail or SMS.
13	Personal Identification Number (PIN)	Used to login in to your website and for telephone services.
14	Security Questions	This Person's preferred security questions and answers to be used in the event they forget their PIN.
15	File URL	A link to the file we keep on this Person. This file is used to store correspondence, notes taken during telephone calls and any other relevant information.
16	First Known Date Time	The date and time that this Person first registered their details with us.
17	Last Known Date Time	The date and time that this Person no longer became an active customer.

Data Item 14 – Person.

The Business data item is very similar:

Data Item 15 – Business		
ID	**Name**	**Description**
1	Business ID	The unique identification number assigned to this Business by the tolling system.
2	Business Name	The name of this business as registered with the Government Regulators and Tax Authorities.
3	Business Number	The number allocated to this business by the Government Regulators and Tax Authorities.
4	Division or Group	Divisions within large companies may operate their own accounts.
5	Trading Name	The name this organisation actually uses to conduct business.
6	Date of Incorporation	The date the business was established.
7	Credit Check and Contract URL	A link to the documentation created if a credit check was performed on the business and the account contract documentation itself.
8	Registered Business Address	The address at which this Business is registered.
9	Alternative Address	An alternative address such as a Post Office Box. The Business may prefer to receive mail at this address.
10	E-Mail Address	The Business e-mail address, preferably of somebody in the Accounts department who can pay invoices.
11	Telephone Number	Again preferably the telephone number of somebody in the Accounts department who can pay invoices.
12	Preferred Communication Channels	Describes how the Business prefers to receive communications from you be it by regular mail, e-mail or SMS.
13	File URL	A link to the file we keep on this Business. This file is used to store correspondence, notes taken during telephone calls and any other relevant information.
14	First Known Date Time	The date and time that this Business first registered their details with us.
15	Last Known Date Time	The date and time that this Business no longer became an active customer.

Data Item 15 – Business.

I'm making another subtle but important design decision here. People can be both an Account Owner of their personal account and an Authorised Agent for their employer. But I want to keep track of the actual person who is doing things in the tolling system. Therefore I'm taking the decision that when a Person logs in to our website to complete a transaction for a Business they have to identify the Business and themselves, and use their own PIN.

You also have to be careful and identify the actual business. MegaCorp may have three quite distinct divisions operating in your city, each of which has a sales team that are regular customers. However, hell will freeze over before MegaCorp Professional Services pays the tolls for MegaCorp Corporate Solutions so always be quite pedantic in finding out who you are actually dealing with.

It's very important for every business that we keep data on our customers up to date. The tolling system should make it as easy as possible for people to update an address or a telephone number. It follows that we keep a history record of all of these changes.

Next, the Tolling Account. I'm intending my Tolling Account to be a multi-purpose data item, one that can support a number of arrangements:

- A standard pre and post paid account,
- A time based pass product,
- Trip passes,
- The NATP customer – someone who is unknown to us at the moment.

The Tolling Account pulls together many things – People, Tags and Vehicles. It provides us with the crucial Account ID number that we use to mark trips as belonging to the account identified through the Tag and Vehicle IDs associated with the account. In doing so it lets us create an on-going account balance and based on that fire off automatic account top-ups, using a Payment Method, or notifications relating to account activities. It drives the status of our Arrangement to Pay data items. It provides us with the structure to create statements and invoices. The Tolling Account and Statement data items follow.

Data Item 16 – Tolling Account		
ID	**Name**	**Description**
1	Account ID	The unique identification number assigned to this Account by the tolling system.
2	Account Owner ID	The ID of the Person or Business that owns the account.
3	Authorised Agent IDs	The IDs of all the Authorised Agents who are allowed to access the account. Could be none, could be many depending on your business rules.
4	Payment Method ID	A link to the payment method for the account. This could be a credit card or a direct debit instruction.
5	Vehicle IDs	The IDs of all the Vehicles registered on the account.
6	Tag IDs	The IDs of all the Tags registered on the account.
7	Toll Product	The Toll Product applicable for this account.
8	Toll Product Personalisations	You may allow customers to vary some of the parameters within a standard toll product. For example they may set up their own minimum top-up amount, statement frequency etc..
9	Account Current Balance	The financial value of the account's current balance.
10	Account Status	For pre-paid accounts this includes "Active", "Low Balance", "Suspended". For post-paid accounts this includes "Active", "Invoice Overdue".
11	Pass Start Date Time	For temporary pass products, the start date time of the pass.
12	Pass End Date Time	For temporary pass products, the end date time of the pass.
13	Number trip passes Remaining	For trip passes, the number of passes remaining.
14	Voucher Expiry Date	The pass expiry date.
15	First Known Date Time	The date and time that this account was first opened.
16	Last Known Date Time	The date and time that this account was closed.

Data Item 16 – Tolling Account.

Data Item 17 – Statement		
ID	**Name**	**Description**
1	Statement ID	The unique identification number assigned to this Statement by the tolling system.
2	Tolling Account ID	The Tolling Account ID to which this statement belongs.
3	Statement Start Date Time	The start date and time of the Statement. Trips made after this date time will be included in the Statement up to the end date time.
4	Statement End Date Time	The end date and time of the Statement. Trips made after the start date time will be included in the Statement up to this date time.
	For your road and each relevant Interoperable Partner:	
5A	Value Tag Trips	The financial value of all the tag trips.
5B	Value Video Trips	The financial value of all the video trips.
5C	Adjustments	You may make adjustments to the statements to compensate for adjusted trips or trips that are in dispute.
5D	Image Processing Fees	The financial value of all the image processing fees applied to trips.
5E	Other Fees	The financial value of any other fees applied to the account.
5F	Total	Total trips for a road.
6	Taxes	The value of any taxes applied – things like Goods and Services Tax (GST), Value Added Tax (VAT) or Sales Tax.
7	Payments	The financial value of all the payments made to the Tolling Account.
8	Statement Balance	The current balance of the account [opening balance + payments – (trips, fees, taxes)]

Data Item 17 – Statement.

As with the Interoperability Invoice, the bulk of the data associated with a Statement are the Trips allocated to this account and marked with a unique Statement ID based on the time period covered by the Statement. How you actually lay out your statement is up to you and the requirements of your concession deed. In the data item above I'm assuming that we want to break down travel for our customers by Tag and Vehicle, and the roads travelled. I think of a statement as belonging to a pre-paid account. Its purpose is to give our customers details of their account movements for a period of time, but we don't expect them to do anything when they receive a statement – except if they think we've made a mistake. With the Invoice, for post-paid accounts, we do expect them to make a payment based on the Invoice amount. The Invoice will be very similar to the Statement with the big difference being that the Invoice has to clearly show the amount to be paid and the payment due date.

A note on payments

One of the most important things your tolling system has to do is maintain Payment Methods and manage payments, and it sounds obvious but you have to know:

- Who a payment comes from, and
- What it is actually supposed to be paying for.

With regards to the first, it is important not to allow people to make anonymous payments by electronic funds transfer into one of your bank accounts. The customer will think everything is fine because they just paid you money. You'll be scratching your head wondering where the money came from, meanwhile the customer account slips into a suspended state because the money didn't make it onto the account. The rule here is make as easy as possible for people to make payments, but restrict it to channels that always inform you as to who is paying.

The second bullet point becomes an issue when customers want to part pay for things, or have paid for something and then want some of the money back as a refund. Or you've given them a NATP Invoice and they agree to pay for one trip out of three because the other trips belong to Uncle Samba. Again it comes down to your own business rules which have to determine to what extent the tolling system needs to track payments against trips, fees and charges. To what level of granularity do you go? The short answer is the more information, and the more accurate that information the better it is for you. The downside is that building that kind of system is complex, expensive and time consuming to test.

Ultimately whatever you decide to do the tolling system will have to have the capability to:

- Cancel or write-off trips, fees and charges,
- Apply credits or refunds to accounts,
- Keep audit logs as to who is making these changes, and why, and
- Ensure all these movements are reflected back into the financial system – that chart of accounts and the credit and debit process.

One possible way of dealing with these situations is to have a Financial Event data item. You can use a Financial Event to mirror all the usual data items that affect the financial system such as trips, fees, payments, write-offs and refunds. The Financial Event can also be the mechanism used to manage those credit and debit movements.

NATP Invoice

The NATP Invoice data item takes us into the murky world of enforcement and debt collection and, as I mentioned before, this process really does differ between jurisdictions, states and countries.

Data Item 18 – NATP Invoice		
ID	**Name**	**Description**
1	NATP Invoice ID	The unique identification number assigned to this Invoice by the tolling system.
2	Tolling Account ID	The Tolling Account ID to which this invoice belongs.
3	Invoice Start Date Time	The start date and time of the invoice. Trips made after this date time will be included in the invoice up to the end date time.
4	Invoice End Date Time	The end date and time of the invoice. Trips made after the start date time will be included in the invoice up to this date time.
5	Value Tag Trips	The financial value of all the tag trips.
6	Value Video Trips	The financial value of all the video trips.
7	Image Processing Fees	The financial value of all the image processing fees applied to trips.
8	Local Vehicle Registration Authority Look-up Fee	We pass on the cost of the licence plate look-up fee to the customer.
9	First Administration Fee	The first administration fee we charge the customer for producing the invoice.
10	Second Administration Fee	The second administration fee we charge the customer for producing the invoice.
11	Taxes	The value of any taxes applied – things like Goods and Services Tax (GST), Value Added Tax (VAT) or Sales Tax.
12	Invoice Total	The total financial amount owing.
13	First Due Date	The date by which the invoice should be paid to avoid incurring the second administration fee.
14	Second Due Date	The date by which the invoice should be paid to avoid the matter becoming a civil offence to be handled by the State Authorities.

Data Item 18 – NATP Invoice.

Following the Victorian model, you can end up with a NATP Invoice for two reasons:

- You have an account but you haven't kept the balance up and so the account is suspended,
- You have made no effort at all to get any kind of Arrangement to Pay.

In the first instance the tolling company knows who you are – because you have an account. They send you the NATP Invoice. They can do this based on the contact information from the account, although strictly speaking they should go through their local vehicle registration authority. The value of the invoice is added to the outstanding balance of the suspended account, increasing the account debt.

In the second case the tolling company probably doesn't know who you are. All being well they have a licence plate read and use that to request contact details from their local vehicle registration authority. If that authority is able to return good name and address details, then the tolling system can create a Tolling Account based on that data, an NATP Invoice and link the two together.

The design of this data item allows for a two strike process. When it is first issued it includes the First Administration Fee #9 and a First Due Date #13. If the invoice isn't paid by the First Due Date it is re-issued with the Second Administration Fee #10 added. If that isn't paid by the Second Due Date #14 then the matter becomes an offence which is handled by the State. The NATP Invoice has to identify the specific trips which form the subject of the invoice. This enables the customer to identify and then dispute some or all of those trips via a Nomination, which is the final data item we'll consider.

The Nomination allows a customer to nominate another person as being responsible for a trip. You can think of it as part of your customer service offering which is great, but it is the source of many of those adjustments which can end up being quite tricky to manage.

This relatively simple data item actually leads us into a number of quite complex scenarios which will require that you think through your business rules carefully. To start with do we need the Nominee Drivers Licence Number #5 and Nominee Telephone Number #6 to accept the Nomination? We need to get clear the level of supporting information we require. To what level do we allow people to nominate? The obvious one is down to the trip level. In some cases the Nominator won't have a known Account ID #2 with us. They may simply be responding to an NATP Invoice in which case all they will have is that invoice reference number. Internally we may have created an NATP Tolling Account for them, so we have to marry those pieces of information together. If we accept that a Nomination is valid, then the system has to reallocate trips and potentially issue a new NATP Invoice. And then what happens if the Nominee decides to argue about the nomination? To what extent are you willing to pursue the matter?

The frustrating part about this process is that more often than not you're dealing with Nominations whose value is a few dollars but people can get upset, belligerent and dig in. You can end up burning many tens of dollars of internal cost trying to bring the matter to a resolution. Ultimately you have to weigh up:

- The value of the trips versus,
- The amount you are spending on the process, and,
- Really irritating customers to the extent that they get the Ombudsman involved versus,
- Ensuring that your enforcement processes are effective i.e. not getting a reputation that says "if you nominate they always let you off".

Another reason to employ really good customer service people.

Data Item 19 – Nomination		
ID	**Name**	**Description**
1	Nomination ID	The unique identification number assigned to this Nomination by the tolling system.
2	Tolling Account ID	The Tolling Account ID of the Nominator i.e. the person doing the nominating.
3	Nominee Name	The name of the person being nominated.
4	Nominee Address	The address of the person being nominated.
5	Nominee Drivers Licence Number	The drivers licence number of the person being nominated.
6	Nominee Telephone Number	Preferably the personal mobile telephone number of the person being nominated.
7	Trip IDs	The trips that are the subject of this nomination – taken from the NATP Invoice.
8	Nomination Created Date Time	The date and time the Nomination was created.
9	Nomination Reason	Useful to try and capture a reason for the Nomination, especially if the Nominator sold a vehicle and didn't tell us about it.
10	Nomination Status	"In progress", "Accepted", "Rejected". Basically the status of our internal processing.
11	Nomination Status Date Time	The date time recorded when the Nomination Status changes to help us track workflow.
12	Nomination File URL	A link to further details about the Nomination. There may be additional correspondence or evidence submitted by both parties.

Data Item 19 – Nomination.

Finally

In these 19 data items I hope I've been able to explain the fundamentals as to how a tolling system works. Obviously in these systems there is a lot more complexity. I haven't really touched on the logistics of moving tags around, nor the whole business of customer service and case management. But if you understood what is there you are well on your way to mastering the art and science of tolling.

I'm glad that's over.

Are you Darling? Go and lie down for a bit.

Tolling System Metrics – Benchmarking

I think it would be very beneficial to the whole of the tolling industry across the world if we could gather and share metrics on our roads and our tolling systems' performance. Operating more or less in isolation as many of us probably do, limits us in our ability to know how to improve – and improve we must. We want the best distributions for our financial partners, we want the best service for our customers, we want to constantly reduce our environmental impact on the planet and we must harness the best and latest technologies to help us achieve these things.

I know that much of what I am going to propose is Commercial-in-Confidence for many toll roads but at least if we start collecting the data we may find a way to share it later which doesn't compromise anybody's tenure of employment.

Physical Sizing

P1. Length of the toll road in kilometres. A simple measurement – if the toll road starts at point A and finishes at point B 23 kms away, the length is 23 kms.

P2. Kilometres of tolled lanes. This is bit more involved, but look at this example. Your road has a section that is three traffic lanes wide and runs for 15 kms, and then another section which is two traffic lanes and runs for 10 kms. The total kilometres of tolled lanes becomes [3 X 15] + [2 X 10] = 65 kms for each direction making 130 kms.

P3. The ratio of tolled lanes and length of toll road – gives an indication as to how "chunky" your road is. [65kms / 23 kms = 2.8]

P4. Open or closed – simple declaration of the tolling system type.

P5. Number of toll points. Not perhaps what you are thinking. By this I mean the number places, based on lanes, that you can toll a vehicle. So if you have a gantry that spans four traffic lanes, that counts as four toll points.

P6. Number of gantry installations. A front and rear gantry count as one installation. A gantry that spans two carriageways (two directions of travel) counts as two installations.

P7. Number of interchanges – the number of points at which you can enter or exit the road. An interchange with two on ramps and two off ramps counts as one interchange.

Traffic Sizing

All of the following metrics are to be calculated for a day, but separately for working days and weekend and holidays, based on an average taken over the previous twelve months.

T1. Tag Passages – the number of tag passages recorded by your tolling system.

T2. Vehicle Passages – the number of vehicle passages recorded by your tolling system.

T3. Transactions – the number of transactions produced by the tolling system.

T4. Trips – the number of trips produced by the tolling system.

T5. The ratio of Transactions to Trips – gives an indication of average journey length.

T6. Peak transactions – the number of transactions created by the tolling system between the hours of 7am and 9am.

T7. Average speed – the average speed at which vehicles travel along the road based on distance covered divided by time spent as measured by Transactions.

Financial Sizing

All of the following metrics are to be exclusive of any taxes, based on an average taken over the previous twelve months.

F1. Total toll revenue for the previous 12 month period.

F2. Total fee and charge revenue for the previous 12 month period.

F3. Average value of a trip – derived simply by the summed value of the all tolled trips (excluding any other fees and charges) divided by the number of trips.

F4. Average cost to create and bill a trip – derived from the cost of everything involved in operating the tolling system and serving customers, excluding depreciation on hardware and software applications. If you're tolling system serves more than one road, apportion it based on the number of transactions for each road. BUT THIS NUMBER IS ONLY TO BE QUOTED WITH THE NEXT ONE:

F5. Number of complaints per trip – the number of complaints received where a complaint results in some action that needs to be taken by the organisation be that a refund, trip cancellation, withdrawal of an NATP Invoice or a referral to the Ombudsman, divided by the number of trips, over a 12 month period. Obviously if you just don't allow people to complain you can't claim a really low number – you have to say that you don't tolerate complaints.

F6. Earnings generated per kilometre of toll road – tricky but looks like this, all based on a 12 month period: [Total toll revenue + Total fee and charge revenue - the cost of everything involved in operating the tolling system and serving customers, excluding depreciation on hardware and software applications] / the total number of kilometres driven by customers.

Service and Technical Sizing

S1. Percentage camera downtime – the total number of hours in a year that any roadside camera was not working due to fault (not scheduled maintenance) divided by [the number of cameras out on the road X the number of hours in a year].

S2. Percentage tag transponder downtime - the total number of hours in a year that any roadside tag transponder was not working due to fault (not scheduled maintenance) divided by [the number of tag transponders out on the road X the number of hours in a year].

S3. Percentage roadside read failures – the number of roadside passage messages that are never sent to trip reconstruction for whatever reason divided by the total number that are sent over a twelve month period.

S4. Human Image Processor Average Handling Time – the average time it takes a Human Image Processor to read an image and record the licence plate string, state or country of registration and vehicle class over a twelve month period. BUT THIS NUMBER IS ONLY TO BE QUOTED WITH THE NEXT ONE:

S5. Percentage Human Image Processor error rate – the number of images that are manually read incorrectly divided by the total number of images read over a twelve month period. Very tricky to work out accurately.

S6. Percentage Machine Image Processor error rate - the number of images that are automatically read incorrectly divided by the total number of images read over a twelve month period. Again, very tricky to work out accurately.

S7. Percentage of customer contacts by channel – of all your customer contacts, what percentage come through on the telephone, via the IVR system, through the website or your tolling app? BUT THIS NUMBER IS ONLY TO BE QUOTED WITH THE NEXT ONE:

S8. Customer Service Operator customer call Average Handling Time – the average time it takes a CSO to complete a customer query or interaction on the telephone.

S9. Percentage of tolling loss transactions – the total number of transactions that have to be discarded for whatever reason divided by the total number of transaction for a twelve month period.

S10. Percentage tolling system downtime – the total number of hours in a year that the tolling system is unavailable due to fault (not scheduled maintenance) divided by the number of hours in a year.

The Future

The future is always bright for those that want to make it so. But to paraphrase Andy Weir's brilliant line from his book The Martian, given all the damage we've already done, and given the strangleholds that vested interests have in the status quo, to make real progress we're going to have to science the shit out this.

I really hope we make that comprehensive move to renewable energy sources. I really hope we start buying electric cars in large numbers and charge them using that renewable energy. And I hope I still have roads that let me get somewhere in a reasonable amount of time. There's the rub – if I'm not paying for roads out of my petrol taxes, where is the money going to come from? Road tolling, or road user charging I think will be an inevitable part of our future.

My biggest concern with this future lies in the social justice of the frameworks we establish. I can see the need to involve private money in the construction of infrastructure and in a western style market based economy that money has to produce a return, or it goes elsewhere. But at the same time freedom of movement is a human right in such an economy. So whatever structures we create to pay for roads have to take into account a person's ability to pay and their desire to travel.

In Australia we seem to be able to turn a paddock into a 500 house estate in six months, but it takes twenty years if you're lucky to connect it to a bus route, let alone the rail network. Why is that? In the meantime the crappy old road that serviced the farmer and his tractor is now groaning under the weight of hundreds of new car trips every day. And then you want to start charging people to use that road? The only reason they bought the dog box houses on that estate in the first place is because they couldn't afford to live anywhere else! So we do have to be very mindful of our future actions.

But we can build an equitable free-flowing future: private money, a decent long term return on investment, the user pays principle but with people paying proportionately what they can afford. It's going to be the Mother of all tolling systems but given where we are now we can build it. I'll leave you with an adapted quote from the great Douglas Adams via the majestic Deep Thought:

> *"I speak of none but the Tolling System that is to come after me. A computer whose merest operational parameters I am not worthy to calculate – and yet I will design it for you."*

Appendix A – Directed Graphs and Road Topology

In this section I'm borrowing the ideas of vertices and edges from Graph Theory[29] to define the tolling topology of the road. Why would you want to do this? Well, if you make tolling systems the chances are you want to sell more than one and thus don't want to hard code the topology of a road into your system. Ideally you make the road topology configurable so that you can change it easily for different customers. It's in this situation that using something like Graph Theory and applying mathematical definitions to software based rule engines can give you flexibility.

In this case:

- The vertices are our toll points,
- The edges are the toll zones between toll points.

With reference back to figure 10, the "Peninsula freeway" the directed graph for the open road version ends up looking like figure A1.

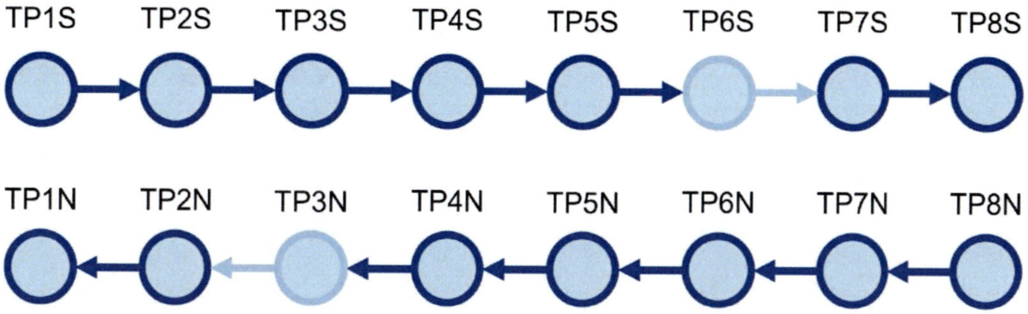

Figure A1 – The directed graph for the "open" Peninsula Freeway

This directed graph can then be translated into a table of vertices and edges:

Vertex set southbound =>	V(S) = {TP1S, TP2S, TP3S, TP4S, TP5S, TP6S, TP7S, TP8S}
Edge set southbound =>	E(S) = {(TP1S, TP2S), (TP2S, TP3S), (TP3S, TP4S), (TP4S, TP5S), (TP5S, TP6S, TP7S), (TP7S, TP8S)}
Vertex set northbound =>	V(N) = {TP8N, TP7N, TP6N, TP5N, TP4N, TP3N, TP2N, TP1N}
Edge set northbound =>	E(N) = {(TP8N, TP7N), (TP7N, TP6N), (TP6N, TP5N), (TP5N, TP4N), (TP4N, TP3N, TP2N), (TP2N, TP1N)}

Table A1 – Vertices and Edges for the "open" Peninsula Freeway

In figure A1 notice that two of the toll points (vertices) are greyed out. They are genuine toll points, but we know that, for those directions, a trip cannot end after those toll points. This is reflected in the edge definitions where two of the edges are actually defined by three vertices.

This notation reveals a big difference between open and closed configurations. The equivalent set of directed graphs for the closed Peninsula Freeway, for the southbound direction only, is given in figure A2.

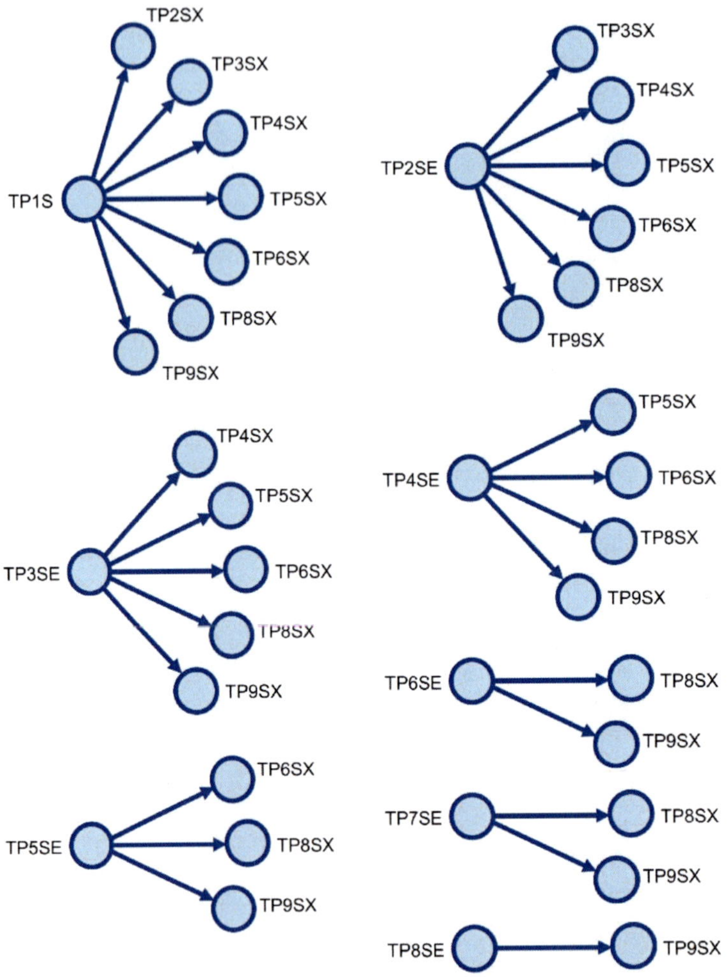

Figure A2 – The directed graphs for the "closed" Peninsula Freeway

Then each one of the graphs in figure A2 can be described in terms of its vertices and edges. Table A2 below shows this just for the graph starting at TP1S.

Vertex set TP1S =>	V(S) = {TP1S, TP2SX, TP3SX, TP4SX, TP5SX, TP6SX, TP8SX, TP9S}
Edge set TP1S =>	E(S) = {(TP1S, TP2SX), (TP1S, TP3SX), (TP1S, TP4SX), (TP1S, TP5SX), (TP1S, TP6SX), (TP1S, TP8SX), (TP1S, TP9S)}

Table A2 – Vertices and Edges for the "closed" Peninsula Freeway

Once you define your road topology in terms of a mathematical model, you can put it into a format that a computer can interpret, and suddenly it becomes useful as a way of specifying topology for your tolling system. You can convert table A2 into XML along the lines of the following:

```
<?xml version="1.0" encoding="ISO-8859-1"?>
<infrastructure_topology>
   <infrastructure_identification>
      <name>Peninsula Freeway</name>
      <code>M42</code>
      <type>Closed toll road</type>
      <location>Mornington Peninsula</location>
   </infrastructure_identification>
   <common_vertices>
   </common_vertices>
   <graph>
      <vertices>
         <vertex>
            <identifier>TP1S</identifier>
            <name>Frankston Mainline South</name>
            <location>
               <coordinates>-38.161311, 145.136338</coordinates>
               <distance_from_start>0.232</distance_from_start>
            </location>
         </vertex>
....
....
      <edges>
         <edge>
            <start_vertex>TP1S</start_vertex>
            <end_vertex>TP2SX</end_vertex>
            <zone name>Frankston Baxter</zone name>
            <zone>1S</zone>
            <length_km>5.1</length_km>
         </edge>
....
....
      </edges>
   </graph>
</infrastructure_topology>
```

Figure A3 – Vertices and edges for the "closed" Peninsula Freeway in XML

So an idea for you to consider. My guess is that if you're building tolling systems, you're already doing something very similar.

Appendix B – State transition diagrams

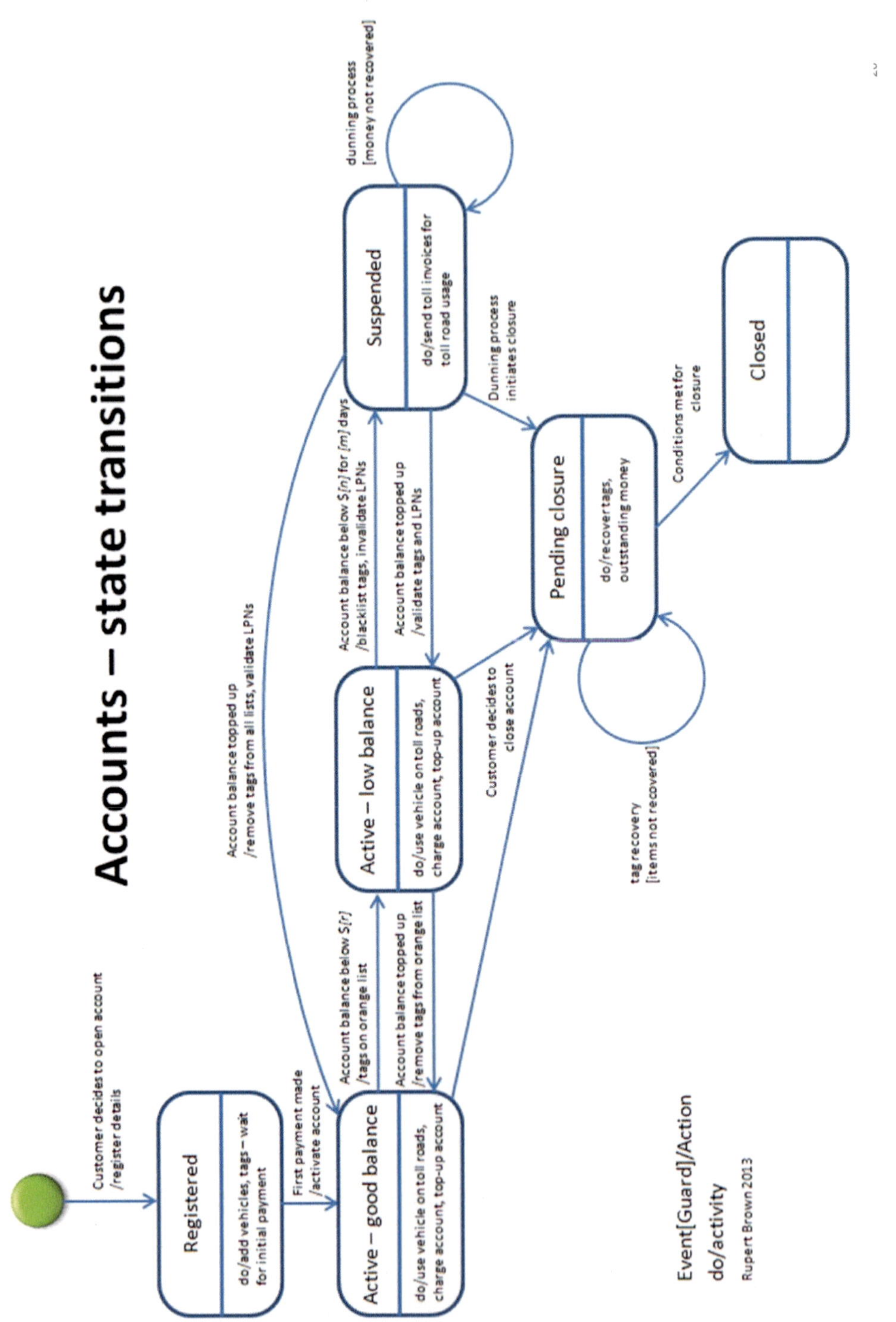

Figure B1 – State transition diagram for tolling accounts

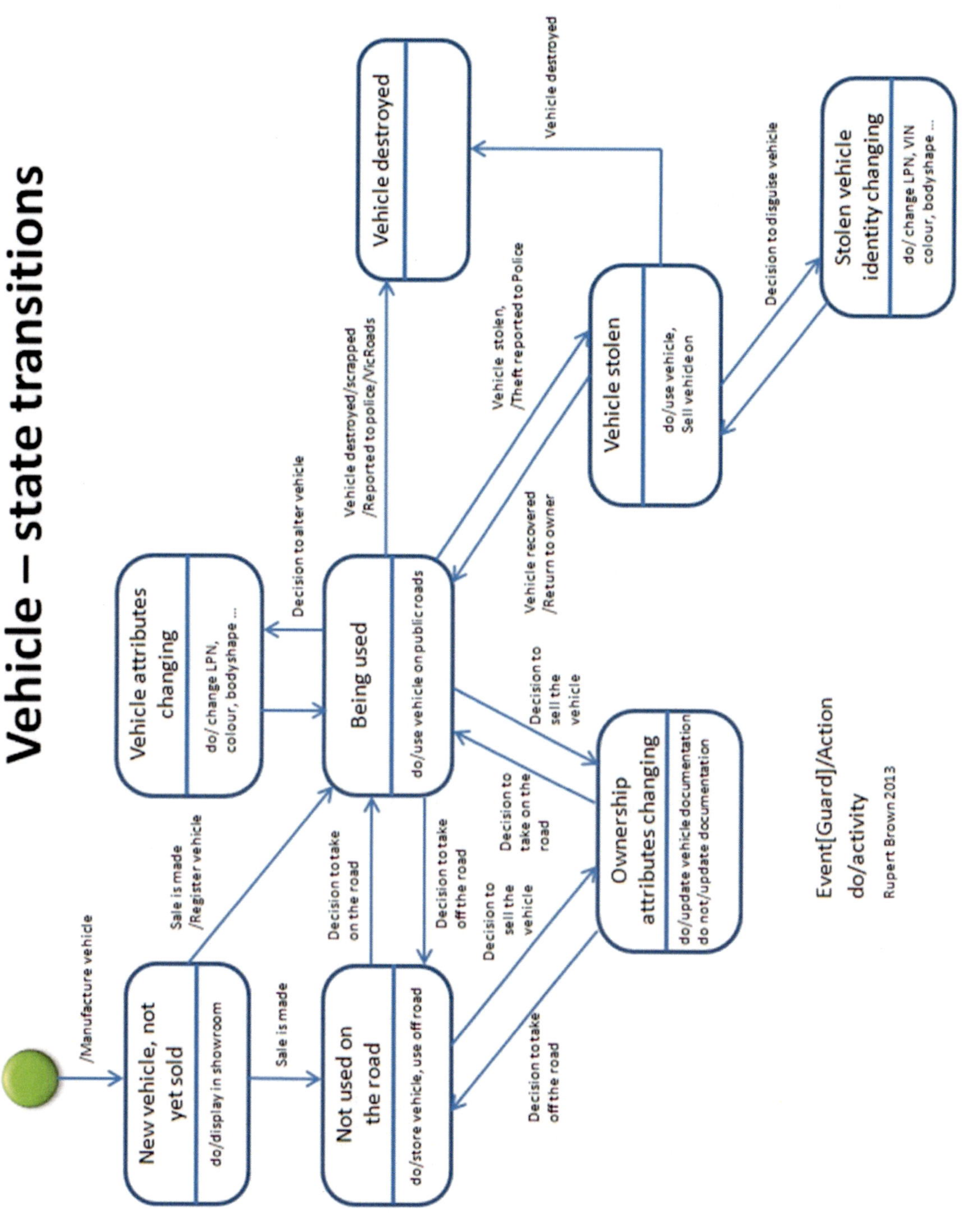

Figure B2 – State transition diagram for vehicles

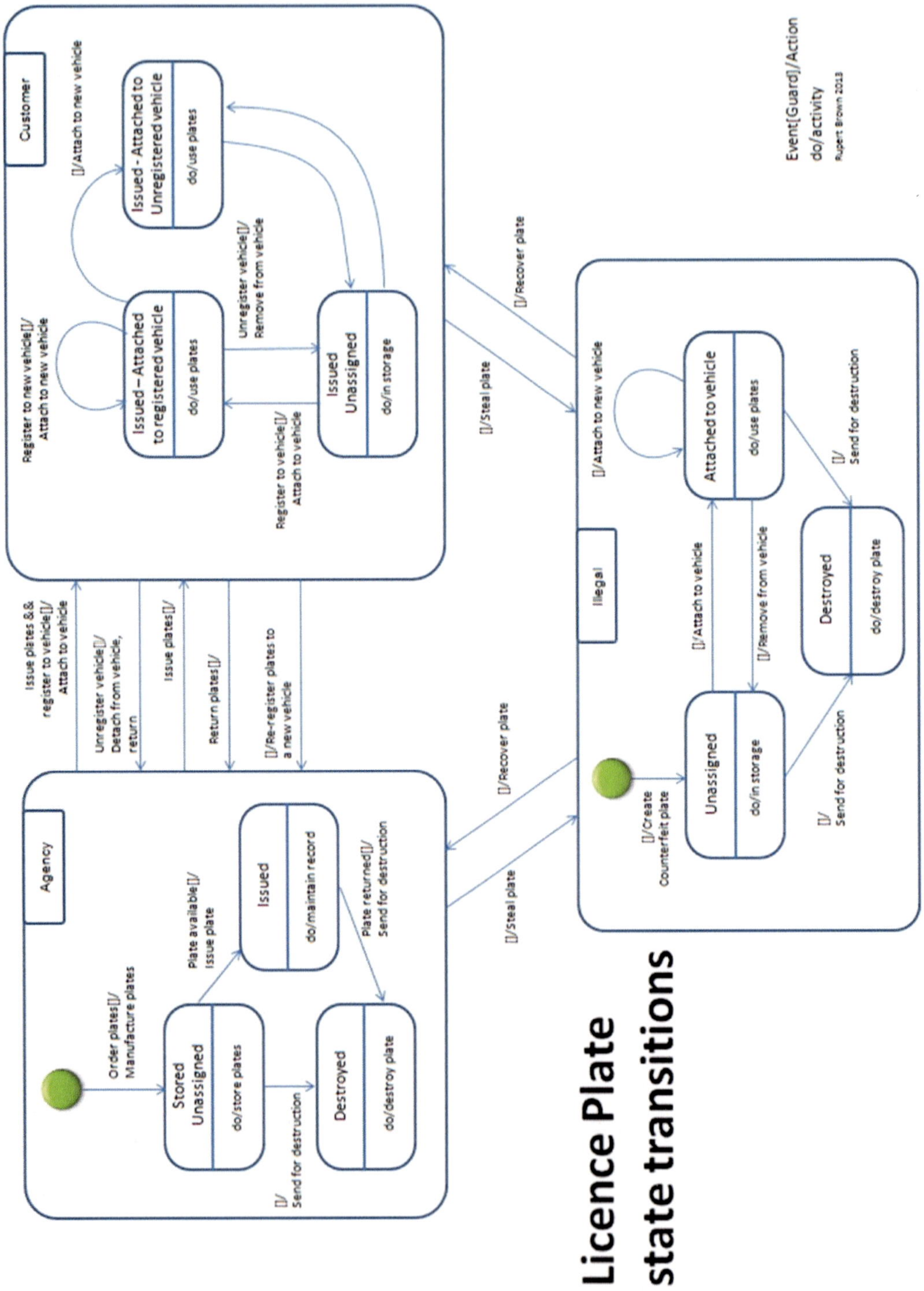

Figure B3 – State transition diagram for licence plates

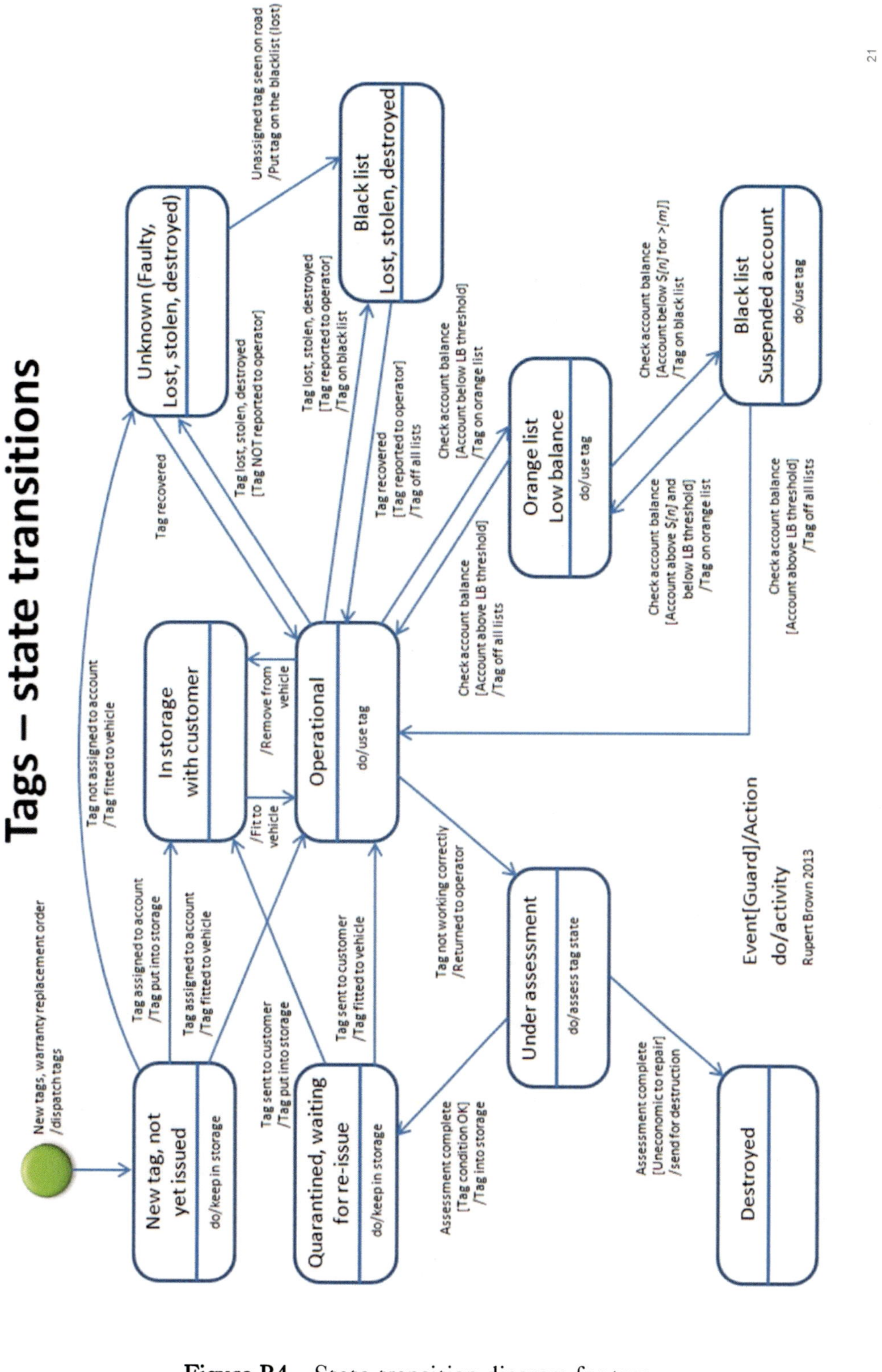

Figure B4 – State transition diagram for tags

References

1 - For a map of Sydney toll roads have a look at:

http://www.rms.nsw.gov.au/sydney-motorways/toll-calculator/index.html

There are more new toll roads on the way.

2 – UN Report on Road Deaths

http://www.un.org/en/roadsafety/report.shtml

3 – "M4 opening eases road congestion in Sydney" from SBS News.

https://www.sbs.com.au/news/m4-opening-eases-road-congestion-in-sydney

4 – "Burning Investor Billions" by Tom Stone in the 2016 edition of Transtoll.

http://www.TrafficTechnologyToday.com

5 – Stephen Mayne's Crikey article on how Transurban uses its concession deed.

http://www.crikey.com.au/2014/10/10/mayne-transurban-out-plays-victorian-governments-of-all-stripes/

6 – ABC News website: "Melbourne's West Gate Tunnel, cooked up by Labor with Transurban, deserves scrutiny" by state political reporter Richard Willingham. Updated Wed 13 Dec 2017, 10:07am.

http://www.abc.net.au/news/2017-12-13/melbournes-west-gate-tunnel-cooked-up-with-transurban/9251712

7 – Sydney toll roads vehicle classification scheme.

http://www.rms.nsw.gov.au/sydney-motorways/toll-charges/index.html

8 – Queensland toll roads vehicle classification scheme.

https://www.govia.com.au/web/ssp/toll-costs-by-tolling-point

9 – Australian Government history of rail infrastructure in Australia.

https://infrastructure.gov.au/rail/trains/history.aspx

10 – "One size fits all" by Jan Stojaspal in the 2016 edition of Transtoll.

http://www.TrafficTechnologyToday.com

11 – French motorway companies.

http://www.autoroutes.fr/en/french-motorway-companies.htm

12 – Sanef European toll offerings to the UK.

https://www.saneftolling.co.uk

13 – Santa Clare Valley Transportation Authority - How to Use Silicon Valley Express Lanes

http://www.vta.org/getting-around/using-express-lanes

14 – California Department of Transport

http://www.dot.ca.gov/

15 – Wikipedia page on Slugging

https://en.wikipedia.org/wiki/Slugging

16 – Slug-Lines.com

http://www.slug-lines.com/Index.htm

17 - Far Eastern Electronic Toll Collection Co. Ltd. (FETC) received the 2017 WITSA Global ICT Excellence Awards- Private Sector Excellence Award at 2017 World Congress on Information Technology (WCIT) held in Taipei.

http://www.taipeitimes.com/News/biz/archives/2017/09/15/2003678442

18 – Taiwan Area National Freeway Bureau

https://www.freeway.gov.tw/english/Publish.aspx?cnid=1628

19 – Number plate collectors clubs.

http://www.npcc.org.au/

https://www.alpca.org/

http://plaque.free.fr/index-english.html

20 – The magnificent but complex I95 from Wikipedia.

https://en.wikipedia.org/wiki/Interstate_95

21 – The Wikipedia page on the Rebecca Riots.

https://en.wikipedia.org/wiki/Rebecca_Riots

22 - Have a look at the Age article: http://www.theage.com.au/victoria/toll-road-fines-ballooning-debt-turning-motorists-into-criminals-20160107-gm17wy.html

23 - Tolling Customer Ombudsman. http://tollingombudsman.com.au/

24 – Transurban's annual report for 2017.

https://www.transurban.com/content/dam/investor-centre/04/2017-Annual-Report.pdf

25 – Wikipedia's entry on double-entry bookkeeping

https://en.wikipedia.org/wiki/Double-entry_bookkeeping_system

26 – The Crimson Permanent Assurance

http://www.imdb.com/title/tt0215685/

https://vimeo.com/111458975

27 – "Who Dares Wins" – the Regimental motto of those charming but ruthless chaps in the Special Air Service

https://en.wikipedia.org/wiki/Special_Air_Service

28 – VINs in Wikipedia

https://en.wikipedia.org/wiki/Vehicle_identification_number

29 - For more information on Graph Theory have a look at "Introductory Graph Theory" by Gary Chartrand, published by Dover, New York.

Figure Credits

Figure 1 – Brad and Marsha. Royalty free image from Corel.

Figure 2 - Main system components in an MLFF tolling system. Author's own work.

Figure 3 - System components of an MLFF tolling system in the context of their physical locations. Author's own work.

Figure 4 – Typical two gantry configuration of roadside vehicle detection equipment. Author's own work.

Figure 5 – A simple toll road topology. Author's own work.

Figure 6 – The basic (Australian) Interoperability process. Author's own work.

Figure 7 – Differences between Open and Closed toll roads. Author's own work.

Figure 8: Toll gantries on the Tullamarine Freeway section of Melbourne's CityLink – by Marcus Wong Wongm (Own work) [GFDL (http://www.gnu.org/copyleft/fdl.html) or CC BY-SA 3.0 (http://creativecommons.org/licenses/by-sa/3.0)], via Wikimedia Commons

Figure 9: Highway 407 and Derry Road, facing southwest - By SimonP (Own work) [CC BY-SA 3.0 (http://creativecommons.org/licenses/by-sa/3.0) or GFDL (http://www.gnu.org/copyleft/fdl.html)], via Wikimedia Commons

Figure 10 – The Peninsula Freeway. Author's own work.

Figure 11 – Taiwan toll road network pricing scheme – see http://www.freeway.gov.tw/english/Publish.aspx?cnid=1628

Figure 12 – A web based toll calculator from RMS http://www.rms.nsw.gov.au/sydney-motorways/toll-calculator/

Figure 13 – Tolling class rule outcomes. Vehicle profiles were taken from the manufacturers' vehicle brochures. The assembled image is the author's own work.

Figure 14 – Main interoperability file formats. Author's own work.

Figure 15 – Liber-t tag lanes on French Autoroutes. Image from a website I believe was created by ASFA, the French professional association representing all the toll roads in France, no longer available.

Figure 16 – Big Jag and his interoperability experience. Author's own work.

Figure 17 – A Norbit DSRC 5.8 GHz tolling tag. Image supplied courtesy of Norbit.

Figure 18 – the FasTrak flex tag from the wonderful website http://www.vta.org/getting-around/using-express-lanes/how-fastrak-works

Figure 19 – California Highway Patrol. Picture taken from http://scvnews.com/2016/12/20/dec-23-26-chp-maximum-enforcement-period/ but the original source is not known.

Data items

Data Item 1 – Tag Passage.

Data Item 2 – Vehicle Passage.

Data Item 3 – Image Package.

Data Item 4 – Vehicle Type.

Data Item 5 – Licence Plate.

Data Item 6 – Vehicle.

Data Item 7 – Tag.

Data Item 8 – Interoperability Partner.

Data Item 9 – Transaction.

Data Item 10 – Trip.

Data Item 11 – Licence Plate Arrangement to Pay.

Data Item 12 – Tag Arrangement to Pay.

Data Item 13 – Interoperability Invoice.

Data Item 14 – Person.

Data Item 15 – Business.

Data Item 16 – Tolling Account.

Data Item 17 – Statement.

Data Item 18 – NATP Invoice.

Data Item 19 – Nomination.

Made in United States
Orlando, FL
04 November 2026

90201114R00136